# So, We're Still Here.
# Now What?

# So, We're Still Here. Now What?

SPIRITUAL EVOLUTION AND PERSONAL
EMPOWERMENT IN THE NEW ERA

Gwilda Wiyaka

Swan•Raven & Co.
P.O. Box 1429
Columbus, NC 28722

Library of Congress Cataloging-in-Publication Data

Wiyaka, Gwilda, 1950-
So we're still here, now what?: spiritual evolution and personal empowerment in
a new era / Gwilda Wiyaka. -- 1 [edition].
    p. cm. -- (The path home series; v. 1)
Includes bibliographical references and index.
ISBN 978-1-893183-57-5 (alk. paper)
1. Shamanism. 2. Spiritual life. 3. Human evolution. 4. New Age movement.
I. Title.
BF1621.W59 2013
201'.44--dc23                    2012044068

**Series Information:   First in the The Map Home Series**

Cover and interior artist: Gwilda Wiyaka

Original book and artwork preparation: Trixie Phelps

Photographers: Laura Curtsinger and Heather Miller

Manuscript Editor: Brian L. Crissey

Manuscript Designer: Pamela Meyer

Address all inquiries to:

Swan • Raven & Co.

an imprint of Granite Publishing

P.O. Box 1429

Columbus, NC 28722

granite-planet.net


Printed in the United States of America.

# DEDICATION

To my children—
Laura & Jason Curtsinger and Mark and Heather Miller,
for their unwavering love, faith, and support.

To all of my friends, clients, students, and spiritual teachers
without whom this book could not have been written.

# ACKNOWLEDGEMENTS

To my publishers, Pamela Meyer and Brian L. Crissey,
publicist Eileen Duhné and literary assistant Trixie Phelps,
whose vision, dedication and sheer tenacity
helped birth this book into ordinary reality.

# Table of Contents

# Publisher's Preface

On December 21, 2012, a remarkable thing happened: nothing. Or so some say. Just as if someone blew a dog whistle in your ear and asked you what you heard, you too might say, "Nothing." You would not be lying, but if you had been asked what had just happened, "Nothing" would be incorrect. It is not that nothing happened, because something *did* happen, but you just could not hear it. Actually, something quite remarkable took place at the end of 2012—though many of us have yet to perceive it. The fact that you are reading this book indicates that, on some level, you have a deep-felt sense of transitioning into the long-prophesied Great Shift of the Ages. You heard the dog whistle. You felt the subtle energies rise, and your heart may have lifted. Perhaps it was a peak event in your life or perhaps even a challenging one, but you heard the call.

Many, however, expected some horrible disaster to befall the Earth, wasting those who were on some designated black list and lifting those who were on some preferred white list. As that failed to take place as predicted, such people may choose to focus their discontent, as many have before them, on the next Armageddon or the next Earth-change disaster. One has to wonder why.

A 1956 book titled *When Prophecy Fails*[1] concerned Dorothy Martin, a Chicago housewife who produced automatic-writing messages allegedly from the Planet Clarion that predicted that the world would end in a great flood before dawn on December 21, 1954. Clearly the world did not end then. Her followers, some of whom had left jobs, schools, and families, gave away everything they owned in preparation for their immanent midnight departure on a flying saucer that surely was coming to rescue the true believers. The group removed all metal and stayed up all night awaiting rescue, which never came. Martin then reported another message that stated, "The little group, sit-

---

1. *Festinger, Leon et al. (1956). When Prophecy Fails: A Social and Psychological Study of a Modern Group that Predicted the Destruction of the World.* University of Minnesota Press. ISBN 1-59147-727-1.

ting all night long, had spread so much light that God had saved the world from destruction."

The event provided much fodder for sociologists, but its lessons seem to have gone unnoticed by the unending series of cultish groups that time and again have predicted the end of the world, some of which carried out violent and bizarre acts when their predicted catastrophes did not materialize. Shoko Asahara, for example, founder of the Aum Shinrikyo cult, declared himself to be Christ, borrowed the term "Armageddon" from Revelations 16:16, and then predicted an imminent nuclear World War.[1] When peace persisted, his followers attacked the Tokyo subway system with Sarin nerve gas on June 27, 1994, in an apparent attempt to hasten the Apocalypse. In 2000, the Movement for the Restoration of the Ten Commandments of God carried out a mass murder in Kanungu, Uganda, after its leaders' doomsday prophesies failed to come true.[2] There have been many others.

It is not only radical extremists who get caught up in apocalyptic beliefs. It is also ordinary citizens who store food and weapons and prepare for the worst. It is prudent to be prepared, but we must ask, "What is it within people that so often leads them to believe that the world is ending?" Are they looking for some escape from the unbearable reality of their daily lives? Do they seek some utopian paradise that may never be achieved here on Earth? Do they feel that the current system is too warped and compromised to ever change for the better? Or do they hope that some immense, angry power will come to punish the wrong-doers on this planet and rapture the chosen ones into heaven?

In late 2012, Chinese authorities detained 500 people from a quasi-Christian religious group called the Church of the Almighty God for spreading rumors that the world would end on the winter solstice of 2012. Throughout the world, millions of others focused on that same date, expecting that the ending of the Mayan Calendar would herald the end of the world. Of course, the world did not end on December 21, 2012, just as it did not end on December 21, 1954, or at any of the other prophesied endpoints. Indeed, again, *we are still here. Now what?*

The Mayan calendar, thought by many to have heralded the end of humankind, seems instead to have been merely a beacon, a turning point, a

1. Lifton, Robert Jay, *Destroying the World to Save It: Aum Shinrikyo, Apocalyptic Violence, and the New Global Terrorism.* New York: Macmillan (2000).
2. Snow, Robert L. (2003). *Deadly Cults: The Crimes of True Believers.* Praeger/Greenwood. pp. 70, 79, 108, 111. ISBN 0-275-98052-9.

beginning of something better. The ancient Hopis long expected the "Fourth World" of greed, war and competition to begin to transform into the "Fifth World" of love, balance and spiritual strength at about this point in time. It is that Fifth World that many believe has now been born.

Something has changed for the better, according to many, but we are embarking now upon brightly lit but uncharted seas. How do we find our way, now that much of the guidance of our recent past has led only onto the shoals? How did ancient peoples find guidance in the darkness of their pre-industrial eras? They turned to their shaman[1], those special people who walk between the worlds, seeing in the dark and hearing the unsaid. In times of great change, they tuned themselves into the vibrations of the Earth and stars in order to keep themselves in balance with the ever-changing frequencies of the universe. Today, modern science is returning to old ways, concluding that what we perceive as reality is but a projection cast by the true reality that lies in the unseen probabilistic realm of the quantum universe, where the shaman roam.

And so, we turn to a remarkable shamanic practitioner of the modern age whose unique abilities illuminate our modern darkness and shine much-needed light upon the untrodden path before us. We present to you for your consideration and enjoyment a proven practitioner of galactic shamanism—a woman who pierces the obscurity of our confusion with the clarity of her inner light, a woman whose immense power and knowledge is undeniable, a woman whose wisdom derives from ancient practices, honed by a deep and compassionate understanding of the labored path we have each followed to get here. We give you Gwilda Wiyaka.

---

1. The term *shaman* is both singular and plural.

# Introduction

We haven't been abducted by aliens, eaten by reptiles, nuked by atomics, struck by an asteroid, carried off by angels, or blown up by the sun. So, we're still here, now what? First, we need a voice of reason in these tumultuous times.

*So, We're Still Here. Now What?* is that voice. It provides down-to-earth, grounded guidance to get through these dynamic changes minus the hype and hysteria. Yet, it is not a stick-your-head-in-the-sand refusal to acknowledge the facts. This book openly recognizes we are currently going through massive upheaval and intense transformation.

This is not what I would call a channeled work but rather a co-creation with Spirit. While I could never have dreamed of writing it on my own, I have been an essential and indispensable component of the process. It has taken no less than all of my life and experience to provide the translation point for the information so generously provided by life itself.

There have been many wonderful teachers along the way, but no one of them gave me this information. Instead they would offer a piece, a small portion preserved through the ages that still had light shining through it. Each of these pieces often posed more questions than answers, but it would intrigue and engage me enough to keep me looking for the ultimate truth.

For over 60 years, I have searched for the teacher or book that had this illusive ultimate truth, only to find small shards, like the shard of a shattered mirror, reflecting the sunlight or the moonlight. My teachers evolved from human ones to those in spirit form, from earth-dwelling ones to friends from the stars, and eventually to life itself. Yet, I have been destined to fail in my quest.

There is no ultimate truth but rather an ever-evolving one. Truth is an ever-expanding frequency—one we must ourselves evolve to embrace. I discovered that one cannot find truth, or possess it, but rather must become it. We can only let it shine through us into the world, for it is too boundless to contain, and everyone we encounter can only embrace a limited portion of it.

Truth is an organism, and those who bear it are simply single cells of a much greater whole.

I have been called a spiritual teacher, and yes, I suppose I am. But life is *my* teacher, and as I share what it offers, I myself am taught.

## TRUTH IS NOT POPULAR

One discovery I have made over the years of my quest is that truth is rarely popular or well received. People think they want it, but ultimately it shines light on the shadow of their denied worlds. Many decide embracing their shadow is too great a price to pay and will project their denials on the source of the light—thus persecuting many a fine prophet.

Am I a prophet? I would have to say no, but the truth, by its very nature, is prophetic. If you are willing to sacrifice your denials enough to embrace truth, it will surely set you free, for you are the truth you seek.

> ~ *AND YE SHALL KNOW THE TRUTH,*
> *AND THE TRUTH SHALL MAKE YOU FREE.* ~
> ~ *JOHN 8:32* ~

Upon receiving my book proposal, Pam of Granite Publishing contacted me saying, "The only thing wrong with your book is that it is not out there yet." After some head scratching, she suggested I break it into two books so we could offer it in a more timely form. I agreed.

*So, We're Still Here. Now What?* will be followed by book 2: *These and Greater Things: Unlocking Your Power to Manifest and Thrive through Shamanism.* Each book will also have an accompanying workbook designed to further help readers build their own map home in a more personal and detailed way.

## HOW TO USE THIS BOOK

I am not a linear thinker. I tend to pick up a book and bounce around in it rather than read it cover to cover. It is ironic that I was destined to write a book that needs the front-to-back approach. This subject matter builds upon itself much like mathematics and therefore does require a more linear approach. At the same time, the material within also deepens in meaning with each reading, so reading it more than once will strengthen your foundation.

Truth is also a multidimensional process of evolution and therefore must build upon itself while remaining cyclic and circular in nature. This has had me struggling with how to present my humble offering in order to best assist you to engage in your own process.

Because the information is so dynamic, it is written in a multidimensional format to appeal to your visual, verbal, and kinesthetic pathways. Detailed graphics, utilizing the energy signature of the subject matter and designed to appeal to the subconscious, appear throughout. Parables, poems, song lyrics, and anecdotes are all woven in to engage your emotions.

For your mind, I have included analogies, scientific facts and illustrations that tie the information together following a logical progression. Most importantly, you will find it laced with humor, heart and optimism. You can't take this subject too seriously or it will make you crazy.

Not only will the application of the principles outlined in these books give you answers to ancient spiritual questions, it will also offer practical, empowering solutions. The information within is not just a mental exercise in spirituality, but it is also a primer of solid principles designed to enable you to manifest change at all four levels of life—physical, emotional, mental, and spiritual.

Better fiction based in reality than a reality based in fiction. In order to protect the privacy of the people involved, many of my anecdotes are composites of real events. However, they are all comprised of actual experiences I have had throughout the course of my life.

Included in "Shamanism 101" are detailed instructions on how to perform your own shamanic journey. In my humble opinion, learning to conduct your own shamanic journey is the single most personal empowering skill you can learn, for with this technique alone you can access the Akashic Records and commune with Spirit. Through performing your shamanic journey, you will be able to access personal answers and design your customized map home to your spiritual evolution and personal empowerment.

As we move from one age of influence to another, even our language begins to fail us. Our current language is by necessity, linear and polarized while spiritual information tends to be more unified. However, as we move into the new era, we are increasingly moving into that unity. Periodically I will need to clarify how I am using particular words to avoid confusion. Therefore, when I am using a particular word or phrase in an a typical way, some of the text will include definitions for your clarification. Additionally, definitions for words that I am often asked to define in my talks have been placed in a glossary.

Throughout the book you will find quotes from music written and performed by myself and Cody Wigle from the musical group—StarFaihre, which is a unique musical group who performs ancient and original world/

shamanic music. This music is designed to assist during these times of intense shifts and deep transformation. As we find ourselves at the precipice of life changing revelations, this music is healing and transformative. For more information on this group, please refer to the Appendix.

Thank you for joining me on the journey of a lifetime—our journey home.

Many Blessings,

# Section I

## Worlds in Transition

# 1

## Wheels Within Wheels

We stand at the precipice of a remarkable adventure—the adventure of human evolution. We may have been here before, but never in recorded history and never exactly like this. By simply being alive during these potent times, we have become the chosen ones to steward an entirely new way of being.

The wheels have turned, the cycles progressed, and we are moving from a polarized existence into unity consciousness. What does this mean to us as individuals and as a people? We have the opportunity to move beyond the current system, which has served us well in the past, but is becoming increasingly restrictive. We can now become the co-creators of our experience, and we can work magic on the physical plane. In unity consciousness there is no war, because there is no cause for war. There is no loneliness, because there is no separation. There is no poverty, because we can manifest at will.

But I get ahead of myself. Without first building the foundation of understanding, this concept may appear at the very least, a pipe dream, if not the ravings of a lunatic. Bear with me.

In order to see where we are going, it is necessary to reframe where we have been. It's important to make clear that there is nothing wrong with our past. As we expose the underbelly of past and current existence, the information may seem a bit negative, if not paranoid. This is not the case. All has been perfect, given the lack of expansiveness we've had to work with, but now we are moving into a time of greater light.

*~ FEAR NOT—EVERYTHING IS TRULY IN DIVINE ORDER.*
*IT IS SIMPLY A MATTER OF PERSPECTIVE. ~*

Please join me as we map out the adventure of a lifetime. You may very well find this to be your personal Map Home. The Map Home is a set of teachings and techniques designed by the Path Home Shamanic Arts School to aid the individual in moving beyond their restrictions and limitations on the physical, mental, emotional and physical levels. Through this process people can regain balance, return to their natural expression, increase their overall frequency, and come home to their rightful place in the circle of life

## FLIGHT OF THE RAVEN

Raven came calling. She flew in from the west making a great show of flaring her wings as she landed on the light post just outside my dining-room window, where I sat with my cup of morning tea. The sun glistened off her blue-black feathers as she cocked her head and looked in at me through one shining, ebony eye.

"Hi Sister Raven," I greeted her. "Do you have something for me?"

She opened her massive beak and cawed loudly in response, while looking directly at me.

"Well, let me finish my tea and I will journey to you, so you can show me," I said, while taking another blissful sip.

Apparently, this time, that wasn't going to be good enough for her. She took off from the light post with an impressive downward sweep of both wings and flew directly at my window. Just when I was sure she would hit the glass she banked, circled, and landed on top of my bird house directly in front of the bay window. The bird house has a steeply pitched copper roof on which she shuffled and slid, unable to find purchase with her talons. Undaunted, she continued her dance on the roof and insistently cawed directly at me.

"OK, OK," I gave in, giving my fresh cup of tea one last longing look as I set it back on the table and got up. She took to the air again and resumed perching on the light post, clearly impatient for me to join her.

I went into the room I reserve for journeywork with my clients. I lay down, and put on my drumming music. I covered my eyes with my trusty camo bandana and went into trance. My power animals came and took me just outside my house, where Raven waited on the light post. She took to the air as I arrived, so I followed her as she banked and headed north as the crow (or in this case Raven) flies.

We flew rapidly, the landscape a blur, as we went from Colorado to Wyoming. Soon we banked again and flew directly into my mother's front door. My mother was sitting in her recliner still in her red robe. She was unaware of me, as I was in spirit form. Her lips and fingers were blue and her face and ankles so swollen that I hardly recognized her.

"Your mother needs you," Raven's voice said in my mind's ear.

We returned as rapidly as we had gone, and before I knew it I was seeing my spirit rejoin my body, back in my journey room. I thanked Raven and my spirit helpers, got up and went directly to call my sister.

"Gad, Gwilda, I hate it when you do that. You are so uncanny it gives me the willies!" my sister exclaimed when she answered before the phone rang. "I had just picked up the phone to call you. Mom is not doing well, but we can't get her to go to the doctor. Dad and I are beside ourselves, and we hoped you could talk some sense into her."

"Give me about three and a half hours. I will be there," I responded. Then I hung up and called downstairs to my son, Mark, who was living with me at the time. "Mark, your grandmother is sick, and I need you to get me to Casper pronto."

"I can do that," he simply responded, and we were in his car and on our way in less than five minutes.

Now a word to the wise—you don't tell a 16-year-old boy in a 280Z to "just get me there." When the highway patrol pulled us over, he had clocked us at 120 mph. No sooner had the ticket been issued and the patrolman disappeared over the hill in the opposite direction, than we were back up to speed, so to speak. We were in Casper in under three hours.

When we pulled into the drive, four ravens were perched in the majestic pines that bordered my parents' house. They started calling as soon as I got out of the car and headed toward the front door. Not bothering to ring the bell, I opened the door and stepped inside. There, sitting in her recliner wearing the same red robe I had seen her in during my journey, sat my mother, face swollen, lips blue, fighting for every breath.

"I knew you would know. I knew you would come," she gasped.

"Yeah, it's what I do," I responded.

## DEATH OF A MOTHER

I helped my mother die. After a life lived in avoidance, indulgence, isolation and pain, a life in which she increasingly collected things and avoided people, I watched her succumb as her body could no longer bear the burden of her denials. She loved me—of this I have no doubt—but she loved her things more, at least until the end, when she slowly started letting go of all her treasures and clung to me.

I had no illusions. I was well aware that she had traded me for the life of wealth and privilege she had never known. Like Scarlett O'Hara, somewhere along the way she vowed that no matter what the price, she would never be hungry again. I was the first price of many, as she left me at four years of age to tour the world and live abroad with her new husband. Then later she chose to ignore his abuse of me, rather than lose the privileges he provided.

Years later as she lay dying, while I watched her body fade, I saw her spirit build and grow above it. No longer tethered to the mundane, it could truly shine. No longer fueling her defense mechanisms, running her programs, or limited by the illusion we call reality, her spirit's glory emerged. It was then, for a brief time—a matter of hours—I got to know, connect with, and love the mother I had lived without. Then she was gone. I will treasure those few hours for all time.

I helped her cross—showed her the way to the gate. It was an honor, but in truth, I think she indulged me. In the end, she knew her own way and needed me not at all. I watched my mother die, and for the first time, I saw her truly live.

I know more of death than of living, yet I know more of life than most. I am a shadow walker by nature, Scorpio by sign, woman by gender, and shaman by trade. Death and life are my business.

Now it is my time to die. I see all the signs. I am letting go of all my possessions, friends, beliefs, and dreams. I am dying, of this I have no doubt, but my body is not failing, nor am I about to leave it behind. To the old world, I am soon quite dead. I am already a mere specter that haunts the "living," a shadow soon to fade and, for the most part, to be forgotten.

But that's only half of the story. There is a new world, a new heaven, and a new Earth into which some are being birthed already incarnate. This is the place of ascension, the "garden" of the old myth and legend. As the age changes, we are no longer on the old track, even though we occupy the same space as before. In this new place, old laws need not apply. As I dispassionately watch the old ways fail, I increasingly disengage.

Should we choose, we are no longer subject to the illusion. However, we are indeed subject to the way life works, since only the true laws of nature apply—laws long forgotten. The challenge is in learning to navigate this new world, we may discover formidable new gifts and powers we do not yet know how to wield. In order to become capable of true co-creation—first, we must learn to walk in this new terrain before we can fly.

## CHILDHOOD'S END

As a spiritual teacher there is one main law that stands—those who "know it all" cannot be taught. What I know and can do come from a lifetime of introspection and processing. Many have seen the result of my years of study and want this "power" for themselves. At first, they seem to be earnest students, but in the long run they are seeking power and glory, not truth. They are unwilling to let go of what they consider to be their already formidable spiritual knowledge. There is the misbegotten belief that they have arrived and just need a few more techniques to perfect their magnificence.

The concept that they may need to reevaluate their stance is out of the question, much less the idea that they might need deep personal growth and processing. Investigating their own shadow is never considered because they believe they do not have one. When it rears its ugly head, it is seen as belonging to someone else.

I was just this sort of student when I started with my first teacher, who was Native American. Take it from one who knows—you can't get here from there. The first part of my path was horrendous, amounting to nothing more than being beaten up by my own ego, arrogance and denials, and then blaming my teacher. How he found the patience to deal with me at all, I have no idea.

I was surely a disappointment to him. I was the wrong race, color, and gender. I knew nothing of the proper treatment of an elder or spiritual leader, and my denials and damage ran deep. At one point, he indicated to me that he did not choose me, but I was chosen for him.

While he always treated me with a sort of distant kindness, at times I could see that he found me humorous, and to this day I'm not sure if he liked me, but he did teach me. In the end, it saved my life and may very well save yours.

The first step to evolution is cracking your personal cosmic egg of western knowledge and arrogance. Let go of everything you think you know, let go of who and what you think you are, and then let go on a deeper level. That's the price of entry.

The second step in evolution is realizing that it is entirely an inside job and no one can do it for you. I do have a carrot for you, though—you are ever so much more than you think. But to come home to all that you are, to all you can be and do, you

> ### Ashes
>
> *I emptied the fireplace today. The ashes of many long dead fires had piled up, covering the grate*
>
> *It was a job that he used to do so I was very careful to get it right*
>
> *As I put shovel after shovel of the light grey ashes into the black pail, a fine dust rose up in the air*
>
> *It danced in the rays of morning light that came in through the east windows, like ghosts of evenings spent last winter*
>
> *I could almost hear the crackle of those long dead fires as they warmed the room*
>
> *The quiet room, where two people sat and stared into the flames, one afraid, the other unwilling to break the silence*
>
> *It is not good to remove all the ashes, you know. Some must be left or the new fire won't burn well*
>
> *I did that once to a wood burning stove. I vacuumed it out until it was shiny clean. I don't think it ever burned well again*

must let go of who you are not. This is a process, not something we can just declare and make so. Humility and openness are the key, and childlike wonder is the stance. Willingness to be infants in a new way of being is paramount.

Yet, all you have lived and learned is not wasted. Its value and purpose remains; it just needs to be set entirely aside for a while to make room for your new life. If a baby does not learn to crawl, part of its development is stunted. Once we learn to walk, we rarely crawl, yet the skill is useful in scrubbing floors, sneaking up on game, entering a sweat lodge, or playing on the floor with babies.

## NEGATIVE NUMBERS

When I was in grade school, the agreed-upon method of teaching math was to deal with addition, subtraction, multiplication, and division of positive numbers only. At the lower-grade levels we were kept unaware of the existence of negative numbers—zero was the end of the line.

I loved math. Unlike history, it made sense to me. There were predictable rules that, if learned and applied properly, would get the right answer every time.

I will never forget when my math teacher introduced negative numbers. Like a wizard with a deep secret, she cunningly and delightedly informed us that we had been lied to all along. We had only been given half the facts. There was another world of math that existed—as massive as the one we'd been taught.

I never trusted a teacher again. I decided that they all withheld information in order to feel superior to their students. In my math teacher's case, it was probably true. She exhibited fiendish delight in watching her poor students trying to twist rigid, left-to-right conditioning inside out and backwards.

Our math realities had been shattered, and many of my classmates never recovered. I was one of the fortunate ones. My brain, for whatever reason, works inside out and backwards as easily as the norm, so the switch was not so challenging. I did learn to question whether anyone possessed, much less shared, all the facts. I learned that, while rules may appear to apply, there are often deeper laws that can change the entire picture, and I decided to seek the deeper laws.

Early on, I found that rules are subject to life; life is a process; and process by its very nature, changes things. At the same time, I observed that within the constant change, certain patterns or rules seemed to pertain. I concluded that true laws could be relied upon, but a larger picture was needed, and no one seemed to have it. I made it my business to find it.

The current view of reality is fragmented, compartmentalized, and linear, while in nature, everything fits together and follows cyclic, universal laws that we seem to have forgotten. By observing nature, I was able to discern truth from someone's great idea. Nature became my litmus test. If what was presented did not align with natural law, it was probably not true.

In following this premise, I discovered, to my dismay, that much of our reality is a myth built upon a foundation of lies. Like castles of sand, the old reality is falling. These are the days when the truth can't hide.

In the old reality we think in linear and polarized absolutes—good vs. bad, light vs. dark, them vs. us, and so on. Things have a beginning, middle, and an end, period. There is a right way to act or believe, and anyone thinking differently is wrong. Now, we have the opportunity to evolve beyond these limited perceptions.

Since change begins within, the first step in our evolution is to move beyond the limited view of our potential. Reality is no more than a reflection of our belief systems and intent, conscious or unconscious. In the long run, we are not changing our true selves, but rather evolving into who we really are, into our true nature.

## THE AMAZING POWER OF DENIAL

One of the contradictions of a polarized view of reality is that, even if we choose to perceive certain aspects as separate, everything is subject to natural law, and therefore, interrelated.

Any time we judge against anything, we are judging against something in ourselves. If we judge against the dark and only value the light, whatever in us that is of the dark (50% of our expression) must be firmly shoved into denial. This not only detaches us from half of our

*Nagi*
*(Lakota: ghost/shadow self)*

*Trapped in the dungeon of my own definitions,*
*I can hear the tortured screams of my raw potentiality as it tries to break free*

*Disowned, unrecognized, invalidated, distorted by the lack of interaction with the whole, it fights for its life*

*The very struggle further identifies it as the enemy of the status quo*

*Hideous writhing brands it the source of pain rather than the sufferer*

*I brutally stamp it down again. Crush it back into the shadows of my denial*

*I rise above its base promptings. Regain my stability*

*But it shall rise again as surely as the sun on the morrow*

*For it is the greater part of me*

personal power and expression but also puts that same amount of power outside of conscious control, and under the direction of the unconscious-ness. The more denied we are, the more unconscious we are.

Now, I don't know about you, but I'm not fond of the idea that half my power is outside of my conscious control, running amuck, messing up my life.

## GUILT AND SHAME

When we judge against part of ourselves, we experience guilt and shame. Most of our emotions have purpose, even those we judge against. An example of this is rage, which results from denied anger. Anger is natural and necessary to set boundaries.

The mother bear is formidable in her protective behavior. She has no qualms about expressing anger in all its snarling glory. Yet, when her cubs are no longer threatened, she doesn't hold a grudge, and she simply goes on about her business.

Humans, on the other hand, feel less free to express anger. It is not civilized to growl at someone crossing our boundaries, so we stuff it. While anger is not expressed in the moment, neither is it forgotten. Instead we tend to hold grudges.

Stuff anger into denial enough times, and we become full of rage. Subsequently, the unfortunate person who unwittingly gets on our last nerve is blasted. After we have vented, it becomes obvious, even to us, that the response was over the top for the stimulus, and we experience guilt and shame.

---

> **The Trap**
>
> *When we judge others we are actually projecting a denied part of ourselves onto them*
>
> *This weakens us and burdens others*
>
> *In judging, we are caught in a trap of our own making*
>
> *As we project our power to change upon another*
>
> *We end up expending personal power to maintain the projection that results in our own disempowerment*

---

Guilt and shame are not natural expressions. They're not found anywhere except in the presence of judgment and denial. These foreign energies are so toxic that they can only be endured for so long before we have to get out from under them.

The usual method is to project judgment and blame upon the poor hapless person who triggered our rage. The part of us which knows that we were out of line is then shoved into denial. As a result, we are even less conscious, present, and in control.

I once had a conversation with a woman about guilt. She felt, in the absence of guilt, people would do bad things. I believe people are intrinsically good and want to do good things in order to belong. Guilt and shame force people to act against their nature by judging against themselves, causing them to fragment from that which they judge against.

The worst crimes result from the projection of self-judgment onto another, then attacking the object of that projection. The vicious circle of judging against ourselves, then feeling guilt and shame, which we project and further deny, results in extreme compartmentalization.

> ~ *LET HIM THAT WIPES HIS SOILED HANDS UPON YOUR GARMENT TAKE*
> *YOUR GARMENT. HE MAY NEED IT AGAIN; YOU SURELY WILL NOT.* ~
> ~ *KAHLIL GIBRAN* ~

Polarized, compartmentalized reality has us viewing ourselves as separate, not subject to the same laws, and forever alone. This leaves us vulnerable to a consumer-driven society. Anything that promises to relieve the illusion of unbearable aloneness and self-denial becomes extremely desirable, so much so that many of us will gladly mortgage our future for the promise of a moment's relief. This is the pain and suffering we have come to accept as reality.

## TIME LINES: WHAT IS MY FUTURE?

Because we live in this linear, polarized reality, we tend to think of our lives as linear. We start at birth, follow a predestined path of things that "happen to us," and end at death. This is what our lives have become as a result of our history, yet it doesn't have to remain that way.

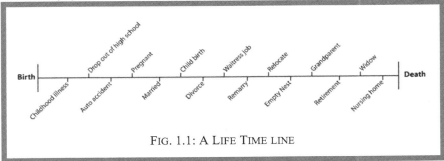

FIG. 1.1: A LIFE TIME LINE

We actually come with a "set" of paths to choose from. We choose or agree upon this set each time we incarnate, depending upon what we wish to experience, learn, or accomplish during a particular lifetime. This is where free will enters in.

When first embarking upon my spiritual path, I, like many others, was looking for what Spirit wanted me to do. What was I supposed to be? It was quite a shock when I discovered that, "Quite frankly, madam, Spirit doesn't give a damn." Every time I asked about my life's path, the answer was, "What do you want it to be?" Talk about no guidance or direction! It's a lonely experience to discover we are the spirit we serve.

Eventually I learned that within my given set, my "great purpose" was simply living my life. How I chose to do it was up to me. It sure took the excuse "Spirit made me do it" out of the picture.

This is my life. The choices and results of those choices are up to me. The buck stops here. So where's the glory? At first I was disappointed that I was not the star of some great plan.

I have since come to realize I am the star of some great plan, but I am the planner. There's a lot of freedom and responsibility in that. On deeper levels, it puts us in the position of being co-creators rather than puppets. Once we get over the shock that we are ultimately responsible for our choices and that the life we are living is entirely the result of our choices, conscious or unconscious, we can truly engage in the process of living.

Let's look at this in a little more detail. As I stated, when we come in, we have a "set" within which we can operate. In this lifetime, I will never be a tall, black, successful basketball player. Wrong race, wrong gender, wrong height, and at this point, wrong age. It is simply not in my set. I suppose I could join a gym and take lessons, but the chance of doing more than spraining an ankle and embarrassing myself is pretty slim. Fortunately (or by design), I have no real passion or desire to be a basketball player.

In Figure 1.2, consider each circle an "option" and the lines between the circles as "paths" from option to option. This represents the set we come in with. In a perfect world, we would have access to all of our options. As things are, we take a bit of a beating, and as a result, we disconnect from some of our options.

When I incarnated this time, I came as a female. Within that set, I had many options, but early on, it was impressed upon me that being a girl meant I was a second-class citizen. If anyone went to college, it would be my brother. If I got to go at all, it would be to find a husband and become a good wife. That's what women did. I would really have loved to have been a doctor, and within my set, I could have been a great one.

But I suffered what is called "soul loss" around my ability to pursue a profession that, at the time, was considered to be for men only. My taking on that belief resulted in my disconnecting from many options. Similarly, we systematically disconnect from our options until what's left is a single path that starts at birth and ends at death, with fairly predictable things happening to us along the way.

My path could easily have been: get married, have children, bring them up, become an empty nester, travel with my husband after he retires, become a widow, and then die. Fortunately, I discovered my set, reconnected with at least some of my original options, and am living the life I choose, rather than the one I was programmed to live

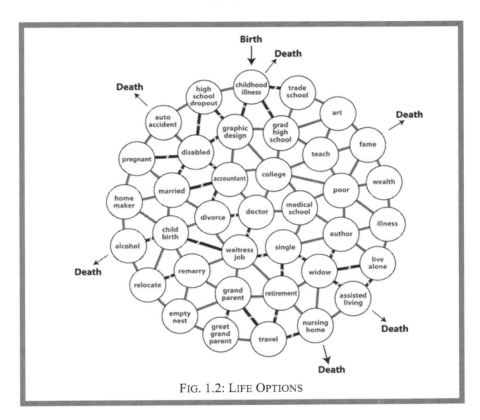

FIG. 1.2: LIFE OPTIONS

## SHAMANISM AND SOUL LOSS

Shamanism is a spiritual-healing practice (not to be confused with religion) at the foundation of all indigenous, Earth-based, societies. If any nationality is followed to its roots, there will be an Earth-based society with its own form of shamanic healing.

In short, shamanism mends where the laws of nature have been broken. The spiritual illness of "soul loss" is a universal shamanic concept. This spiritual or shamanic illness results whenever we disconnect from our true expression or options, thereby breaking our own natural laws. Socialization causes much of this, but trauma is also a contributor.

When we suffer trauma, we do, or circumvent doing, whatever we think is necessary in order to avoid repeating the experience. This limits mobility within our "set."

As we are no longer a shamanic society, we have not had the provision for spiritual healing. The result has been repeated disconnection with no means to reconnect, so we simply change the way we operate without looking too deeply. Our lives go on in a different direction as a result of our limited mobility, rather than choice. We unwittingly end up living in reaction instead of conscious intent.

The systematic disconnect from our natural expression has gone on for generations without the benefit of reconnecting through shamanic healing, so limitations are passed down from generation to generation. We unconsciously impose these limitations on our children and view it as basic socialization.

For instance, through modeling, children are shown: when a woman cares for the children, she is doing her job. When a man cares for the children, he is babysitting. Our realities are constructed through this messaging. Gender roles are but one example of the many limitations passed down.

> **Bondage**
>
> *I found you in bondage,*
> *no room left to move*
>
> *Hands bound, eyes covered, a blinded*
> *owl with clipped wings*
>
> *Your beautiful spirit controlled by*
> *self-serving others with only their*
> *personal interests at heart*
>
> *My gifted one in a cage, heart in pieces*
> *cast to the four winds*
>
> *I found you in bondage. Spirit has used*
> *me to shatter your life and set you free*

In recent years, reality has been evolving and we see parents sharing equally in child rearing and acquiring income. There is also a broader view of gender roles and more acceptance of other races and religions. But in many aspects of life, the old messaging still remains. It is the bedrock of our polarized reality. In addition to the standard-issue fragmentation that has resulted from socialization, each of us is subject to our own particular combination of disconnect. Just living in this polarized world is a bumpy ride. As children and later as adults, we are subject to projected denials and judgments. If we are too young or already too damaged to protect ourselves, we end up letting go of our innate identity and taking on the projection. Not only do we disconnect from more of our natural expression and options, but we also take on guilt and shame, which causes us to act outside of our natural expression. Inauthenticity creates

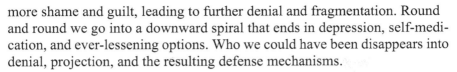

more shame and guilt, leading to further denial and fragmentation. Round and round we go into a downward spiral that ends in depression, self-medication, and ever-lessening options. Who we could have been disappears into denial, projection, and the resulting defense mechanisms.

In truth, few of us have any idea who we really are or what we really want, much less what we can do. Our value becomes attached to what others think of us. Our worth is defined by social status, which in turn is dictated by the ability to acquire wealth. Many of us sadly believe we are no better than the car we drive.

In contemplating the massive amount of disconnect we have all experienced, we can begin to see how much of our natural expression, and therefore our personal power, is seemingly offline. If it were just offline, it would be one thing, but it is online somewhere. Worse, it is not where it was designed to be, doing what it was designed to do, nor is it under our conscious control.

When my mother left me at four and went overseas to live with her new husband, I lived with my father, stepmother, her son and daughter. Her son was several years older than I, and the daughter was older by six months. My poor stepmother was a damaged individual who resented me deeply. I soon discovered that if there was anything she knew I wanted or needed, including having enough to eat, she would insure I did not get it. As a result, I developed the skill of manipulation in order to survive. For instance, I would offer to harvest peas for dinner from the large garden my father grew, eating half of what I picked. I would talk to my stepsister about her favorite lunch until she asked her mom for some so we could both eat.

I became so proficient at manipulation that it became my default setting, and, on some level, I decided the only way to get my needs met was by manipulating someone else and making it beneficial to them as well. All of this became unconscious behavior. Simply asking for what I needed was no longer an option.

This conduct carried into young adulthood when people started accusing me of being manipulative, yet I didn't know what they were talking about, since it wasn't consciously controlled. My ability to manipulate had become a defense mechanism, operating outside my consciousness and without my intent, long after the need for it became obsolete.

I hated being viewed this way, so I firmly set my intent to discover what others were talking about in order to fix it. Once my intent was set, an entire chain of events went into motion. These events included the discovery of my first teacher, and receiving soul retrieval around "deserving to get what I need" by simply asking. I was then able to dismantle the defense mechanism and take manipulation off of default.

This is a clear example not only of how different traits can be used without our knowledge, but how, through the intent to live differently, we can actually find the broken spokes on our personal wheel of possibilities. In order not to be known as manipulative, I had to find and heal my inability to directly state my needs and have them met.

> ### A River Runs Through It
>
> *There once was a man who bought a beautiful property on which to build his house. It had lovely trees and a river running through it. He had just dug the foundation and had the bags of concrete and sand delivered in order to pour the foundation walls when an exceptionally rainy season came. It rained so much the river was leaving its banks and threatening to wash out his fresh digging.*
>
> *In a panic, the man took the sand intended for the foundation concrete and sandbagged the river with it. This worked well, preventing his work from washing out. Later that year, some of the river was redirected up stream which kept his part of the river from leaving its banks in the future.*
>
> *Everything dried out and construction could have easily gone forward but the house was never built. For you see, he had forgotten the sand bags were for the foundation, not to dike the river.*

Soon after my healing, this allowed me to live in a very direct way, hitting everything head on, pulling no punches. I became brutally honest in dealing with others, but I was then viewed as harsh and opinionated.

I discovered that manipulation was not a bad thing when used consciously with good intent. The skill I had spent most of my life perfecting, and then judging against, was actually a necessary component in dealing gently with others. Now, in my practice, I often manipulate situations and information to ease my clients into finding their own truth. Rather than flatly stating what information was given to me and alienating my client, I can use gentle manipulation to help them come to conclusions on their own.

It is not easy looking at what you have been doing unconsciously. Yet, in order to heal and evolve, it is a necessary part of the inside job.

## WHEREVER TO START?

Once we discover how limited we have become due to generations of uncorrected soul loss, it can look like an insurmountable challenge to heal and reclaim our birthright. It took generations to get this messed up, so it won't *all* get fixed overnight. We must look at what we can do in our lifetime to heal what blocks us from the life we wish to live.

The good news is that it is not necessary, or even desirable, to heal all soul loss. A totally whole person could not relate to the rest of society, given the state of our culture. Rather than obsessing on every place we have disconnected, the first step is deciding what we want. However, what we first decide upon may be only what we think we can have, rather than what we really want. It would be better to let what we want be a moving target for now.

Once we have picked a goal, we set the intent to achieve it. This is as simple as deciding upon an action. Every broken spoke in the wheel between us and our goal suddenly becomes visible. "I can't do that, I am not smart enough." "I had better not try to do that, it did not go well for me last time," and so on. At this point we must decide if the effort is worth the bother. Be careful though. All our defense mechanisms will be telling us it is not.

By systematically setting our intent and healing what stands between us and our goals, we can, over time, reclaim the life we desire rather than live what is left to us.

## VICTIM

One of the major challenges standing between us and reclaiming our options is the stance of "victim." Most of us feel more victimized than we realize. The view of our future as a fated continuum along which things "happen to us" is a victimized perception. As long as we believe we are subject to events, rather than proactive, we are viewing ourselves as victims of circumstance.

From this limiting set of beliefs, it never occurs to us to do things differently. We feel we have no other choices, so we never look for them. We keep doing the same thing in the same way and hoping for different results (one definition of insanity).

> ~ *IF YOU DO NOT CHANGE DIRECTION,*
> *YOU MAY JUST END UP WHERE YOU ARE HEADING.* ~
> ~ *LAO TZU* ~

Good ol' guilt and shame keep us in the victim stance. If we are victims of events, we can't be blamed for them. As long as we are powerless victims of fate, we are not responsible. Avoidance of blame makes it difficult for us to come out of victimhood.

In my family of origin, and later in the work place, every time something broke or went wrong, out would come the pointing fingers with a whole lot of ducking going on. "It's not my fault, if you would have (fill in the blank), it wouldn't have happened." This is common in polarized reality.

It's assumed there's a good guy and a bad guy, the innocent and guilty. Much effort is spent finding someone to blame so all can agree on a scapegoat in order to project denied guilt and shame. It's no wonder that we grow up finding ways not to be responsible for our experience. No one is anxious to be blamed and suffer the judgment of others.

## MIND? WHAT MIND? I DON'T MIND

We have become a mind-based culture. In order to perceive the future with our minds, we must base the future on experiences from the past.

Instead, if we can engage our imaginations and view the future as multidimensional with many options, and the past as having been our creation, we can once again take the reins of our lives. Life can be transmuted, becoming ours to create, rather than endure.

It is no longer useful to project the events of the past onto the present, making a rerun out of the future. The alternative is to become conscious of what we intend. Through *conscious* intention, we can then create our dreams.

Yesterday is a distorted matrix of old belief systems, a quagmire of discontent and limitations. Too often many aspects of our lives and histories have been little more than agreed-upon myths rewritten by guilt, avoidance, and shame.

As times change, old beliefs can simply fall away and transmute to greater understanding. When we come to view life as a vision quest full of metaphorical meaning rather than experience set in stone, it will evolve and transform, assisting our evolution rather than preventing it.

There are many paths we may walk, some easier than others, but none better or worse. It's entirely up to the individual to choose the pathways within their given set.

Now there is a new way emerging. Even prophecies indicate that we are approaching the time of "the new heaven and the new Earth." This book offers you a map out of the old illusion, a map to our new way of living as we reenter the circle of life. This is our Map Home.

# 2

# The End of Days

We are coming into a time when the old method of taking the events of the past, superimposing them on the present, and making a rerun out of the future is failing. While this pattern is familiar and comfortable, it is also increasingly dysfunctional, as it ignores life's cyclic nature. Although it is not always evident, life actually operates as a spiral. As a culture we have lost our connection with the larger cycles of life, and we find ourselves floundering without guidance. Staying light on our feet and in constant contact with spiritual information is paramount. The ancients knew how to achieve this, and this book is designed to help you do the same.

Due to our conditioning, change tends to be met with great fear. Yet the very nature of life is one of constant change. The Earth wobbles as it spins on its axis, at about 1,038 miles per hour.

Simultaneously, the Earth spins around the sun at approximately 67,000 miles per hour, while the sun is itself flying through the galaxy. It is no mystery that change is continual.

When things stop changing, they die or fall out of the sky, which is yet another change of form.

Within this constant change lie repeating rhythms and cycles. Some changes we can easily see. It

*Winds of Time*

*This is the end, the night has fallen,*
*I have reached the end of days*

*What's real is not, reason fails me*
*I've gone beyond all known pathways*

*This is the end, the end of reason*
*This is the end, the end of time*

*I am alone, alone and broken*
*I am apart from what was mine*

*I stand now, at the edge*
*Of the abyss, nowhere to go*

*The time has come, I must choose*
*To take the leap or be laid low*

*This is the end, the end of reason*
*This is the end, the end of time*

*I travel on it is my season*
*To travel on the winds of time*

*~ StarFaihre ~*
*Excerpt from the album: "Winds of Time"*

is obvious that the sun rises and sets every day. What is less noticeable in the rising and setting of the sun is that it happens every day in a little different place in the sky with a slight change in the ratio of light to dark. We mark these changing times of light and dark by what we call equinoxes, solstices, and seasons. The equinoxes occur in spring and fall and are times when night and day are exactly the same length. The summer solstice is the longest day of the year and the winter solstice is the longest night. If we track change over longer periods of time, we find additional overarching patterns. To examine these larger patterns that span multiple generations, it is necessary to look into history.

Every culture has its own myths, legends, and prophecies from the ancient past. When dealing with snippets of information preserved from the past, it is hard to tell myth and legend from history or to discern metaphor from literal meaning. Yet within these mysteries lies evidence of larger, recurring cycles.

Never before in our recorded history have we been subject to more change and acceleration. From natural disasters and social upheaval to failing economies, it is difficult to ignore that the rules are changing. What has worked in the past is increasingly inadequate in the face of these rapidly shifting times. With all of this apparent destruction of our way of life, at times it's easy to fall into fear that we are indeed facing the end of days. Through examining ancient ceremonies of various indigenous tribes, I will illustrate the larger cycles that are currently affecting us and provide a greater understanding of the tsunami of change now upon our world. Through this understanding one can choose to be propelled by the current rather than taken out by the undertow. In other words, one can die with the old world or embrace the new one evolving. For generations the ancients have been tracking these changes; yet our modern, scientifically based societies have lost sight of the cohesion of the universe and our ever-evolving place in it.

## A QUESTION OF BALANCE

As far back as we have recorded history, indigenous tribes have had some form of ceremony for balancing Heaven and Earth. Over the generations, many of the ceremonies and their purposes have become distorted from the original intent, which was to align the people with the energies present at any given time at their location on Earth. Note: it is the people being balanced, not the heavens or the Earth. The Earth and stars managed to maintain balance long before humans appeared on the planet, and I strongly suspect they will continue long after we are gone.

In ancient times, a shaman or medicine person would perform ceremony at designated times and places. Through these sacred rites, the shaman would align their people with the entire symphony of frequencies being presented by the universe. Many ceremonies were performed at sacred sites and landmarks on the planet in order to better attune to the movement of stellar constellations. These practices were often held at times of seasonal change such as equinoxes, solstices. Once the frequency calibration was embodied by the shaman or holy person, it was then available for the tribe's people to align with. In this way, the indigenous people remained aligned with, and therefore supported by, the evolving frequencies of the universe.

Ancient record keepers were able to predict many future trends on the planet based upon the long-term tracking of influences of the past. One of the prophesied influences we are now experiencing is the phenomenon of accelerated time. This phenomenon, predicted by many religious texts, including the Bible, is explained by the Mayan Calendar.

## The Mayan Calendar

At the risk of revisiting a subject that has been discussed for decades, it is important that we realize that just because the inter operation of the Mayan Calendar has been subjected to much hype doesn't mean the calendar itself is not accurate and valuable. The Mayan religious practitioners were both mathematicians and shaman. They employed a system called the Long Count Calendar to compute cosmic and historical cycles. The Mayan Calendar placed mathematical values upon the emerging patterns of varying galactic frequencies, thereby creating a model for divining the course of human history.

*Approximation of "World" Ages*

*First World: 18,489 BC – 13,364 BC*
*Second World: 13,364 BC – 8,239 BC*
*Third World: 8,239 BC – 3,114 BC*
*4th World: 3,114 BC – 2012 CE*

The Mayan Calendar is the most accurate calendar of our time, yet it remains a mystery how such an ancient culture with no technology obtained such advanced knowledge of galactic cycles. Many legends surrounding its source indicate that the calendar was given to the Maya by prophets from the Pleiades constellation, who were said to have visited the Earth to impart knowledge to the Mayan people.

The Long Count Calendar contains periods of time referred to as "worlds," or cycles of emergence. The present or 4th World began around August 11, 3114 BC. The beginning or emergence of the 4th World involved a process rather than a singular event.

According to the Long Count Calendar, the Fourth World was scheduled to end around December 21, 2012. There was much speculation that this date would mark the end of the world. Actually, it marked our present point in time as a transition point from the 4th World to the 5th World.

Many myths, legends, prophecies, and scriptures, including the Bible, speak of the "End of Days." Again, some schools of thought interpret this to indicate the end of the physical world. The Old Testament of the Bible was originally written in Hebrew. The Hebrew word "yom" currently translated as "day" (in the King James version of the Old Testament) can actually mean anywhere from 12 hours up to a year, or even a "time period" of unspecified length. The prophesied "end of days," as we will see later in this chapter, is actually a phenomenon that is developing as we transition from the Fourth World to the Fifth World and involves a process covering a "time period" rather than being a singular event.

In many of these prophecies, it is mentioned that during the end days, time will accelerate. The Mayan Calendar offers an explanation of the acceleration of time that we are now indeed experiencing.

I don't claim to have extensive knowledge of the Mayan calendar, as it is extremely involved and detailed. Much of the information we have on the calendar is from ancient paintings on walls created by scribes who themselves may have been puzzling over the complex concepts contained within it. With that said, the Mayan pyramids were built based upon the Mayan Calendar, with each tier of the pyramid representing a single age of the Calendar. These ages differ from what we normally think of as ages, such as the Iron Age and the Industrial Age, which are dictated by human events, or geological eras, but instead are based on the *cyclic* workings of the universe. The Mayan Pyramid is not the calendar itself but will be used as a visual aid to assist our understanding of the workings of the Mayan Calendar. Each "age" is divided into sections or periods of time referred to as "days" and "nights," which do not refer to the daily rising and setting of the sun. Each day and night has unique energies that support different events, types of activities or qualities of movement specific to each "age." Individuals and cultures are equally affected by the energies present within each age.

The Mayan Calendar tracks the varying influences humans are subject to as the solar system moves through the galaxy and the galaxy moves through the universe. The Calendar begins at the base of the pyramid and moves up nine tiers. Each of these nine tiers is divided into segments, which are also referred to as "days" and "nights." There are seven days and six nights per tier, adding up to 13 divisions. Each day and night brings different energies into play in accordance with the Earth's changing position in the galaxy. That is to say, the first day brings into play different energies or influences than the first night, which are both unlike the second day, and so

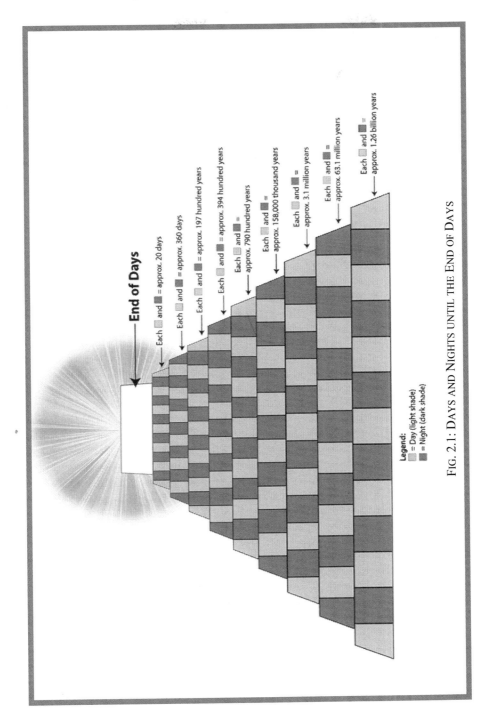

Fig. 2.1: Days and Nights until the End of Days

on. Each tier represents a different age and is divergent from each of the other tiers or ages. The first day on the first tier is not the same as the first day on the second tier.

The amount of time in each age decreases with each rising tier of the pyramid, resulting in a compression of the time spent in each day and each night. The first age represented by the first tier (ground level of the pyramid) began approximately 10.4 billion years ago, at which time each day and each night was around 1.26 billion years long. The ninth tier began around February 2011, with each day and each night in this tier spanning approximately 20 days. While, at the level of the first tier, a single day or night spanned millions of generations, at the ninth tier, movement from day to night occurs approximately every three weeks. This is acceleration of time in massive proportion.

These figures are rough approximations but close enough to give us a working idea of the concept. In Figure 2.1, as you can see, the base of the pyramid has the most time distributed between the days and nights. Moving up one-tier, there is the same number of days/nights, but these are distributed over a shorter period of time. This systematic lessening of the time spent in each day and night, reflected in each elevation of the tiers, results in moving through cycles and energies more rapidly. The faster we move through days and nights, the more expansive the frequency we are subject to, so each generation is exposed to more influences than the previous generation. During the time of the first tier, where each day and each night was 1.26 billion years long, the ramifications of a single action did not have an effect for many generations. This multi-generational delay between action and result is the genesis of the expression that one's actions will affect one's descendants "until the seventh generation." Now, however, we are reaping the rewards of our actions almost immediately—instant karma, if you will.

Another phenomenon of the acceleration of time is the ever-expanding concept of truth. When things were changing very slowly, reality was like a single-frame image or a photograph, as opposed to a motion picture or video. We can apply all sorts of interpretations to a still image that can be proven false when we see the picture in motion. As an example, what do you suppose is about to occur in Fig. 2.2?

FIG. 2.2: YOUR INTERPRETATION?

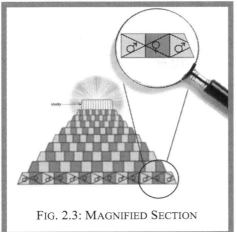

FIG. 2.3: MAGNIFIED SECTION

At left is a magnified section of the first tier of the Mayan Calendar, showing a day, a night, and a day. If we use the analogy of the still photograph, we can see that each day and each night within each of the ages is a slightly different reality like a still-frame photograph. In addition, each day is a positive polarity and a masculine expression, and each night is a negative polarity and a feminine energy.

As we pass from day to night, we undergo a polarity reversal. The faster we undergo polarity reversals, the closer we come to unity. This is much like creating a flip book out of numerous still photographs, then thumbing through the pages very quickly. What was a book of still photos becomes a moving picture depicting an event. The still photograph leaves room to fill in a story that may or may not reflect the truth of the actual event. By living in a time of still photographs, much room is left for individuals and cultures to create their own realities. These divergent realities not only promote alienation but also leave much room for manipulation of the truth. If one can manipulate the truth, one can control the actions of others.

FIG. 2.4: IN THE LEFT STILL IMAGE, ONE MIGHT PERCEIVE THAT THE PERSON ON THE LEFT IS ABOUT TO STRIKE THE PERSON ON THE RIGHT, BUT PROVIDING THE CONTEXT CHANGES THE PERCEPTION.

APOCALYPSE?

The model of the Mayan Calendar most often presented leaves the impression that the Calendar ended on December 21, 2012. Yet, recent discoveries dispute this belief: An astronomical calendar was unearthed from a filled-in scribe's room in the ruins of Xultun in Guatemala that indicates that the Mayan calendar extends well beyond this date.

Since we've established that everything in nature is cyclic rather than linear, I propose that *around* the date December 21, 2012, we entered the tenth tier of the Mayan pyramid, where time is so accelerated as to become unified. This period of unity marks the end of an entire cycle (the 4th World) only to begin again with another pyramid of cycles (the 5th World) upended on the top of the first pyramid (see Figure 2.5).

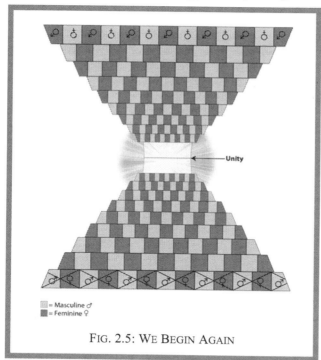

= Masculine ♂
= Feminine ♀

FIG. 2.5: WE BEGIN AGAIN

Instead of Armageddon, the prophesied "end of the world," represented a time when we came to the end of the influence holding the Fourth World together. We are entering the energetic matrix with new frequencies that support the Fifth World. The end of days or end of linear time is when we enter unity or the neutral point as we pass from one polarity to another. The neutral point between polarities is characterized by the eternal present. These repeating, equal but opposite (positive and negative) cycles of ascension and descension and resulting expansion and contraction would follow natural law in accordance with the rest of life.

Why then, one might ask, did the Mayan Calendar not indicate a repeat of the cycle? Who is to say? Eventually, it may be discovered that it did. The Calendar is based upon the interrelated cyclical movements of our planet, the solar system and our galaxy within the universe. As the Earth's position changes in relationship to other heavenly bodies, additional influences came into play after December 21, 2012, which necessitates modifications in the next cycle of the Calendar. In nature, the expansion and contraction of all things is not a repeating circle of events but rather a spiral upward or downward, which depends upon whether we are in a cycle of creation or one of destruction, respectively. For example, every year we have the budding of spring, the growth of summer, the harvest of fall, and decay in winter. Yet, while these cycles repeat each year, there are no two full cycles exactly alike.

Taking all of this into consideration, apparently the "primitive" Mayans had a better handle on the complicated astrological cycles than our "advanced" sciences can master. Go figure.

Later in this chapter and the one following, the astrological perspective will be covered more in depth. Let's now look at the influences created by the acceleration of time.

### SHE'S BREAKING UP CAPTAIN!

An illustration of the effects of acceleration can be found in aviation history. When airplanes were first invented, the original models were somewhat boxy in shape, with exterior rivets, cables, and landing gear, and, in some cases, two sets of wings. In short, the older models had massive amounts of what is now called "drag." Airplanes similar to these original models are still in use today for crop dusting, as these planes are great for slow, low-level flight.

When the decision was made to attempt to break the sound barrier, bigger, more powerful engines were put on the existing model of airplane. It soon became evident that the old models would not do. It was discovered that at higher speeds, wind resistance became a problem. What held together just fine at lower speeds started to shake apart when pushed beyond a certain speed.

FIG. 2.6: AN EARLY JET AIRCRAFT

This is when aerodynamics was discovered. Engineers realized that by recessing the rivets and encasing the engine and cables, they could make the skin of the aircraft smoother. This enabled the aircraft to go faster before running the risk of shaking apart, but it still didn't hold up under the speed required to break the sound barrier. Retractable landing gear was invented, which helped, as did streamlining the overall shape of the craft. The aircraft that finally broke the sound barrier look much like the jets of today. (See Fig. 2.6)

This is not unlike what we are going through today as we are challenged with the intensity of rapidly changing ages. We are moving into a time when the frequency is becoming much more intense. This is like moving faster through the air in an old bi-plane—everything that is of a less expansive frequency becomes drag. That is to say, any place within us that is not resonating with the frequency currently bathing the planet becomes drag. I call these places of restriction *miasms*, which we will examine further in "A Magic Temple." Miasms are blockages or areas that have lost mobility within our physical, emotional, mental, or spiritual bodies. Miasms occur when we have been forced to set aside our natural expression and interaction with the world to compensate for the people and events around us. These compensations limit our natural ability to express a wide range of frequencies.

The disparity between our restricted, compensated expression and our natural, more fluid state is caused by, among many other things, socialization. Children are socialized into behaviors and beliefs that are not necessarily in alignment with their true expression—their original expression having been much more aligned with nature. Constantly responding in a way that is not natural to us takes additional energy—first to block our natural response, then to assume the culturally accepted responses that allow us to fit into society. Our options within our set, as discussed in "Wheels Within Wheels." become increasingly compromised, limiting our mobility, which restricts our ability to align with the ever-changing frequencies of the seasons, the planet, and our position in the universe. Behaving in ways that are alien to our nature results in a configuration that is less flexible, and therefore, less "aerodynamic." In short, we have more "drag."

In the past, when life was moving more slowly, the blockages in our natural expression were not as problematic, but as we are subjected to the acceleration of time, we begin to shake apart, so to speak.

> ~ *AT GREATER SPEEDS OR FREQUENCIES,*
> *WE EITHER INTEGRATE OR DISINTEGRATE.* ~

Each place where we have disconnected from our options or true expression serves as a restriction that causes drag. More pressure is being applied upon those places where we are not in true expression than ever before.

We are being challenged wherever we are not in integrity with nature.

This leaves us with three choices:

1) Reexamine our behaviors and beliefs, in order to heal and release compensatory behavior;

2) Shut down altogether, as any movement puts further pressure on us; or

3) Be turned upside down and shaken until the change falls out of our pockets.

Evolution or devolution is the result, depending upon our personal choices and willingness to face our pain, uncover our illusions, and process through our damage.

My mother chose option number two when she emotionally shut down to the point where she no longer had enough mobility or frequency to maintain physical life.

## LET THERE BE DARKNESS, LET THERE BE LIGHT

Another, more cyclical, approach to the times we now find ourselves in is implicit in the concept of the Photon Band, which purportedly is a band of high-frequency particles existing in a place in our galaxy that our sun periodically and predictably passes through. This Photon Band is linked to the ages of the Zodiac. There are the ages of lower frequency, which are strongest in Scorpio and Taurus. I refer to these ages as the long dark, during which our perceptions are more limited (the horizontal band

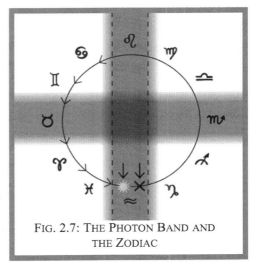

FIG. 2.7: THE PHOTON BAND AND THE ZODIAC

in Figure 2.7). There are ages of high frequency, which support enlightenment and are most intense in Leo and Aquarius (the vertical band). These are related to, but not to be confused with, *multidimensionality*, which is the ability to access multiple frequencies, and therefore multiple realities, at the same time. Also, *light* within the context that I'll be using it refers to the increasing levels of multidimensionality in both the "dark-light" feminine frequencies and the "light-light" masculine frequencies. These are concepts that I will discuss again in "Smoke and Mirrors." then delve into further in "The Natural Law." The long dark refers to the times when our access to both dark-light and light-light are more restricted, while during the times or ages of enlightenment we have greater access to both dark-light and light-light.

Our sun is currently moving into the enlightenment, or higher-frequency, band as we draw closer to the Age of Aquarius. Understanding the movement through the Photon Band helps explain the intensities we are now experiencing.

There are five different methods of spiritual connection that are available as the sun moves counterclockwise through the ages of the zodiac—unity, wise ones, shaman, monk, and dogma. These five levels correspond to the energy, or level of frequency, available when our sun changes position in relation to the Photon Band (see Figure 2.8).

1) *Unity:* The last time we were in the Photon Band was in the age of Leo. This is the age of the legends about the garden when "man was one with God." In the ages of highest (or more expansive) frequency, we become less dense and have more direct access to spiritual information.

2) *Wise Ones:* As our sun started to move out of the age of unity in Leo on its way around the galaxy, only the people who possessed a genetic predisposition for more sensitivity to expansive frequencies remained in direct contact with spiritual information. The rest of the people relied on these wise ones for guidance. I call this the age of the wise men and women.

3) *Shaman:* Moving farther away from the Photon Band, only those with a genetic predisposition who were also *doing ceremony* to further raise their frequency could access spiritual information. I refer to this as the age of the shaman.

4) *Monks:* Along the path into the long dark, only those with a genetic predisposition who were doing ceremony, and who were *cloistered from the general populace,* could access spiritual information. I call this the age of the monks.

5) *Dogma:* Finally, in the age of Taurus, all that was left were the ceremonies and scriptures with virtually no one having direct access to spirit or unity. This is in the center of the long dark—the age of dogma. Those who performed or interpreted the scriptures and ceremonies were the only spiritual guidance available.

The age of Taurus—the time of greatest polarization and least light or frequency—was when the information became greatly distorted and compartmentalized (not to mention exploited). Like a motion picture in freeze frame, much was lost, and the people began to war over the "truth." It was believed that whoever had the "truth" was right, and "might makes right," (as in whoever overpowered prevailed and got to dictate reality).

As the sun continues its path around the ages and moves beyond Taurus, the process reverses. First we reenter the age of the monks, where gifted individuals who are cloistered and perform ceremony can once again obtain direct spiritual information. Then the age of the shaman returns, which is available to us now.

By working with well-trained, shamanically gifted individuals, and undergoing sha-

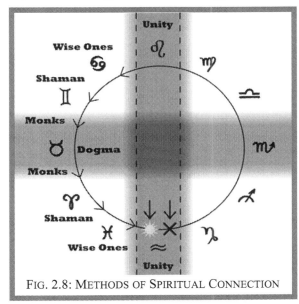

FIG. 2.8: METHODS OF SPIRITUAL CONNECTION

manic healing, we can continue to evolve and catch up with the times. The next step, the age of the wise ones, can be embraced by those who have healed enough to contain the higher frequency (amplified light), which is becoming increasingly available. This age is moving forward very quickly now. Already, wise ones are among us as we move toward the time when all of those who have participated in the evolutionary process have the opportunity to directly access their own spiritual information.

Regardless of the age we are living in, we are not all operating at the same frequency at any given time. There are groups of people in every age that reside in each frequency, creating different realities. As individuals, we can undergo this evolutionary process during any age. This is why we have had prophets (wise ones) during various ages when there was insufficient light to support them. Jesus, who reportedly had direct access to spirit, came during the age of Pisces, which is not fully in the light. Hitler also came in the age of Pisces, which is not fully in the long dark.

We are now coming into an age that supports enlightenment or direct access to spiritual information. At any given time, we have two separate processes going on—one within each individual and the other occurring within the masses. The ages influence the general tendencies of both. The masses control what we view as agreed-upon reality. Radical change can come about when enough individuals come into agreement at a higher- or lower-frequency reality. By creating a critical mass, or the "hundredth monkey theory," first presented by Ken Keys, Jr., the agreed-upon reality of the masses can be shifted. In this way, the choices of the individual affect the quality and quantity of our evolution.

At this point it is easy to judge against the long dark and favor the ages of enlightenment. I would like to point out that there is no wrong or bad age—each offers its own lessons. I would hazard to guess that we each incarnate during the age we choose to participate in and experience.

What is important about this process is the balance maintained by the cyclic movement from unity and wholeness to polarization and compartmentalization and back again. In any given age, all of these energies are alive within each of us. How we choose to use them is entirely up to us.

The cyclic nature of this model is in agreement with my proposal that the Mayan Calendar is a repeating cycle. Furthermore, the cycles continue in a spiral configuration, with each cycle slightly different than the last, according to the differing positions in the universe when each cycle repeats. Our solar system is subjected to an ever-changing symphony of frequencies created by our shift in relative position to the Photon Band as well as to our neighboring galaxies.

I am not saying we are in for a smooth ride—I have never known process to be overly neat and tidy. Much like a chemical reaction, there's a whole lot of destroying and rebuilding going on. How we weather it depends upon how connected we are.

Today, most humans are extremely disconnected from life and all of its cycles, galactic and earthly. During the tsunamis that occurred in Indonesia and Japan, many animals that were not confined moved to higher ground long before the monster wave hit land. Only the humans stayed close to the ocean, either unaware of the impending disaster, or disbelieving how bad it could be even as they watched it coming.

## LIKE A GOOD NEIGHBOR...THE SAGITTARIUS DWARF GALAXY

The discovery of the Sagittarius Dwarf Galaxy (see Fig. 2.9) adds another interesting slant to the overall picture. The Sagittarius Dwarf Elliptical Galaxy, as it is fondly referred to by astronomers, was unknown until 1994, when the main cluster was officially discovered, using stellar brightness density investigations. In February 1998, a team of astronomers headed by Rosemary Wyse of the Johns Hopkins University using a Two-Micron All Sky Survey employing infrared light, mapped the Sagittarius Dwarf Galaxy and discovered that it, in fact, orbits the Milky Way Galaxy. At that time, the Sagittarius Dwarf Galaxy became the nearest known neighbor to our

Milky Way. It is currently thought to be the second closest external galaxy after the Canis Major Dwarf Galaxy.

FIG. 2.9: THE SAGITTARIUS DWARF GALAXY INTERSECTING THE MILKY WAY

The Sagittarius Dwarf Galaxy is noteworthy here as an example of ever-shifting stellar influences. Due to its orbit around our galaxy, the Sagittarius Dwarf Galaxy is thought to have passed through the central region of the Milky Way Galaxy at least 10 times during the Milky Way's lifetime. The extended loop-shaped ellipse of the Sagittarius Dwarf Galaxy is currently extended around and through our solar system's local space. The Sagittarius Dwarf Galaxy is much smaller and less dense than the Milky Way, and as a result, this Galaxy is slowly being absorbed into our larger galaxy. This may lead to many of Sagittarius Dwarf Galaxy's stars becoming part of the Milky Way. If we consider this not only from an astronomer's but also from an astrologer's point of view, stars from another galaxy passing by and possibly even joining our local scene would drastically change the astrological frequencies to which we are subject. While Sagittarius Dwarf Galaxy's influences are not new, having been present for longer than recorded time, the Earth's proximity to, and polar alignment with, the galaxy is always changing, slightly altering the energies brought to bear.

In Figure 2.9, our galaxy is represented by the center spiral. The dot on its outer left is the relative position of our sun. The swooping band running from left to right is the extended loop-shaped ellipse of the Sagittarius Dwarf Elliptical Galaxy. As the picture illustrates, an arm of the Sagittarius Galaxy is currently passing directly through the position of our solar system as it has for millions of years.

As we have discussed, the relative proximity of the Earth to different star systems and other heavenly bodies greatly alters the symphony of frequencies that bathe the Earth at any given time. In light of this, we can only imagine the impact of Earth's interaction with an entire arm of another galaxy, containing countless star systems, virtually passing through our back yard.

While the Sagittarius Dwarf Elliptical Galaxy's orbital period around the Milky Way lasts around a billion years, the Earth's movement relative to it changes on a daily basis. The positioning of the Earth relative to that of the Sagittarius Galaxy is only one example of the ever changing influences that may necessitate an alteration in the Mayan Calendar for the next cycle. While scientists just became aware of the Sagittarius Galaxy in 1994, the Mayan Calendar appears to have taken it and possibly many other factors, yet to be discovered, into consideration. This makes the sophistication of the knowledge base behind the Mayan calendar even more astounding.

The calendars we now use are based upon the Earth's movement around the sun. The Mayan Calendar was based on the wheels within wheels that are created by the movement of our solar system within the Milky Way and its periodic interaction with various star systems and heavenly bodies. This makes the Mayan Calendar the most accurate calendar known today.

The implications here are multifaceted. The proximity of the two galaxies, the Milky Way and the Sagittarius Dwarf Galaxy, changes in a cyclic and therefore somewhat predictable manner. Because the Milky Way Galaxy spins like a wheel, as does the Sagittarius Dwarf Galaxy, these two galaxies virtually never encounter each other in exactly the same way. The Milky Way Galaxy cannibalizing solar systems from the Sagittarius Galaxy results in no two complete identical cycles. This creates a spiral effect within the repeating cycles. While each full cycle can be viewed as a series of wheels within wheels, the repeated cycles create a spiral necessitating a new calendar of events. This modified repeat or spiral configuration is in line with everything else in nature. Every year we have four seasons; each year the seasons are somewhat different.

In Figure 2.10, we see an artist's rendition of the Earth and her neighboring planets as they spin around the sun.

In Figure 2.11, another artist's rendition displays our sun, (the dot on the left) as it spins around the Milky Way Galaxy, (the center swirl), and interacts with the extended loop-shaped ellipse of the Sagittarius Galaxy, (the swooping band).

Figure 2.12 is a drawing from the Mayan Calendar that displays the wheels within wheels and cycles within cycles taken into account by the complex structure of the Mayan Calendar.

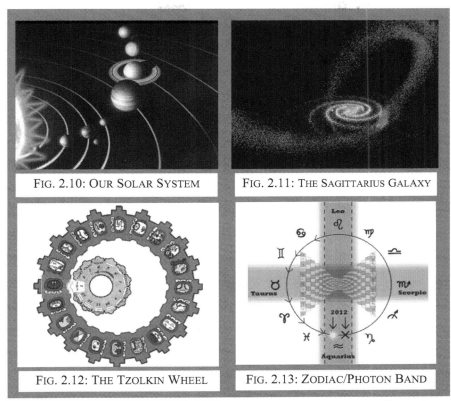

FIG. 2.10: OUR SOLAR SYSTEM

FIG. 2.11: THE SAGITTARIUS GALAXY

FIG. 2.12: THE TZOLKIN WHEEL

FIG. 2.13: ZODIAC/PHOTON BAND

And finally, in Figure 2.13, we see the repeating Mayan configuration superimposed over the ages of the zodiac and the Photon Band model.

The above illustrations provide a dramatic visual representation of the complex and cyclic influences represented by the Mayan Calendar. It also shows the galactic changes occurring that accompany the end of the Mayan 4th World, which indicates that we have simply come to the end of a cycle of influences and are in the process of entering a new cycle.

It would appear that we are in for some exciting times. Let's examine an overview of these wheels within wheels also alluded to in the Old Testament book of Ezekiel (see the text box on pg. 36). The first wheel found in the astrological signs, we call the horoscope. The yearly astrological calendar tracks the Earth's position relative to the sun, based on the sun signs of each of the astrological signs. These signs change approximately every 28 days. For instance people born between March 21 and April 19 in any given year would be born under the sign of Aries. The second "wheel" is comprised of the astrological ages within the progression of equinoxes, which results from the Earth's wobble as she spins on her axis, changing the orientation of her north pole at the time of the equinoxes. This cyclic shift in direction of the Earth's North Pole dictates the astrological ages. Each age lasts approximately 2,160 years. Every individual on Earth is being impacted by their personal sun sign, the current monthly sign of the zodiac and the current astrological age. Additionally, the sun is spinning around the galaxy and the galaxies spin around each other as they in turn spin around the universe. When all of this motion is charted out, it looks like wheels set within wheels.

The movement of our sun within the galaxy produces the different influences of astrological ages. As we pass through different astrological ages we are influenced by the Photon Band in varying intensities. The Mayan Calendar tracks the movement of our galaxy and the resulting influences. As the Earth's orientation changes relative to the Sagittarius Dwarf Galaxy (and possibly many other galaxies yet to be discovered) we are being subjected to additional dynamic frequencies.

At this point your head is probably spinning as well. Rest assured that we will go into a much more detailed explanation of the astrological signs and the progression of equinoxes in the next chapter.

Myths and legends have spoken of repeating cycles. Even if we have been in this portion of the cycles in the past, as most legends indicate, it is unlikely that we have been in this exact configuration before. From a much higher perspective, even these much larger cycles eventually repeat. Yet relative to the unfathomable age of the universe, humans have been around only a short time. We lack the long-term perspective necessary to chart these grand cycles that so touch our lives. While we have no chart of the cosmic scheme, we do have a compass. This compass was and is accessed by shaman and is found in nature.

*I saw a wheel on the ground beside each creature with its four faces. [16] This was the appearance and structure of the wheels: They sparkled like topaz, and all four looked alike. Each appeared to be made like a wheel intersecting a wheel. [17] As they moved, they would go in any one of the four directions the creatures faced; the wheels did not change direction as the creatures went. [18] Their rims were high and awesome, and all four rims were full of eyes all around.*

*Ezekiel 1:15-21*

# 3

# Of Earth and Stars

As long as humankind has inhabited the planet, we have looked to the stars in wonder. Though today most of us spend more time watching television than star gazing, our ancient ancestors were well versed in our ever-changing position relative to the heavens. A common cross-culture practice was one of building structures on the surface of the planet to align with the sunrise on the equinoxes.

Some of these structures were designed to create amazing shadows, such as the temple of the feathered serpent at Chichen Itza (see Fig. 3.1). At this site the shadows cast by the rising sun create the feathered serpent Quetzalcoatl that ascends the nine terraces of the pyramid on the vernal (spring) equinox. Others frame the sun like the ancient Neolithic mound in Ireland or the Mayan site of Dzibilchaltún on the Yucatan Peninsula in Mexico. At this site the rising sun on the spring and

FIG. 3.1: CHICHEN ITZA

autumn equinoxes shines through a central doorway of the temple toward a single erect stone. Yet others were built to face the sun as it rises on the morning of the vernal equinox like the Sphinx at the Giza plateau in Egypt. There is also evidence that during the era of 10,970 to 8,810 BC, the Sphinx gazed directly toward the rising of the constellation of Leo, which would have preceded the sun at dawn on the spring equinox.

Why this widespread uncommon attention to that one day in the year? From basic calendric functions to more esoteric meanings, every culture has its myths and legends around the equinoxes. Most importantly, these structures were built by people in ancient times who had knowledge of the spiritual process that leads to enlightenment. This process has a direct relationship to the Earth's relative positioning in the heavens. These structures were created to house ceremonies designed to focus the cosmic eternal forces that support enlightenment.

The structures, built to focus the energies present on the equinoxes, are only one example of how the ancients sought to maintain balance and spiritual connection. Through establishing alignment to the cycles of Earth and the stars, our ancestors were supported by the power inherent in natural law. Through examination of the myths and legends of multiple cultures we can come to a greater understanding of this primordial knowledge.

## MYTHS, LEGENDS AND PROPHECIES

Every culture has its own myths, legends, and prophecies of the ancient past. These original cultures were Earth/star-based shamanic societies with an oral tradition and specifically assigned record keepers who saved the history in story form. What is fascinating about these stories is that from culture to culture there are similar themes. Ancient civilizations and societies including China, Babylonia, Wales, Russia, India, America, Hawaii, Scandinavia, Sumatra, Peru, and Polynesia all have versions of a giant flood—many occurring in the same geological time frame, and all profoundly similar to the biblical account.

The following is a Creation story told by Lee Brown from his book, *North American Indian Prophecies*.

### Guardianship

*There was the cycle of the mineral, the rock. There was the cycle of the plant. And now we are in the cycle of the animals, coming to the end of that and beginning the cycle of the human being.*

*When we get to the cycle of the human being, the highest and greatest powers that we have will be released to us.*

*They will be released from that light or soul that we carry to the mind. But right now we're coming to the end of the animal cycle, and we have investigated ourselves and learned what it is to be like an animal on this Earth.*

*At the beginning of this cycle of time long ago, the Great Spirit came down and He made an appearance and He gathered the peoples of this Earth together, they say on an island which is now beneath the water and he said to the human beings, "I'm going to send you to four directions, and over time I'm going to*

*give you some teachings, and you will call these the Original*
*Teachings and when you come back together with each other*
*you will share these so that you can live and have peace on*
*Earth, and a great civilization will come about." And he said,*
*"During the cycle of time I'm going to give each of you two*
*stone tablets. When I give you those stone tablets, don't cast*
*those upon the ground. If any of the brothers and sisters of the*
*four directions and the four colors cast their tablets on the*
*ground, not only will human beings have a hard time, but almost*
*the Earth itself will die."*

*And so he gave each of us a responsibility and we call that*
*the Guardianship.*

Anthropologists, sociologists, and historians, in an approach known as comparative mythology, have compared the mythologies of multiple societies in an attempt to discern global history. Immanuel Velikovsky's, *Ages in Chaos,*[1] first published in 1952, is an example of an attempt to identify shared themes and characteristics. Velikovsky's work points to interesting possibilities. By adjusting the time line of biblical and Egyptian history by 600 years, Velikovsky found that the two accounts, the Israeli and the Egyptian, became congruent. Both of these versions of history reported natural disasters or "plagues" which, with the 600-year time adjustment, lined up, creating a historical Egyptian account of the biblical Israelite Exodus.

Velikovsky believed the catastrophes that occurred within the memory of humankind were recorded in the myths, legends, and written history of all ancient cultures and civilizations. He proposed that this comparative mythology evidenced periodic natural catastrophes that were and can be global in scale. Immanuel Velikovsky's earlier work, *Worlds in Collision,*[2] first published in 1950, suggested that asteroids or comets orbiting the sun periodically pass close to the Earth. Velikovsky felt these close encounters may account for the phenomena reported in the Bible stories. If this is indeed the case, it serves as an example of how our relative position within the solar system, galaxy, and universe not only affects the frequency but also physical, geological, and climactic events on Earth. Furthermore, these incidents can be somewhat predictable if one knows where to look and how to interpret what one sees.

---

1. Velikovsky, Immanuel *(1952) Ages in Chaos,* Paradigm, Ltd. 2009
2. Velikovsky, Immanuel *(1950) Worlds in Collision,* Paradigm, Ltd. 2009

While *Worlds in Collision* was initially not well received, new geological and recently uncovered historical evidence lends this work more credence, which prompted a reprinted, unchanged edition to be published in 2009 as a nonfiction work.

Natural disasters are indeed natural, predictable, and recurring. Over the ages, shaman have been able to steer their people to safe passage by tapping into the frequencies and energies emanating from the universe. A biblical example of this level of shamanic mastery is the story of Moses, who led the Israelites out of Egypt.

Let's explore several indigenous teachings and practices from the Americas and Europe. By employing comparative mythology, we can gain a greater understanding of the changes we are currently facing. It is clear that the commonality among most native peoples is the concept of maintaining balance among the Earth, the planets, and the stars. While examples can be found in almost every nationality and culture, for expediency, I have chosen only two American Indian tribes—the Lakota and the Zuñi—and an overview of the ancient European Celtic traditions. But first, let's examine the following Lakota prophecy that eloquently speaks of the trends we are experiencing today.

## THE LAKOTA TRADITION

The Lakota, whose name means friends or allies, are a Native American tribe, descendants of the original inhabitants of North America. Most know them by the name of Sioux, given to them by the French, which was actually a derogatory name meaning throat slitter. They are one of seven related tribes inhabiting the most western portion of the United States including lands in both North and South Dakota. One of their most famous sacred ceremonial sites is Devil's Tower, in the Black Hills.

The Lakota exemplify a culture that rebalances its people with Heaven and Earth by annually performing ceremonies, during which the Earth's shifting relationship with all other heavenly bodies is taken into account by adjusting the people's relationship with the stars. In this way the Lakota people recalibrate annually, enabling them to stay in synch with the ever-changing frequencies of the universe. The Lakota have individuals from special, designated lineages who have passed these sacred ceremonies down their line. Each lineage and ceremony represents a star in a particular constellation. To this day, in the spring of each year, individuals from the Lakota nation go on a pilgrimage following the sun's path through the constellations, performing ceremony at the corresponding sacred sites in the Black Hills.

The following statement from Charlotte Black Elk is an example of the Lakota shaman attuning to the balance of Heaven and Earth and offering it to their people.

> *It is our rule that the pipe is so sacred that it must not be casually drawn. With the Black Hills Ceremonies of Spring, the pipe becomes symbolically present through the tobacco to fill the pipe, Pipestone quarry, the bowl of the pipe, with Devil's Tower, and the fire to light the pipe.*
>
> *As the pattern moves across the sun at daybreak and sunset, creation is filling, lighting and smoking the pipe with the sacred hoop—a hocoka, where all of creation is present, altogether.*
>
> *On Earth, the Lakota participate in this same ceremony of renewal, in the same way, a fulfillment of the Oneness of the entire universe.*
>
> *The ceremony on Earth and in heaven sends a voice that, with the four relations, we may live well in the manner suited to the way the Power of the World lives and moves to do its work that we may all walk with our generations in a dancing manner on the good red road.*
>
> *Charlotte A. Black Elk*
> *From: Ronald Goodman's* Lakota Star Knowledge

## ZUÑI SHALAKOS

The Zuñi people are a tribe of Pueblo Native Americans in the United States. The Zuñi Pueblo, consisting of approximately 12,000 people, is located about 150 miles west of Albuquerque, in the northwestern part of New Mexico. The Pueblo culture is located in the present-day Four Corners area of the United States, comprising southern Utah, northern Arizona, northwest New Mexico, and southern Colorado.

The Zuñi peoples also perform ceremonies to balance Heaven and Earth, the most outstanding of which are the Kachina dances. Shalako, one of the most famous, is a series of sacred dances, songs, and ceremonies conducted in the Zuñi Pueblo at the winter solstice, following the harvest. It celebrates the end of the old year and the beginning of the new year and blesses all of the Pueblo houses erected during the year.

The exact date of the Shalako is calculated annually by Zuñi medicine men, known as Zuñi Bow priests, who use an ancient formula passed down through the generations. Traditionally, the Shalako dance is held on the 49th day past the tenth full moon. This is yet another demonstration of an ancient people's strict adherence to heavenly cycles.

The Shalako dance also exemplifies traditional ceremonies performed by indigenous peoples to balance the members of the tribe with Heaven and Earth. It is understood that all illness is a result of being out of balance with one's environment. These sacred dances are considered essential healing practices for the well-being of the tribe.

The following transcription is from an interview with Clifford Mahooty, Zuñi Elder and member of the galaxy medicine society and the Kachina society:

> *The entire Kachina society is one priesthood that was formed as a representative of space beings or star people.*
>
> *It is believed that these star people used to come to the Zuñi from different star systems for ceremony to make sure they were following the orders given the Zuñi by the Creator.*
>
> *The Zuñi believe star beings are actually here with us but chosen members of the tribe represent the star beings by wearing masks or costumes designed to look like them.*
>
> *The star beings are able to be present with the people, yet remain in the higher dimensions by joining with the dancers, who serve as surrogates. The dancers wear masks and take on the particular energy or frequency of the star beings they represent. Each Kachina in the dance represents a different star system.*
>
> *Ceremony would be performed in the kivas to allow the surrogate to take on the essence of the star being they were to represent for the dance. Songs and dance are performed by the Kachina during this healing ceremony to balance the mind, body, and spirit of the people to that of the universe.*

## THE CELTIC APPROACH

When thinking of the Celtic traditions, we often envision people from Scotland and Ireland, when in fact, the Celts occupied what is now known as Eastern Europe, Greece, Spain, Northern Italy, Western Europe, England, Wales, Scotland, and Ireland. Anyone who has European ancestral roots most likely has some Celtic genealogy.

The Celtic culture goes back over 2,700 years. Like most indigenous cultures, their history and myths were originally preserved through the oral tradition. The earliest Celtic writings paint an ancient Celtic worldview that is poetic and anchored in a deep respect for nature. It views the spiritual and the material worlds as a seamless whole. The Celtic culture was integrated with nature and expressed itself through the principles of the natural world.

Celtic tradition and belief have not remained static, but have continuously developed and progressed without a break over the centuries.

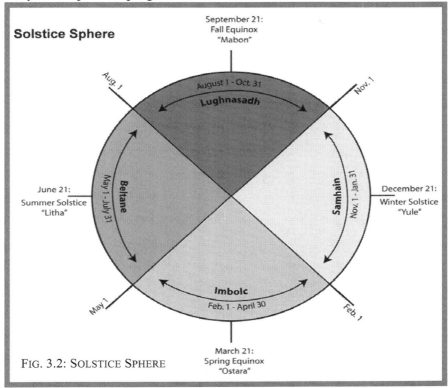

FIG. 3.2: SOLSTICE SPHERE

The Celts understood that all of existence has a cyclic nature, with everything existing on several simultaneous levels. They were aware of the direct continuity between the material world and the "other world" that interpenetrates and affects the visible world. As we will address later, the "other world" is a metaphoric representation of the unseen influences behind the laws of nature, or in other words, the quantum field.

The Celtic tradition is rich and extensive and, like other indigenous cultures, the Celts performed ceremony to honor and hold the alignment between humans, the Earth that sustained them, the stars and the seasons. The four most significant Celtic celebrations honoring the Earth's annual cycles fall at the midpoints between the equinoxes and solstices. In Fig. 3.2, you can see how Samhain (pronounced Sow'en) is the mid-point between the Fall Equinox and the Winter Solstice; Imbolc (pronounced Imm' ulk) is the half-way point between the Winter Solstice and the Spring Equinox; Beltane (pronounced Bell' tane) is the midpoint between the Spring Equinox and the Summer Solstice; and Lughnasadh (pronounced Loo' nassa) is the celebration of the midpoint between the Summer Solstice and the Fall Equinox.

## SAMHAIN

Samhain is the festival of harvest and marks the end of the growing season. The celebration itself is held on October 31 through November 1, while the Samhain season is November 1 through January 31. Samhain, the Celtic New Year, is considered to be the end of the light half of the year. Traditionally a time of inward turning and contemplation, Samhain is associated with the coming of death and remembrance of the ancestors. Bonfires were a large part of this ancient celebration. People would herd their livestock between two bonfires as a cleansing ritual. Bones of slaughtered livestock were cast into the fire to express gratitude.

## IMBOLC

Imbolc is the Celtic celebration performed to mark the beginning of spring. The Imbolc ritual is held February 1 through 2, while the season itself runs from February 1 through April 30. The Imbolc Festival, associated with the goddess St. Brigid, honors innocence, new beginnings, and the sowing of seeds for the coming year.

## BELTANE

Beltane, which takes place on the first day of May, or May Day, marks the midpoint in the sun's progress between the Spring Equinox and Summer Solstice. Its season runs from May 1 through July 31, during which the cycle of youth, passion, procreation and growth is honored. Beltane's infamous bonfires and amorous revelry from pagan times tend to overshadow our modern-day understanding of this sacred holiday.

## LUGHNASADH

Lughnasadh is celebrated on August 1 to honor both the physical and spiritual harvests of the previous months. Its season runs from August 1 through October 31 and is seen as a time to give thanks to the spirits and deities for the beginning of the harvest season. It also involves the offering of prayers and gifts in exchange for protection of the crops that remain in the field. This is considered the time to honor the god Lugh, a deity of storms and lightning. Lughnasadh is the first of the three autumn harvest festivals, the other two being the Fall Equinox and Samhain.

Many other cultures like the Lakota, Zuñi, Celts, and Mayans, understood that humankind would fall out of the natural order to the extreme detriment of the people unless periodic readjustment with the natural order of life was maintained. We are currently experiencing the detrimental effects of living out of balance with our environment. While we are quite impressed with our own advances in "conquering nature," we need only to look around to see that ill health, depression, and disease have reached epidemic proportions in our modern society.

## THE SKY IS FALLING

Cycles within cycles, wheels within wheels—the heavens are truly a mystery. We sit on our little grain of sand gazing out with the aid of our visual optics, and in our arrogance we profess to understand the workings of the universe and our place in it. Suddenly, an unplanned heavenly body pops into view, and our entire reality is shattered. "What do you mean it isn't all spinning around us? We are the center of the universe, right?"

We reach out with the technique of stellar-brightness-density investigations, and an entire galaxy heretofore undetected shows up in our celestial back yard. Scientists, while observing interstellar X-radiation, stumble upon a black hole in the center of our own galaxy. What do you suppose is on the other side?

> ### The Celestial Ballet
>
> *Dressed in gossamer blue and white, Terra pirouettes, her perpetual motion casting her first in light then in shadow.*
>
> *She dances in a counterclockwise circle while Luna, her understudy revolves around her in flawless accord.*
>
> *Together with other dancers they orbit around the golden prima donna who herself circles around the starlit stage.*
>
> *The music is harmonious, complex and ever changing as the dancers spin and twirl to its intonation.*
>
> *They live to dance, they dance to live, never questioning the composition or the choreography.*

In February, 2013, an enormous asteroid, estimated to be about 150 feet across and 143,300 tons, zipped between the Earth and its communication satellites. Its closest point was 17,200 miles away. A day later, a meteor exploded over Russia, breaking approximately 4,000 windows and injuring close to 1100 people. For over 30 seconds, the fireball lit up the sky in broad daylight, before detonating with the force of a 500-kiloton bomb. What was originally estimated to be a 10-ton rock, eventually weighed in at 10,000 tons, after being reevaluated by scientists around the world. Shortly after this event, a bright meteor streaked across the skies of California. It seems that Earth is just a ten-pin in some cosmic bowling alley.

We postulate and theorize in endless, often heated debate as if our knowledge of the universe will grant us dominion over it. Theories are disproven, but the universe continues her dance, undaunted by our feeble attempts to contain her.

With the understanding that we are precariously perched on an electron spinning around the nucleus of an atom in the body of God (see Fig. 3.3), I will not profess to fathom the functioning of the universe. Having stated that little disclaimer, let's play with what we think we may know in order to glean a slightly larger perspective of what is going on around us and the resulting influences upon us.

**You Are Here**

FIG. 3.3: OUR PLACE IN THE UNIVERSE

The Earth spins on her axis at a tilt and with a wobble. This creates our days, nights, and seasons as she travels around the sun in an elliptical orbit. The sun bathes the Earth in a particular symphony of frequencies providing, among many other things, warmth and light. The moon in turn spins around the Earth, creating tides and cycles of fertility, and reflecting sunlight laced with her particular eminence. Other planets also revolve around the sun, constantly yet cyclically changing in their orientation to, and influence on, the Earth, much like our moon.

Further out, other stars, each with a unique set of frequencies group together, forming constellations. Every constellation has a unique song of its own, which is added to the symphony of the galaxy. Each galaxy is but a single musician in the symphony of the universe.

## THE CELESTIAL SPHERE

The Celestial Sphere (see Fig. 3.4) is a model with which we can orient ourselves to heavenly bodies. The Celestial Sphere is an imaginary bubble around the Earth and is an exact reflection of the Earth in that the celestial north pole is aligned with the terrestrial north pole. The celestial equator is directly above and in the same plane as the Earth's equator and so on. I would point out that through the use of the Celestial Sphere, we observe the sky as it appears from Earth, not as it is. The problem inherent in all models, even those designed to map cycles, is that these models, by their very nature, tend to be frozen, while the only constant in the universe is change.

The Celestial Sphere is used by astronomers for various functions from mapping star charts, to constructing calendars and predicting eclipses. The

Celestial Sphere is also used by astrologers to understand the zodiac, create astrological charts for individuals, and to track the ages. For our purposes here, I will use a simplified model to demonstrate the precession of equinoxes through the ages of the Zodiac.

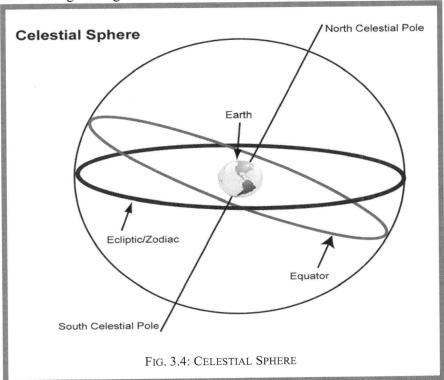

FIG. 3.4: CELESTIAL SPHERE

## THE ZODIAC

There are as many differing views on the zodiac as there are people to take them. We will limit ourselves to the traditional zodiac which dates back at least as far as the last age of Leo, running approximately from 11,000 to 9,000 B.C.E. (an interesting note aside, this is also the age of the great flood as recorded by Sumerian clay tablets).

The traditional zodiac resides on a band of the Celestial Sphere known as the Ecliptic, which is the imaginary line on the Celestial Sphere charted by the path that the sun appears to take around the Earth as viewed from the surface of the planet. (Note: the Celestial Sphere model has the sun appearing to orbit the Earth whereas we know the Earth actually is in an orbit around the sun.)

The Ecliptic is divided into twelve equal 30° segments, each representing one of the twelve houses of the zodiac. These houses, or signs of the zodiac, are each named after a constellation. While directly related, there is a distinct difference between signs of the zodiac and the constellations after which they are named. Each constellation is a group of stars, while its corresponding zodiac sign is one of the 30° segments located on the ecliptic band.

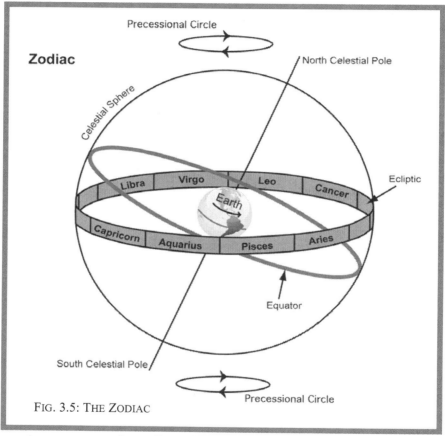

FIG. 3.5: THE ZODIAC

As we can see, the zodiac has numerous functions. For now we will be examining it as a calendar that marks beginnings and ends of ages, the twelve-month years, and the seasons.

Before I lead you to believe that we are about to set off on an interstellar trek requiring star maps, let me clarify. Every star puts out different color, light, radiation, gravitational pull and so on. Each constellation is a unique symphony of influences that affect us here on Earth in differing ways. We are using the zodiac as a map of the ages. Each age brings to bear different energetic influences created by Earth's relative positioning to vari-

ous heavenly bodies at any given time. The zodiac maps out these influences so accurately that it has been used by numerous cultures as a
divination tool with impressive results. Though we have regrettably lost
some of the original science, astrology continues to be used today.

## THE PRECESSION OF EQUINOXES

The straight line passing through the Earth represents its axis. At present,
the north axis points to Polaris, which we refer to as the North Star. While
we may think of the North Star as a constant, it is not—5,000 years ago, the
Earth's axis pointed to a star known as Thuban.

The wobble in the Earth's rotation causes its axis to trace two imaginary
circles (see Fig. 3.5) one at each end of the axis. These circles appear to
revolve counterclockwise from the Earth's perspective and complete an
entire revolution approximately every 25,700 years. It is this singularity that
causes the shift in the orientation of the planet's North Pole and creates a
phenomenon called "the precession of equinoxes." On Earth, these are the
times in spring and fall when day and night are equal in length. The Earth's
wobble is caused by gravitational forces of the sun, the moon, and other
heavenly bodies as each act upon the Earth's somewhat spheroid shape.

## IN A NUT SHELL

The Earth's relative position to the sun on her annual elliptical orbit creates
the monthly zodiac whereby we are under the influence of each sign for
approximately 30 to 31 days each year.

The zodiacal age is determined by where the Earth's wobble causes her
axis to point along the ecliptic at the time of the vernal equinox. Each of
these ages lasts approximately 2,150 years.

A person's sun sign or what we commonly think of as their sign of the
zodiac is determined by the triangulation created by the exact time they
were born, precise location on the planet and the position of the Earth relative to the sun. To do a person's chart, astrologers also take into account the
positioning of the moon and the other planets, but this gives us a general
idea of the mechanics involved. The significance of a person's astrological
sign is that it maps the particular frequency or harmonic they were attuned
to at birth and will personally be subject to throughout their life time.

At any given time each individual on the planet is under the influence of
their personal birth sign as well as the monthly sign and the overlording
influences of the current age that affect the entire planet.

If we consider the numerous and varied influences of different stars and
constellations at any given time, it stands to reason that any change in our

orientation to them creates a change in our overall experience on many levels. It is this shift in influence that is the basis of astrological charts and the differing global influences charted by the ages reflected in the Mayan Calendar.

## GALACTIC CENTER

While there are many galaxies and therefore many galactic centers, we will be concerned with only the rotational center of the Milky Way Galaxy, which purportedly contains a black hole, whose mass is nearly three million times more than the Sun.

A black hole is a region of space-time so massive and compacted that not even light can escape its astonishing gravity. In fact, it is called "black" because it absorbs all light. Yet, paradoxically, black holes glow, unsteadily flickering, at all wavelengths from radio to gamma rays, emitting radiation so powerful that it is detectable from Earth. Black holes also eject impressive jets of charged particles into space. It is thought that this flickering and spewing is a result of the black hole consuming matter that is drawn in by its formidable gravitational pull.

When matter is pulled into a black hole, it results in what is referred to as the "silent scream," which is an explosion that produces shock waves, accelerating electrons near the black hole to nearly the speed of light. All this belching and screaming impacts everything in our galaxy and beyond in ways we can't even imagine.

The energy of each age is associated with major evolutionary and cultural shifts of the species. We are currently entering the Age of Aquarius when the Earth's axis passes from the 30° portion of the ecliptic that represents the constellation Pisces to that of Aquarius. As we enter the Age of Aquarius, the frequencies that characterize the Aquarian Constellation begin to rain down on Earth, bringing a new set of influences. Concurrently, for the first time in approximately 12,960 years, the Earth's axis is also leaning in the direction of galactic center, where all that belching and spewing is going on. Moreover, we're dancing with the Sagittarius Dwarf Galaxy and therefore subject to additional shifts in stellar influences. According to the Photon Band model (see Fig. 3.5), our sun entered the Photon Band of high-frequency particles, and around that same time, the 4th World of the Mayan calendar ended.

All of this activity changes the very rules we have previously been able to rely on, and it puts the Earth and all who live on her under greater pressure. When we look at the rapid evolutionary and cultural development of the species over the last 200 years, it becomes clear that we have been increasingly under this pressure our entire lifetimes, but things are now coming to a head, so to speak.

*~ YOU CAN ONLY PUSH THE BOUNDARIES OF AN AGREED-UPON
REALITY SO FAR BEFORE THAT REALITY SHATTERS,
LEAVING DESTRUCTION IN ITS WAKE. ~*

This is the true nature of life—expansion and contraction, building and destroying. Our bodies do it on a moment-by-moment basis, or we would die. The universe does it as well, so why not realities? Yet, realities are simply a set of frequencies that don't cease to exist just because we move beyond them. Some individuals will stay in the *old* reality to hold that frequency as a springboard for the next reality. Like a multiple-story building, if the foundation is not maintained, the structure will fall. When you get on an elevator and go from the ground level to the third floor, your reality alters to the one held by the third floor. Yet, the ground floor doesn't cease to exist just because you are now on the third floor.

Another way to view shifting realities is by comparing them to a chemical reaction. In a chemical reaction, only the elements drawn together to create the reaction change form. Soap, for instance, is formed by a chemical reaction called saponification. By combining lye and lard, among other things, and changing the frequency by adding

> **The New Heaven**
>
> *For, behold, I create a new heaven and a new Earth: and the former shall not be remembered, nor come into mind.*
>
> *Isaiah 65:16-18*
> *The Holy Bible*
> *King James Version*

heat, a chemical process takes place, creating soap. However, all the lye and lard in the world doesn't become soap just because the lye and lard we put into the pot undergoes a chemical change.

## UNITY CONSCIOUSNESS

While the energy of each age is associated with a major evolutionary and cultural advancement, the nature of that advancement is dictated by the age. Whereby the Age of Pisces typified the development of religions, the Age of Aquarius will bring enlightenment, personal freedom, and unity consciousness.

The more unified we become, the more we are in touch with All-That-Is, which will increasingly enable us to commune with the frequencies from both the Earth and the stars. Each of us has varying access to this guidance and information, depending upon where we are vibrating or at what frequency we reside. Again, we can refer to the ancient texts for the wisdom that still resides there. On page 52 in the box, "On Gifts," Corinthians 4-10 speaks beautifully about the many gifts that are available for each of us once we reach the frequency required to perform them. The closer we are to unity consciousness, the more we can be directed by these gifts.

Later in this work I will offer instruction in a technique that has been used over the ages known as the shamanic journey or trance, which is an easily learned, reliable method you can use to access and decode higher-frequency information. Even as we train ourselves to tap into the changing frequencies of the universe, many of us may find it most expedient to consult with shaman or wise ones to validate and translate the new information coming to us in order to be guided through these times of upheaval and change.

Just because we have almost eradicated shamanism on our planet doesn't mean shamanically gifted people have stopped being born. However, because we have nearly lost the ancient art under the grinding wheels of religious dogma, reliable shamanic training is hard to find, so many of our gifted channels lack the hard-to-find shamanic training that would help them accurately translate their information or discern its source.

> ### On Gifts
>
> *Now there are diversities of gifts, but the same Spirit.*
>
> *And there are differences of administrations, but the same Lord.*
>
> *And there are diversities of operations, but it is the same God which worketh all in all.*
>
> *But the manifestation of the Spirit is given to every man to profit withal.*
>
> *For to one is given by the Spirit the word of wisdom; to another the word of knowledge by the same Spirit;*
>
> *To another faith by the same Spirit; to another the gifts of healing by the same Spirit;*
>
> *To another the working of miracles; to another prophecy; to another discerning of spirits; to another diverse kinds of tongues; to another the interpretation of tongues:*
>
> *Corinthians 4-10*
> *The Holy Bible*

Channeling and divination are shamanic skills and there are many gifted individuals with us today who have a genetic predisposition to shamanic skills that allows them access to spiritual information. Some of these individuals are bringing valid channelings, with profound information to aid us. Many of these offerings are a mixed bag, as the light is only as clear as the window through which it shines. We are all limited by our level of processing and understanding at any given time.

~ *THERE IS NO ULTIMATE TRUTH. INSTEAD,*
*THERE ARE INFINITE LEVELS OF THE TRUTH,*
*DEPENDING UPON OUR FREQUENCY OR LEVEL OF REALITY.* ~

As we enter the Aquarian Age—a time of more direct access to spiritual information—it becomes necessary to acquire the skills needed to access and accurately decode this valuable material. Yet each of us is unique, and none share the same track in the evolutionary process. Spiritual information is, by its very nature, multidimensional—many truths are contained in one small piece. The truth that will pertain to any given individual at any given time depends on his or her level of reality. With this in mind, we can see why it is up to the individual to discern what spiritual information is valid and useful for them personally at any particular time. After you increase your skills using the shamanic journey (see page 161), you can use these ancient skills to receive and translate these profound messages from the Earth and the stars.

## THE WINDS OF CHANGE

There is considerable scientific evidence of the drastic changes that are upon us. There is much talk of global warming, yet there is strong evidence that all the other planets in our solar system are warming also. The magnetic north pole of the Earth is moving and aircraft are no longer able to land safely or reliably with "autopilot navigation." There is also evidence that the fluctuating magnetic north of the Earth is responsible for the increasing incidence of migrating birds losing their way. There has been a marked and measurable increase in the frequency and strength of earthquakes. Recent solar flares, observed by scientists on the space station, actually slowed the rate of radioactive decay. This discovery has challenged the existing scientific belief that the rate of radioactive decay is a constant. Even the Earth's ley lines and spiritual centers are in flux. The process of evolution can be a bumpy ride.

For humans, evolution is and always has been an inside job, affected by each person's personal path and choices. The Earth will make the necessary adjustments to accommodate the pressures brought about by the changing ages, with or without us. Individuals who have chosen to evolve with the Earth are responding according to their gifts. Some are being drawn to different acupuncture points on her surface where their very presence will provide an anchor for the rest of us during these shifts. Others are bringing forth spiritual information to help us surf the tides of change, while still others, through their own process, are providing the blueprint for the physical structure of the new human being.

From a shamanic standpoint, Earth spirits, animals, and our stellar ancestors are working overtime to provide much protection and guidance for the humans who have chosen this path. I have no doubt that each of us has an opportunity to make a difference. Rest assured that we need simply to follow the lead of our spirit guides and our own promptings.

While this shift into the new era progresses, there is no one "safe place" to be—it is different for each of us at any given time. We will be distributed to where we are needed, when we are needed, and we will be protected there. The new interplay of energies emerging is creating new sacred sites and de-activating the old ones to correspond with the changing heavens. These sites will provide us with the balance of frequencies we need to carry in order to be in alignment with our changing world—this organism we call Earth.

What is beneficial to remember is that at any time, the only constant seems to be change. I can't say that I know our future. I can say it is unprecedented and that I would rather find out as we go. Now is a time to let thought and prediction go and live by instinct and intuition. Today, more than ever, the "now" is the only thing we can be sure of. It is a grand adventure, is it not?

# 4

# Smoke and Mirrors

We have established that each age in the Zodiac and the Mayan Calendar carries a different configuration of frequencies. These varying frequencies support differing events and experiences on the planet. They also sustain diverse organizational formats. Different species thrive in various ages, and as ages change, some species evolve, while others dissolve. This is also true of all organizations, including our current societal structure.

*~ IN UNITY THERE IS NO "GOOD" NOR IS THERE "EVIL"*
*BUT VARYING DEGREES OF BALANCE. ~*

## THE FOOD CHAIN

In the denser/more polarized ages, we are less multidimensional—that is to say we have less access to multiple frequencies and therefore multiple realities at the same time. We require balanced light—levels of multidimensionality in both the "dark-light" feminine frequencies and "light-light" masculine frequencies to sustain us. Without the availability of direct access to this balanced light we have to find sustenance elsewhere (more on this in Chapter 5: The Natural Laws). For now suffice it to say that this decrease in multidimensionality necessitates killing to live and living to kill. Our very sustenance comes at the expense of others—plants, animals, human beings, and the very Earth herself. In short, the denser ages, during the long dark, promote physical, emotional, mental, and spiritual parasites. The machinery of our society has developed accordingly.

## WELCOME TO THE MACHINE

Though our current society served us in the past, it is unable to stand in the increasing velocity of the evolving age. Like a bi-plane trying to break the sound barrier, it is losing integrity, starting to shake apart, and its ugly underbelly is being exposed If we are to embrace the new world at hand, we must be willing to disentangle ourselves from the old, which requires a parasitical cleanse of sorts. To free ourselves of parasites, it is important to understand how they function in all their various forms and stages.

> Welcome my son, welcome to the Machine
>
> What did you dream?
> It's alright, we told you what to dream
>
> You dreamed of a big star,
> he played a mean guitar
>
> He always ate in the Steak Bar.
> He loved to drive in his Jaguar
>
> So welcome to the Machine.
>
> ~ Pink Floyd ~
> "Welcome to the Machine"

Know thy enemy. Yet, just like a parasitical infection, the enemy is within you as well as around you. Know thy self.

I am not recommending that we spend undue time scratching around in our past, nor do I advocate polarizing against parasites. The status quo is simply what thrived in the preceding frequency; we now have the opportunity to evolve beyond it. We do need to unveil enough of our current system to extract ourselves from it and reclaim our personal power. Only by pulling our power back from the exploitative system can we redirect it to create what we want in our lives. One of the first places we need to collect our power from is the universal lies perpetrated upon all of us by our culture.

There was a movie some years back that provides a great metaphor for this lie we have been living, "The Matrix." One great line from this film is: "The Matrix is the world that has been pulled over your eyes." In "The Matrix" the agreed-upon reality was actually generated by a computer program. All humans were hooked into this program to occupy their minds, while their bodies were being farmed for energy to feed aliens.

How does this relate? The consumer-based system we live in is designed to tell us lies and sell us a false reality. Through this false reality our personal power is appropriated to run the system rather than sustain our personal lives... "Welcome to the Machine."

## THE PYRAMID SCHEME

Once again using the pyramid configuration, let's look at our current societal structure based upon frequency and evolving realities.

At the base of the pyramid we find our hard-working masses. If we set aside the damage and patterns from which many operate, most people try to put in an honest day's work for an honest day's pay, aspiring to live a good life while providing for their families. They believe what they are shown, do what they are told, and to the best of their abilities, relate to each other honestly. They tend to believe in the basic benevolence of those above them. At this level, information is doled out from the tiers above on a need-to-know basis. If they only need to know positive numbers to function and serve, then negative numbers are not brought into the picture. After all, knowledge is considered power, and the more powerless they are in the bottom tier, the easier they are to control. The next tier up is in charge of the bottom tier, much like managers in a corporation. These "managers" enjoy the power of their position, but for the most part, are munificent to those below them. The managers are afforded more information than they share with their charges. They would not want to panic their employees with rumors of layoffs or mergers, for they might look elsewhere for employment before management is ready to surplus them.

At the management level it is still believed that the higher-ups will provide good severance packages for those being let go, so ultimately all will be well. The employees just don't need to know yet, and it is important to keep things operating smoothly. This is the manager's reality.

In the next level up, we have the supervisors who manage the managers. They have even more inside information. They know the

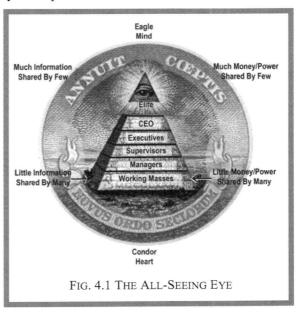

FIG. 4.1 THE ALL-SEEING EYE

company needs to trim the fat. After all, what are a few older employees, when they can get someone younger to do it for less? They must look at the big picture—the company has to make a profit to survive, and competition is stiff. Let the managers be all warm and fuzzy with the little guy. The supervisor has a more important job to do—a job that insures the company's well-being. This is the supervisors' reality.

This continues up the tiers through executives and CEOs until we reach the all-seeing-eye at the top of the pyramid. Here the social elite run the show by manipulating the realities, finances, and lives of those below them in order to feed off of the masses. After all, they are the elite, have been for generations, and it is their birthright to rule. This is the elite's reality.

This basic pyramid scheme is the structure underlying every organization in our current society, from schools and corporations to the government. The people in the bottom tiers are pulled around by their emotions or heart, which is characterized by an imbalance resulting from aligning more to the "dark-light" feminine frequencies. Those in the top tiers are controlled by logic or the mind, and aligned more to the "light-light" masculine frequencies. This imbalance is characterized by mental delusions and emotional disconnection. As we recall, *enlightenment* is the increasing levels of multidimensionality in both the "dark-light" feminine frequencies and "light-light" masculine frequencies. Any increase in one without an equal but opposite increase in the other results in the imbalance outlined above. The reference to light-light and dark-light is not to be confused with the *ages* of greater enlightenment, Leo and Aquarius, and *ages* of the long dark in Taurus and Scorpio. In the ages of greater light both light-light and dark-light are equally increased while in the long dark both light-light and dark-light are diminished. At the same time one is diminished more than the other, creating either a masculine or feminine imbalance.

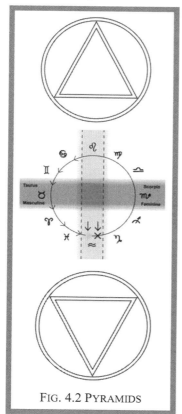

FIG. 4.2 PYRAMIDS

The top of the pyramid has evolved toward the masculine light without the counterbalance of the feminine. At the bottom tier there is little information, power, or wealth spread among many, while at the top there is much information, power, and wealth shared by few.

This is the pyramidal structure that develops in times of extreme polarization. Everything is pulled apart by this polarization and is taken to its most extreme point of distortion. This is not evil; instead, it is the simple expansion and contraction—breath in breath out, that is necessary for movement and therefore necessary for life.

The single pyramid we are currently examining (Fig. 4.1, top) was developed during a time of an extremely polarized masculine age, as we moved into the long dark in Taurus (left, middle. In times of extreme masculine polarization, the mind rules, ungrounded by the heart.

Directly opposite the age of Taurus (Fig. 4.1, middle) we find the age of Scorpio, which is also in the long dark, but it is a feminine age. In times of extreme feminine polarization, passions rule ungrounded by logic (Fig. 4.1, bottom).

## Programming

Before we get into a discussion on programming, it is important to note that it is not necessary or desirable to remove all of our programming at this time. To do so would produce individuals so refined that they could not survive in the current system. We are all addicted to something—it is just part of the equation. It is not a matter of removing all of the things that compromise our frequency, but instead becoming aware of those compromises and choosing which ones to address. In short, if while reading this, you discover you have a sacred cow that is a deal breaker for you—just hang on to that bovine as long as you like. There are many other things you can choose to address in order to evolve.

During times of a single pyramidal hierarchy, it is relatively easy to manipulate the masses. This manipulation is achieved and maintained by careful and systematic programming, which is designed to control the energy or frequency of individuals and groups. If frequency can be controlled, realities can be dictated, and tiers on the pyramid can be established according to the agendas of the ones in control.

> *"Everything is energy, and that's all there is to it. Match the frequency of the reality you want, and you cannot help but get that reality. It can be no other way. This is not philosophy; this is physics."*
> *~ Albert Einstein ~*

In order for this programming to be effective, the masses must be recalibrated on all four levels—physical, emotional, mental, and spiritual. One basic example of such programming can be found in our military "boot camps."

Physically, our recruits are compromised through poor-quality processed food, dangerous "immunizations," harsh living conditions, and exhausting rigorous exercise. This imbalance puts the body under extreme stress, which draws energy from all other levels in order to survive. After all, there is no point having a sharp mind without a body to carry it.

Emotionally, recruits become challenged by the physical stress and are ill prepared to defend themselves against the critical humiliation and shaming techniques employed by their superiors, which results in shattered self-esteem, a shutdown of the emotional realm, and a continual state of fight or flight.

Mentally, without a strong sense of self or emotion, they lose grounding in their former reality and more readily accept the now-agreed-upon "logical" reality being forced upon them. It is clearly demonstrated that resistance is futile. If they hope to remain safe, they had better toe the line dictated by the hierarchy. When in fight or flight mode, one does whatever is necessary to find safety. Flight is impossible without being hunted down for being AWOL, and fight is hopeless against such overpowering numbers, so compliance is the only remaining choice. "Yes sir!"

If the physical, emotional, and mental levels have been hacked into and are under siege, our overall frequency becomes so restricted that we have no conscious connection to the higher frequency or more unified realms. We then can no longer connect with universal guidance, sovereignty is compromised, and we are now totally subject to the will of the system in order to get what we need. Rather than following our intuition, we do what we are darn well told in order to survive. "Welcome to the Machine."

So how does all of this apply to our society, you might ask?

## PHYSICAL PROGRAMMING

Shortly after birth we are subjected to *mandatory* immunizations that have been proven to be quite dangerous.

Upon the birth of our first child, my then husband and I were deciding where we stood on immunizing our baby. Having had a friend whose infant died in her sleep following her first set of infant immunizations, I vigorously researched the subject. I had to dig fairly deep, but what I found horrified me.

There was a huge correlation between SIDS and immunizations. Furthermore, immunizations had been shown to compromise the child's immune system. Trying to understand why, with such risks, immunizations were *mandatory* I dug deeper. Apparently there was a "needs of the many vs. the lives of the few" mentality behind the law.

My husband and I decided to forgo immunizing our baby. Should there be a time when the disease posed a greater risk to her life than the immunization, we would revisit our decision. At that time, parents who had personal reasons not to immunize their children were legally allotted a personal exemption. We signed the necessary paperwork and refused immunizations.

Several years later when I had both of my children in the doctor's office for their *mandatory* school physicals, our physician apologetically informed me that the personal exemption had been rescinded, so only a medical or religious exemption was available. Because he could find no clear evidence that either child was allergic to immunizations, he said he regrettably could not give me a medical exemption. All that remained was a religious exemption.

I stared at him silently while he squirmed. Then placing one wrist dramatically against my forehead and my other hand over my heart, I threw my head back. In a resounding, thickly southern accented voice that would have done my Baptist minister grandfather proud, I declared "Ah feel the spirit a-comin' over me!"

I have since discovered that there is an even more sinister motivation behind *mandatory* immunizations and strongly recommended flu shots—lining the pockets of the drug companies while compromising the immune systems and physical frequency of the general population.

## Sugar in the Gas Tank

As I mentioned above, during times of decreased light/frequency, we must look to the life found in other things to sustain us. This requires a diet of organisms that were once alive. The major challenge we all face in maintaining a healthy diet is locating and procuring things with at least a little life left in them. The further a thing gets from its natural expression, the less its integrity and the more its drag; the less integrity, the less frequency; the less frequency, the less life.

The fact is—unless your grocery store carries organic, non-GMO, un-irradiated produce, there is probably nothing in the entire store that isn't long dead. Our food is so altered, manipulated, chemicalized, preserved, and polluted that it is no longer food at all, but counterfeit. It takes more energy/frequency to digest and assimilate this counterfeit food than we can possibly draw from it. As a result, we are consuming a diet of diminishing returns—literally starving to death while becoming obese with toxic overload.

Additives such as salt, processed sugar, corn syrup or genetically modified wheat are in virtually everything, starting with baby food. Chemical dyes and flavor enhancers lace nearly all packaged food, including many "fresh" meats. These additives not only seduce the palate, but they also compromise frequency. As an added bonus, they are quite addictive, so you keep coming back for more. This is very expedient—control and commerce all in one. Great Marketing!

*~ Strange, the desire for certain pleasure*
*is the source of my pain. ~*
*~ Kahlil Gibran ~*

If, by chance, there happens to be a small amount of contraband life-force left in the food you bring home, by all means microwave it. Microwaves—commonly used in almost every home and restaurant—alter the atomic structure of food to the point that the human body is unable to recognize or absorb it. Microwaves also alter the frequency of anything near when they are running, further compromising frequency. What results from consuming microwaved food doesn't bear thinking about, so let's just not think about it. We wouldn't want to have to go back to the messy affair of actually cooking, now would we? Ping! *Bon appetit.*

While we're avoiding things, let's not look too closely at school lunches either. Talk about child abuse! Chemical additives, dyes, sugar, and corn syrup have been linked to ADD and ADHD. Why do we have candy and pop machines in schools? Where is the FDA when we really need them? Why, out approving Ritalin, of course. While the placement of soda machines in our schools has decreased considerably since 2004, other sugary, high-calorie fruit and sports drinks are still readily available. There has also been a concerted effort in recent years to make more healthy food available in school lunches. Salads and fruits have been added to the menu among other more healthy choices. Yet, the fact remains that all the food offered is still laced with sugar, salt, chemical additives and preservatives that create addictions, compromise health and lower frequency.

> ~ *IF THERE IS ONE THING YOU CAN BE SURE OF ABOUT THE FDA,*
> *IT IS WHAT IT POLICES—ANY THREAT*
> *TO THE FOOD AND DRUG COMPANIES' BOTTOM LINES.* ~

And exercise? What exercise? We are probably the most sedentary society on the planet. Yes it is important to note that overuse (such as extreme sports and rigorous exercise programs often associated with dieting) and lack of movement (as in too many of our schools and workplaces) equally stress the human body. Yes, a great amount of lip service is given to the benefit of diet and exercise. You can sit in front of a television and watch it all day. They also will tell you about all the fake food and drugs that will supposedly help you lose the weight you gained due to fake food and drugs in the first place. What do they say about fighting fire with fire?

EMOTIONAL PROGRAMMING

From the concept of original sin and "good boy/bad boy" parenting techniques to circumcision and premature potty training, children soon discover that they are not considered worthwhile the way they are.

Parents are under pressure to bring up "good" children who will "make" something of themselves. The favored method is reward and punishment. If you are good, I will love you and give you candy and toys. If you are bad, I will withdraw my love, take away your toys, and deny you candy. In lieu of (or in addition to) corporal punishment, love, approval and goodies are bartered for compliance. While seen as socialization, the currently recommended parenting practices are actually a very effective form of programming that equates food and possessions with love. This is perfect grooming for the ultimate consumer.

Emotional programming is a process of replacing self-esteem and confidence with guilt and shame. From being told we are bad if we don't obey our parents, to comparing ourselves with the Photoshopped icons in the media, we are constantly being judged by ourselves and others. Guilt and shame feel so awful that most people will do anything to avoid feeling them. Anything people avoid can easily be used to direct their actions.

*~ IF YOU DON'T WANT THEM TO GET YOUR GOAT,*
*DON'T HAVE ONE. ~*
*~ PUBLIC DOMAIN ~*

Early in childhood we are taught to judge against our natural emotions and encouraged to stuff them rather than express them. By stuffing our emotions, we immobilize our emotional realm so that it can no longer participate with the rest of us. If we are emotionally numb, we cannot feel or sense truth from lies, nor can we access our true desires, rendering them more easily influenced and controlled. At the same time, we start to build a backlog of emotion that can and will be exploited.

## PROPAGANDA

There are hidden (or not-so-hidden) forms of programming we actually pay to experience. How many of us spend untold hours sitting in front of a television set being "programmed?" Loss of self-esteem and worthiness, coupled with being conditioned to earn love in the form of toys and candy, has completely set us up to be exploited by advertising and marketing. Subtle messages found in every aspect of the media dictate what is necessary to be considered worthy of love; then they offer to sell it to us.

The news, which has deteriorated to endless drama trauma, pulls us around by our denied emotions. It is so easy to control the reality of a person who is ashamed of what they feel. Simply paint a villain worthy of all that denied rage and fear. You can have an entire nation up in arms against anyone you wish to demonize. The truth of what is really going on is rarely addressed. Why address truth and confront the lies when there is no money or control in it?

The media, which we voluntarily expose ourselves to, actually dictates our reality. It is also quite addicting. Just take the television away from a person who is really into it, watch how long it takes them to begin pacing the floor like a junkie needing a fix. Television can actually become a form of self-medication used to ease the unbearable pressure of unprocessed, backed-up emotions.

Now you don't really think such a valuable tool is overlooked by the elite do you?

## MENTAL PROGRAMMING

Most of us believe our *mandatory* educational system is designed to educate. Actually, it is designed to bog down our minds and program obedient drones. Education follows the basic pyramidal structure of realities with its content and extent being dictated by the top tier. Higher education is seen as a privilege that will move us up the ladder of success and power. It is also expensive, which often insures that only the most privileged ever reach the sought-after positions of authority, while too many begin life with a huge debt. As one moves up the tiers, the mind is revered, while the heart languishes and logic rules all. In the absence of heart, the mind can be manipulated through "logic" into or out of almost anything.

> I was preparing an after-school snack for my two children when my son, a second grader, calmly informed me, "Mom, I have decided; I am not going to school anymore."
>
> "Oh? Do tell, son," I responded.
>
> "Well mom, all they do is make you sit still all day, tell you lies, and expect you to memorize them." He defended his well-thought-out position.

Opposed to popular belief, the mind was not designed to be a storage device nor was it designed to establish realities and run the show. The true functioning of the mind is to access and translate information stored in the Akashic Records, or as some physicists call it, "the field."

Our current educational system bogs the mind down with so much stored misinformation that it can no longer function according to its design. This leaves us disconnected from truth and subject to what the system feeds us.

## SOCIETY'S CHILD

Basic socialization, which is the process of learning one's culture and how to live within it, is actually a form of generational programming. Starting with our family, friends and local neighborhood, we are taught the accepted reality and our place in it by this subculture. This reality is established by the generational conditioning of both parents and is policed by the beliefs, conditioning, damage, and denials of our parents and siblings. As we grow older, we are introduced into the larger subculture—the school system—where the reality of the established school system is combined with that of our teachers and peers. We continue up the pyramidal social structure until we are well indoctrinated into the subculture of our country.

I had the dubious advantage of growing up in multiple families and cultures. At the ripe old age of seven I was shipped off to Saudi Arabia to live with my mother and stepfather. As I grew older, I was confronted with some very interesting discrepancies. When I was in "camp," the small fenced-in American compound owned and maintained by Arabian American Oil Company, it was alright to run around in shorts and a t-shirt with my hair loose and face exposed. If, however, I went to the Arab market place just outside of the compound, dressed the same way, I was stared at as if I were naked. If I traveled further afield into the desert with my stepfather when he was checking pipelines, I had to completely cover up my hair and veil my face. Now at 120° in the shade, that was more than a little uncomfortable. I was not allowed out of the American encampment unescorted by my stepfather, nor were women allowed to drive.

One day my mother sent me to the small grocery store the oil company maintained within the encampment. The encampment was very small, so I would walk to the store, but in order to get the groceries home, I would take a cab. The taxis were driven by Arabian men. On my way home the cab driver asked me when my father was going to arrange my marriage. Shocked, I said he wasn't.

"How old are you *memsaab*?" he asked not unkindly.

"I'm eleven." I responded.

"Oh *memsaab*," he declared, clearly concerned for me, "He must arrange for you soon, or you will be too old."

Not long thereafter another Arabian man who worked with my stepfather started showing up at our house with gifts for the family. He gave my little brother a wrist watch and my stepfather, who had started an ivory collection, a beautiful ivory box. He seemed like a nice man, but he acted strangely around me. He would glance at me then look quickly away. He never spoke directly to me, so I decided he didn't like me. Once when he was visiting, I offered him a glass of water and as he took the glass, his hand shook so badly I feared he would drop it. I wondered if he was unwell.

One evening he came calling and asked to speak with my father. He was clearly unsettled and shook more than usual. Thinking something must be terribly wrong at work, I invited him in and went to get my stepfather. Before I left the room, he spoke directly to me for the first time. The words were softly uttered in Arabic, but I was fairly fluent. I was confused, as it sounded as if he suggested that I pack my belongings. I wondered if the country was at war with Israel and we were being evacuated.

My stepfather went to talk to him while I stood out of sight in the hall and wrung my hands, listening in. He said something quietly to my stepfather in his deeply accented English and slid a fat envelope across the table to him. My stepfather opened it and I could see a large amount of Saudi currency inside, learning later it was probably the young man's life savings. My stepfather, who did love his money, smiled a secret smile, closed the envelope, and with no little regret, I imagine, slid it back to the young man.

"I am sorry Jaul. This is an impressive amount, and I understand how important this is to you, but it is not our way to sell our women."

"Then what is your way? How can I obtain your beautiful daughter for my first wife?" Jaul wanted to know.

My stepfather went on to explain that by our standards, at eleven, young girls were considered way too young to court.

That was only the first offer of many over the next years of my life. Once when I was 12 we were approached by a representative of a Saudi prince who had been visiting the encampment and had seen me in the swimming pool playing with my friends while he was touring the clubhouse. He promptly had me followed home. The offer was exorbitant. I could see the greed and contemplation in my stepfather's eyes. You can bet I was on my best behavior.

By the time I finished college I had lived in eight different countries, often with local families. I learned to comply with the norms of each culture. In the American encampment a woman was considered ungroomed if she didn't shave her legs. When I moved in with a Swiss family before going to boarding school in Switzerland, I was firmly informed that only prostitutes shaved their legs. At 14 it puzzled me how I could go from well groomed to a prostitute by changing locations.

I soon came to realize that how I was viewed had very little to do with me and everything to do with the norms of the culture. While I learned to adapt from culture to culture by recognizing each had a different reality, I also observed that the people in each culture truly believed their reality to be the only one. Being totally indoctrinated into their culture, they were thereby identified with and controlled by it.

## SPIRITUAL PROGRAMMING

By the time the masses have been subjected to these physical, emotional, and mental compromises, their frequencies become so low, that the spiritual realm is reduced to a dogmatic adherence to a limiting set of rules in a last-ditch effort to find safety. These very rules are used to control and exploit the individual through fear, shame, and guilt.

## THE POWER OF PROGRAMMING

Programming creates physical weakness and addictions, promotes shame, guilt and fear, dictates reality, and isolates the individual from spirit. This is the perfect set up. Frightened, sick, and addicted people spend their money on insurance, pharmaceuticals, and the very foods that promote their addictions. These foods and drugs make them fatter and sicker. Mental programming tells them that being fat is bad, so they turn to the diet industry, which advocates more drugs and fake food, which in turn makes them even fatter and sicker, which creates guilt, shame, low self-esteem, depression and despair. Not to worry, there are always psychotropic drugs.

So far I have been outlining your basic garden-variety programming common to us all. There are other forms of programming—extremely dark and perverse forms that are designed to serve an even more sinister purpose.

*~ WHEN WE ARE LIVING OUT OF PROGRAMMING,*
*WE ARE LIVING OUTSIDE THE CIRCLE OF LIFE,*
*AND WE ARE THEREFORE POWERLESS. ~*

## ANOTHER LOOK AT PARASITES

Everything expresses according to frequency. Every organism has frequency ranges in which they feed and thrive, beyond which they die. This describes the very nature of parasites, who need to live on or in a host and derive their food from that host. It is in their best interest to keep their hosts in a weakened, but alive, state, thereby frequency compatible and beneficial to the parasite. A dead host is of no use at all, and if the host is allowed to raise its frequency too high, its immune system will oust the parasite. Parasites also make themselves as invisible as possible so the host doesn't detect their presence and take measures to be rid of them. Parasitic infestations tend to produce brain fog, making it easier to hide their presence from their host. Most parasites, like the tape worm, can actually secrete chemicals into their host that cause the host to crave whatever it is that the parasite needs to live and to avoid what would be harmful to it. In short, it is the mushroom method—keep them in the dark and feed them BS.

As below, so above. Parasites are present on all four levels of our beings and beyond. They also take all four forms. There are physical parasites. There are parasitic emotions such as guilt. Thought forms can be parasitic, drawing from and diminishing other thought forms in order to survive. The spiritual realm has parasites as well, feeders, demons, possessing spirits and things that go bump in the night.

> **Stirring the Pot**
>
> *I used to watch my step-father prod my mother by intentionally saying things that he knew would insight her ire.*
>
> *He would be relentless in his harassment until she would go into a full blown rage, then he would walk away with a satisfied look on his face while she raved.*
>
> *It was a very insightful moment for me when I realized he actually gained power from her loss of control.*

On the physical level our bodies are actually communities of organisms living in symbiosis, or an interdependent and mutually beneficial relationship that is necessary for life. The friendly bacterium found in our gut is an example of a symbiotic organism. Other organisms feed off of us to our detriment—the physical parasites. Some physical parasites reside outside our bodies, such as ticks, mosquitoes, and leaches. Others, such as hook worms, round worms, and tape worms live within our bodies. Technically, almost every living thing is a physical parasite because we all have to feed on other living things.

Emotional parasites feed on the frequency of emotion. We all need love in order to survive, yet at the current frequency we are unable to connect with universal love, so we do whatever is necessary to get it from each other.

Deep empathy can actually be a form of feeding. We all have known someone who is totally preoccupied with the suffering of others. Some misguided prayer groups have been known to be guilty of this.

The community is stalked for a hapless person in suffering (the prey). From a lofty place of haughty superiority, and without permission, it is decided what the prey needs to ease their perceived suffering (group agreement on a common reality). Then the Lord is petitioned to provide it. In this example, the group is actually unwittingly feeding from the very suffering they wish to alleviate. Mental parasites feed by creating and controlling realities, which they do by procuring group agreement (campaigning).

Please note I am not trying to condemn prayer or prayer groups. I view it as a wonderful modality. The good news about prayer is that it really works: the bad news is that it really works and if misused or used without permission, it can work to the detriment of the one being prayed for.

LIVING IN GLASS HOUSES

Once we become aware of these feeding patterns, it is common to start observing them in the behavior of all the people around us. The temptation often arises to point to this or that person and say, "Oh, look, he is an emotional parasite," or "She is a mental parasite." Parasitic feeding patterns are the currency of our existing system. By necessity, all of us dance any number of these parasitic positions at any given time. Again, the enemy is within you as well as around you. Our parasitical feeding patterns are being prompted and directed by yet other parasites higher up on the pyramidal food chain.

To transcend the current exploitative system, you must know yourself. If, instead of recognizing and owning our participation, we choose to deny our involvement in any portion of this system, we put that involvement into denial. In order to keep anything firmly in denial, it is necessary to project our denials onto others, create a reality substantiating our position and campaign for agreement. A stunning example of this denial and subsequent projection taken to its most extreme can be found in the life of Adolf Hitler.

## THE FEEDING FRENZY

As we look a little further into advertising, it becomes clear that no one really cares if you need what they are selling or even if it may hurt you. They do whatever is necessary to get you to buy it. This runs deeper than it may appear at first glance. Our entire system is based upon the game of whoever has the most money and stuff when he dies, wins. We are so deeply involved in this game that it underlies everything, and the only ones winning are the ones at the top of the pyramid—the social elite—not the little guys at the bottom fighting over toys. These are the very toys, Jaguars and such, that we have been programmed into believing that we must have in order to have value and power in our world. It is through having money and power that we have come to believe that we can gain love.

## PYRAMIDS WITHIN PYRAMIDS

Every organization in our current reality is a pyramid with well-meaning hard-working individuals in the bottom tier. Because we are just coming out of a time of extreme masculine polarization, the pyramids of our society are polarized toward the mental realm. As one moves up the tiers of a masculine-polarized pyramid, one finds that people on each higher tier become increasingly detached from their hearts and driven by their minds.

When not counterbalanced by the heart, the mind goes quite mad creating ungrounded and distorted realities. Again, Hitler was a stunning example of this phenomenon being taken to its extreme, which explains how the German people could remain virtually ignorant of the holocaust taking place in their own country. The citizens of Germany were the well-meaning people on the bottom tier of the pyramidal structure that was the German government at that time.

Individuals populating any given pyramid naturally (or by design) gravitate to the tier that best suits their conditioning and feeding patterns.

These pyramids don't stand alone—all are interrelated in some way. There are also symbiotic relationships among various pyramids. As an example, we will pick on the auto-insurance industry and its relationship with our laws, law enforcement, and banking pyramids.

## PROTECTION MONEY

Years back I was in an auto accident. When I first called my insurance company, the woman who handled my case was kind, sympathetic, and helpful. It was clear that she was a caring, compassionate soul who wanted to help. I really felt that I was in good hands. She was a member of the first tier of the pyramid.

A month later, after repeated visits to my doctor and subsequently finding that I was more injured than we first thought, I was given a different case manager who was less sympathetic and more judgmental. She made it clear that she thought I was making more of my injury than what was warranted. That was her reality. We had moved up a rung and into the hands of an emotional parasite who fed herself by invalidating the suffering of others.

After being diagnosed with a severe closed-head injury, I was handed off again to another woman who dealt with me through liberal doses of guilt and shame. Looking down from yet a higher rung, her reality was that I was trying to milk the insurance company, and she was dedicated to exposing me as a charlatan. She was a more extreme form of an emotional parasite, feeding on the self-esteem of others by imposing guilt and shame.

Soon my personal doctors were judged by the insurance companies and found wanting. Never mind they were the top in their field—this clearly required a second opinion—so I was sent to an independent medical examiner (IME), aka insurance-company puppet.

IMEs are members of a subculture of medical doctors who create and maintain their own reality. In this reality they are the heroes, protecting the noble insurance companies from unscrupulous medical doctors in private practice.

In this symbiotic relationship, the insurance companies pay the IME to see a steady stream of patients. In exchange, the IME gives the insurance company the words they want to hear—words like malingerer, maximum medical improvement, or non-compliant.

My short-term memory was still severely impaired. I mentioned to my primary-care physician that I was concerned that I would be unable to remember what the IME said, so my doctor suggested I make a recording of my visit.

As the time neared for my appointment, it became clear that my mother was dying. I called the insurance company, explained the situation and asked if I could reschedule my appointment with the IME.

Once again I rose up the pyramid from Ms. Guilt-shame-suspicion, to the full-blown gestapo. Ms. Gestapo informed me if I did not show up for my appointment, I would be deemed non-compliant and my insurance would be canceled. She was convinced I was lying about my mother just to get out of the exam. That was Ms. Gestapo's reality from yet higher up the proverbial pyramid as a completely heartless, full-blown mental parasite, feeding by distorting realities.

Still too head injured to drive, I had a friend drive me the five hours from my mother's house in the middle of Wyoming to downtown Denver in order to make my appointment. He and I sat in the waiting room of what appeared to be a hastily thrown together office while I attempted to fill out reams of paper work. Due to my closed-head injury, my eyes still didn't work well together and I soon became overwhelmed. I told the receptionist that I was head injured and I was having trouble with the paper work. She informed me it was *mandatory,* and if I did not fill it out, I would be non-compliant.

"What is in the box?" She interrogated me some time later when she came to get my forms.

"A tape recorder. My doctor suggested that I tape the IME's instructions because I won't be able to remember them," I answered. She turned sharply on her heel and disappeared into the back office. Soon she reappeared, armed with said IME.

"I do not allow *my* exams to be taped," he shouted at me, without preamble.

"My short-term memory is still impaired; I was hoping to record what you recommend so I can refer back to it." I was wondering why I was feeling guilty and defending myself in the first place.

"You don't need a tape. You already brought *him* as a witness," he huffed at me, pointing at my friend, who blushed crimson at the thought of witnessing my exam.

"Witness? No, no, he's my ride. I can't drive. What on Earth are you going to do to me in there, that I would need a witness?" I wanted to know.

"I am sending a report to your insurance company stating that you have been non-compliant." He stated turning to go.

"Non-compliant? I'm not refusing to be examined. I don't understand."

"You brought a tape recorder." He stated as if that explained it all. "Yes?"

"You are non-compliant." He turned and stomped back into his office and, as God is my witness, he slammed his door. To my utter embarrassment, I burst into tears.

Ms. Gestapo lost no time gleefully writing me a nasty letter informing me that my insurance benefits were canceled due to non-compliance. Yet, my insurance bills kept coming every month, like clockwork. The rates had been raised because I had been in an accident, and other insurance companies would be as high for the same reason. Yet the law dictates that I must have auto insurance. I had just been chewed up and spit out by the parasitical pyramid known as the insurance industry.

So let me sum up this pyramid and its symbiotic relationships for you:

❖ Laws are set by those with the most lobbying dollars (symbiosis the with legal-system pyramid).

❖ There are laws in place mandating that every auto and person driving on the roads must maintain auto insurance.

❖ Compliance with these laws is enforced by our law-enforcement agencies that our tax dollars pay for (symbiosis with the law enforcement pyramid).

❖ Violation of those laws can result in fines that support the law enforcement pyramid (symbiosis with law enforcement pyramid).

❖ It is difficult to hold a job if you cannot drive. If you cannot work, it's hard to live.

❖ Prompt payment of insurance premiums is strictly enforced by insurance cancelation policies (symbiosis with the banking-industry pyramid).

❖ Should an individual be unfortunate enough to have an accident and actually need to use this *mandatory* insurance, his/her premiums go up.

❖ An insurance company can refuse to insure anyone they deem a "poor risk."

❖ Guilt, shame and pressure are put on accident victims by insurance company "case managers" in an attempt to discourage or delay them from getting the treatment they need and have paid for.

❖ Payment of benefits are postponed through elaborate delaying tactics routinely employed by the insurance companies.

❖ There is a staggering amount of interest earned every hour by insurance companies on these unpaid benefits that are invested in the banking pyramid (symbiosis with the banking-industry pyramid).

❖ This provides plenty of funds to cover more lobbying and any law suits filed by the customers they are routinely cheating out of their benefits (did I mention that there are the legal equivalent of IMEs who make a mighty fine living defending the insurance companies?)

❖ The employees at the bottom of the pyramid are just honest, hard-working people trying to provide a good service. Sadly, these are the ones to whom we are funneled when we want to scream our heads off at the company for exploiting us.

Lest we demonize the poor insurance companies, it is important to remember that this exploitative system is firmly in place to one degree or another in every organization in our consumer-driven society, and all of us participate in it one way or another. I have known countless individuals to exploit the insurance companies by making false claims or remaining in the victim stance rather than heal and get on with their lives. These people often choose to collect disability long after the support is necessary, which only perpetuates this system.

There are massively complex symbiotic relationships between the various pyramids comprising our consumer-based society where everything is driven by money. In a system driven by money, one just follows the money to unveil it.

## Food, Drug, and Diet Industries

As demonstrated above, and discussed before, we have been programmed to equate food with love, which creates food addictions. Addicted people spend money on these addictions, which in turn, compromises their health. Money must then be spent on drugs to treat the resulting illnesses. Obesity is the result of the imbalanced nutrition caused by addiction to counterfeit food. The diet industry advertises pills and processed foods that promise to solve a problem originally created by drugs and processed food, which drives us to the health industry.

## The Hostile Takeover

While the doctors were busy trying to save lives, the insurance companies were lobbying to take over health care. People actually die waiting for clearance from their health-insurance provider to give them permission for procedures their doctors have deemed necessary. Now people, often with no more than a high-school education, are telling our doctors what the insurance companies have decided we need. Taking a page from the auto-insurance companies' book, the health-insurance companies base this decision on how little money they can get away with investing in your life vs. how much more life you may have to live to pay premiums and not need health care. Our good neighbor has us in good hands all right. These same hands squeeze us until we are used up and then raise our premiums when we do get ill and need coverage. God forbid that they would have to pay out what they have promised and what we paid for in a timely manner.

## WANNA, NEEDA

We are programmed early on to equate toys and other acquisitions with love, which sets us up to be extremely vulnerable to advertising. Commercial advertising sets us up for the credit-and-banking pyramid. We cannot live without love. We now believe that if we have the right stuff, drive the right car, wear the right makeup, or own the right home, then we can be loved. Soon, we can no longer afford all the wonderful things that promise to make us lovable or fill the empty hole inside, where we long for love.

## FUNNY MONEY

Not to worry, there is this wonderful thing called credit. Credit card offers are routinely mailed to high-school students about to enter college. The policy is to get the young in debt and hopefully keep them paying interest for the rest of their productive lives. School loans promise a bright future, but, in reality, many graduates pay on them for a good portion of their adult lives, reducing their income to something less than they could have brought home before their grand education. The vicious cycle of programming our wants and desires and then offering to fulfill our immediate needs through loans and credit cards leads us to yet another lie—money. Like our food, our money is actually counterfeit—paper backed by nothing, printed and controlled by the social elite at the top of the financial pyramid.

## OUR GOOD UNCLE

If you think for one moment that we have any idea where our outrageously high tax dollars are going, think again. While we are engaged in the acquisition game, so is everyone else, including our government. The more money involved and the higher up the pyramid, the more heartless and the deeper the corruption. In truth, war is nothing more than a money-making scheme. Elections are polarized dramas solely designed to give us a false sense of control while keeping us distracted from what is really going on. As Mark Twain said,

~ *IF VOTING MADE ANY DIFFERENCE, THEY WOULDN'T LET US DO IT.* ~

The few who have the real story are above it all, happily pulling strings and jerking chains from the top of the proverbial pyramid. Our good president, regardless of whether he/she is a democrat or a republican, is far from the top—his or her strings are being pulled by the elite while engaging us in a deadly game of Russian roulette with nations.

This pyramidal dance continues its interwoven pattern until we find the over-lording pyramid of physical reality. The bottom tier of this monster is actually populated by nations. Who is the eye at the top of that puppy, you might ask? Ever hear the term global elite?

Don't despair. Even this monstrous overlord is at the bottom tier of a larger pyramid somewhere in the big scheme of things. This extreme pattern of polarization is not restricted to our physical reality or even to our little spot in the galaxy. Life itself is a pattern of polarization and unity, breath in/breath out, as our galaxy expands and contracts while it merrily spins around the universe.

Right about now you may be thinking that I am a conspiracy theorist. When I first started uncovering this, I doubted it myself. If you stop believing everything you are told and follow the money, it is appalling what comes to light. Again, these are the days when the truth can't hide. All that is required is a willingness to reexamine the "facts" and face the lies we have been living, which is the key to the first of the doors leading to our personal power and freedom.

It is important to note here that I am not telling you not to watch television or that you can't have health insurance and evolve. Nor am I saying that we can expect to change the system or that we should not be involved in it. We can only become conscious of what we are involved in and discern what our next steps are in order to disengage from the aspects of the system that do not serve us. The goal for now is to live in the system without being overly influenced by it. Everyone has a different path out of the "matrix," if they choose to leave it at all. It is all about personal choice and intent. The system is not evil. It is simply what developed during the long dark and, for some of us, it outlived its usefulness. It is the old Heaven and the old Earth in which some will rightly choose to remain.

## THE POWER BEHIND THE THRONE

Imagine that we have been living in a small cell eating bread and water, for generations, restricted to a mono-dimensional world. We've been led to believe that this is all we can hope to obtain. In order to even be granted our moldy bread we must put our belief in and power behind our all-powerful jailers who own our world and everything in it. These jailers live in abundant luxury in the rest of the grand multiple-story mansion under which we are restricted to four-by-six foot cells.

Then one day, the lights come on, and some of us discover that we are the rightful owners of the entire mansion. The jailers have no real power except to put us under a spell of hopelessness, lack, and fear in order to trick us into creating for them. In truth, all we need to do is to find our way out of our self-created cells.

This is the truth behind the lies—the power behind the throne. Our current belief system has us locked into a narrow band of what some call 3-D (or ordinary/physical reality), while there are actually an untold number of dimensions we could be surfing at will. Our realities in 3-D are created by our group-belief systems. We are the only ones who can create our reality, yet we have been manipulated into creating for the "elite" and the entities behind them, who cannot manifest in 3-D on their own. This has been going on for generations. Now, as we move into the greater light of the Aquarian age, we have an opportunity to wake up to the power and glory of our birth right. We can reclaim what is rightfully ours—our reality and everything in it.

## MONEY CAN'T BUY ME LOVE

With all this talk of money, power, conspiracy, and realities, it is easy to lose sight of the fact that money is not what we are really after, nor is power. The true underlying motivation behind all of our parasitic feeding patterns can be found back at the beginning of this chapter.

Yet, paradoxically, we really can't get love from others. The only way to truly obtain love is to heal and evolve beyond the blockages that prevent access to our multidimensionality. For only through this multidimensionality can balanced light—and therefore love—be channeled into our lives.

It is our birthright to be the link between Heaven and Earth, between masculine and feminine light. It is our nature to be channels of the divine. All that is required is that we find our way out of our self-imposed cells and reenter the circle of life. How? Come dance with the fairies. The spirits of nature hold the key.

~ *LIGHT IS THE ULTIMATE SUSTENANCE—*
*LOVE THE ULTIMATE LIGHT.*
*IT STANDS TO REASON THAT ALL OUR ASPIRATIONS*
*CAN BE CONDENSED*
*TO A PURSUIT OF LOVE.* ~

# Section II

## The Science of Spirit

# 5

# The Natural Law

From Celtic fairies and Seidh people to Native American Earth spirits, every culture has a mythological representation of the spirits of nature.

Spirits of nature express in the Middle World, which according to the Shamanic view, is the reality we live in, but it exists outside of time and space. These spirits also express in non-ordinary reality. This may sound a little strange, but it will make more sense in later chapters on Shamanism and journeying.

### Dance of the Seidh

*We lived long in silence*
*Stilled by your fear*
*You have forgotten us*
*kings and queens*
*And yet we hold you dear*

*We balance the light and*
*the darkness*
*We balance the night and day*
*We hold together heaven and earth*
*For you we hold the way*

*Dance awake the land of your heart*
*Dance awake your soul*
*Dance tomorrow into today*
*Dance and make us whole*
*~ StarFaihre ~*

These nature spirits are not to be confused with helping spirits. Unlike helping spirits, the spirits of nature have their own agenda—that of maintaining balance in the natural world. Some Celtic myths and legends warn against trusting the Earth spirits known as Fairy Folk or Seidh People. It is believed they will trick you and appropriate you to correct the imbalances in the natural order that are being caused by humans. In the larger scheme of things, this is not an idle threat. The natural order will correct imbalance one way or the other.

*~ YOU CANNOT BREAK THE LAW—*
*YOU CAN ONLY BREAK YOURSELF AGAINST THE LAW. ~*
*~ THE TEN COMMANDMENTS (1956) ~*

In actuality, these "spirits of nature" are a metaphoric representation of the differing divinations of the power found in the natural order and the laws they follow. That is not to say that they are imaginary. They are, in fact, quite real.

## RESISTANCE IS FUTILE

The law of nature *is* the way things work together in perfect ever-moving balance—the ebb and flow of cycles and seasons as they dance in perfect consort and accord. This law applies from the subatomic level to the movement of the universe and beyond. It only makes sense that cooperating with this law supports us and working against it is an exercise in futility. I would even suggest that the biblical references to the punishment of "sinners" refers to "sinners" as those who attempt to work against natural law and the "punishment" the natural result of attempting to live against the flow.

## IT CAME FROM BENEATH THE SWAMP

I would like a moment to discuss the difference between dogma and the deeper meanings that can be found in all spiritual texts. Spiritual texts were originally a means of preserving techniques to align with the way life works. During the long dark, direct access to spiritual information was extremely limited. In a spiritual vacuum, the metaphorical language of these texts was interpreted literally (or misinterpreted altogether) and used as mandatory dictates. This reduced the scriptures to religion or man-made belief systems, as opposed to being a means of understanding natural law. It was taught that the violation of these supposed dictates would send one to a fiery hell. These man-made decrees were then used to control the masses. For this reason, many of us have an aversion to quotes from religious texts. Please bear with me while I attempt to extrapolate some valuable truths that have been preserved in these ancient scripts. I am not claiming to be a theologian, nor am I offering my interpretations of these writings as "gospel." Rather I will examine them as they apply to natural law, rather than to religion.

*~ MANY A DOCTRINE IS LIKE A WINDOW PANE.*
*WE SEE THROUGH IT, BUT IT DIVIDES US FROM THE TRUTH. ~*
*~ KAHLIL GIBRAN ~*

## GENESIS

Every culture also has its own creation myths or stories of how nature formed itself, or its beginnings. For insight into some of these myths and how their principles apply to natural law, let us consult one fairly close to home—the Holy Bible. When looked at from a different perspective than the usual religious interpretation, the Bible contains some interesting principles of manifestation.

Genesis 1:1-4 of The King James Version reveals these basic principles outlined quite clearly. In verses one and two it is pointed out that all creation begins in a void, total neutrality. Creation is initiated in the quantum level—spirit. Next "will" (in this case the will of God) is engaged to initiate movement.

*[1] In the beginning God created the heaven and the earth.*

*[2] And the earth was without form, and void; and darkness was upon the face of the deep. And the Spirit of God moved upon the face of the waters.*

Verses three and four establish polarization—light and darkness or positive and negative. This outlines the basic elements of power—positive and negative moving around neutral.

*[3] And God said, Let there be light: and there was light.*

*[4] And God saw the light, that it was good: and God divided the light from the darkness.*

This is the basic principal behind the generation of power, and it can be found in every electric generator, from the one in your car to the monster turbines that power our cities.

The generation of electricity creates an electromagnetic field around the generator. These toroidal fields are in the shape and form of the torus and can be found around everything from the human body to the Earth herself.

## THE TORUS

A torus is a surface generated by a closed curve rotation around, but never intersecting or containing, a vertical axis in its own plane. There is much speculation that, under the right circumstances, some toroidal fields have the potential of perpetual motion. There is technology based on this propensity that would render our current reliance on fossil fuels obsolete. This does not please the elite at the top of the energy-industry pyramid. No, this does not please them at all. It is no mystery why this technology is currently being carefully suppressed.

The perpetual-motion potential of the toroidal field is dependent upon balance, which is dependent upon freedom of motion. Even the longevity of the human body is determined by this freedom of movement. The enemy of this freedom is "drag."

*~ AN OBJECT THAT IS IN MOTION WILL NOT CHANGE ITS VELOCITY UNLESS AN*
*UNBALANCED FORCE ACTS UPON IT. THIS IS KNOWN AS UNIFORM MOTION. ~*
*~ FROM NEWTON'S FIRST LAW ~*

Anywhere we do not express according to our true nature, we create drag, which is the true motivation behind the systematic programming (covered in "Smoke and Mirrors,"). If one can impose drag on a toroidal field, one can create a torque, through which energy can be appropriated.

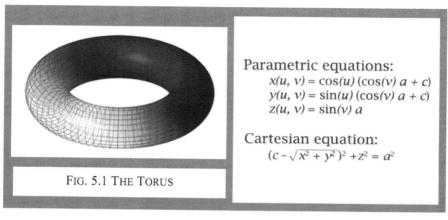

Parametric equations:
$$x(u, v) = \cos(u)(\cos(v)\, a + c)$$
$$y(u, v) = \sin(u)(\cos(v)\, a + c)$$
$$z(u, v) = \sin(v)\, a$$

Cartesian equation:
$$(c - \sqrt{x^2 + y^2})^2 + z^2 = a^2$$

FIG. 5.1 THE TORUS

## ELEMENTAL, MY DEAR

While teaching a wilderness program for Path Home Shamanic Arts School, I was demonstrating the shamanic art of working with the fire element. I was using drumming to focus my intent during the ancient healing ceremony. I gathered the "spirit" of fire around the group of students to reestablish balance through the use of fire's toroidal field.

The Wilderness Program falls in the first year of the Shamanic Practitioner Program, at which point students are at varying levels of mastery. Most are still unable to see or experience the quantum level outside of the formal journey or trance state, which grants the practitioner the ability to access information at the quantum level by representing it through metaphors formed in the imagination.

As the director of the Wilderness Programs for the school, my daughter Laura was present on a particular retreat. Though quiet about her abilities, Laura is quite capable of "seeing" the quantum level without the aid of a formal journey trance. She was standing in the trees some distance away while I did my demonstration. Laura happened to hear one disgruntled pupil express her doubt that I was doing anything beyond drumming around a camp fire and making a spectacle of myself. Laura pulled her small camera out of her fanny pack and, with uncharacteristic disregard of the rules of ceremony, snapped a picture of the proceedings. Upon our return from the trip she showed me the picture, which had captured the "orbs" created by the fire "spirits" as they worked to rebalance the group. These orbs are actually toroidal fields created by the element of fire as it changes matter from one form to another. During this process it has all the right stuff—neutrality, positive charge, negative charge, and motion. All I needed to supply was my will, which I directed through the ceremony.

When I asked her why she had taken the picture, she said it was to send to the particular student who apparently needed physical validation. Laura had sent the doubting student a copy of the picture with no accompanying note, feeling that the picture is well worth a thousand words.

FIG. 5.2 CALLING THE FAIRIES

## THE ELEMENTS

No discussion of natural law is complete without contemplation of the elements. It is the interaction of these elements as they transmute from one form to another that creates movement and the building blocks of life.

Different cultures consider different things to be elements. Some, like most Native American traditions, honor water, air, earth, and fire. Some eastern traditions consider metal and wood to be elements as well. For our purposes, we will use the basic four, considering wood to have evolved from a combination and metal to be part of the earth.

Some Celtic and Native American traditions teach that the Fairy folk or Earth spirits can be found within and around each of the four elements. Each of these elements is active. For example, running water tends to create positive and negative ions that move around a neutral field. This in turn creates happy little toroidal fields like the "orbs" captured in the photograph, so it is easy to see where this belief comes from.

Myths of water sprites or other elemental spirits are actually metaphorical representations of active principles found operating at the quantum level. Through conscious, intentional interaction with these four elements, a shaman can affect desired changes on the physical plane.

POLARIZATION

In "The End of Days," we discussed the "day's" masculine/ positive polarity and "night's, feminine/negative polarity concept, as it applies to the Mayan Calendar. We saw that as we pass from day to night we undergo a polarity reversal. The faster we undergo these polarity reversals, the closer we come to unity. The more time spent in either day or night as on the lower tiers of the pyramid, the longer it takes to get from one charge to another. During these times we experience more extreme polarization or a less unified existence. Conversely, the less time spent in either day or night as on the upper tiers of the pyramid, the less time it takes to get from one charge to another and the less extreme the polarization resulting in a more unified experience.

Our solar system is in the greatest polar extremes during the ages of Taurus and Scorpio, when the sun is the farthest away from the Photon Band. During these ages it takes the longest time to move from one pole to another. The least polarized existence occurs during Leo and Aquarius, when the sun is immersed in the Photon Band. These are the ages when polar shifts happen very rapidly.

*Judge Not*

When we judge another
We condemn ourselves
To the same judgment

Judgment freezes us in place
We stagnate
Our spirits die

Furthermore,
We are caught in a trap
Of our own making

In casting judgment
Upon another
We have become victims

As we have projected
Our power to change
Upon the actions of another
Which we cannot hope
To control

There truly is no judgment
Other than self-judgment

"Judge not
Least ye be judged"
Makes perfect sense

It is simply *THE WAY*

Again, this is represented on the Mayan pyramid where the base shows the slowest movement from positive or "days" to negative or "nights." The top of the pyramid represents the fastest movement from "days" to "nights." Each pass from the Mayan "day" to "night" or "night" to "day," represents a shift in polarity or polarity reversal. The more of these shifts we experience in a lifetime the more diverse, yet unified, our experience will be.

Polarities don't cease to exist at the top of the Mayan Calendar—they just switch so rapidly as to allow for a unified experience and the seeming end of linear time. Total unity is not the goal. If we did not live in a state of polarities, we would not live at all. Even our cells draw in nutrients through positive and negative charges. Electricity is generated by revolving a positive and negative pole around a neutral center. The Earth herself has poles that create her protective magnetic field.

Polarization is inherent in and necessary for physical life. The key here is movement. When we judge against any experience or state, we avoid it, taking up residence in its opposite expression, and movement ceases. In our physical world where everything, by its very nature, is in motion to polarize *against* something, free movement from one pole to the other stops, which creates drag against the way life works. It doesn't take rocket science to figure out who will be on the losing end of that equation. "You cannot break the law; you can only break yourself against the law."

The faster we are moving, the more readily and more intensely we experience the effects of this drag. We are currently in very rapid movement from one pole to another as we pass the apex of the Mayan pyramid and enter the Age of Aquarius, resulting in the rapid disintegration of anything not in cooperation with life. In the light of this, it only makes sense to figure out how life works and get with the program before we become   collateral damage.

*~ IT IS EASIER FOR A CAMEL*
*TO GO THROUGH THE EYE OF A NEEDLE,*
*THAN FOR A RICH MAN*
*TO ENTER INTO THE KINGDOM OF GOD. ~*
*~ MATTHEW 19:24 ~*

The eye of the needle was reputed to be a gate in Jerusalem through which a camel could not pass unless it first had all its baggage removed and crawled through on its knees. There is much debate, among our literal thinkers, whether the eye of the needle ever existed. As far as I am concerned, it doesn't really matter. Dogmatically speaking, this scripture is often used to convince the devout that it is not righteous to be wealthy, so it would be best to hand your riches over to the church.

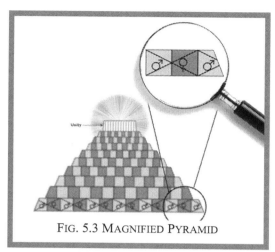

FIG. 5.3 MAGNIFIED PYRAMID

If we treat the story as a metaphor, like most other spiritual information, a much deeper meaning emerges. Every time we pass from "day" to "night" or from "night" to "day" in our progression through the ages represented by the Mayan Calendar, we experience a polarity reversal. These polarity reversals occur at the X in the center of the magnified section. It is at this point that the most pressure is brought to bear wherever we have polarized against something, thereby losing our mobility. These locked-down places are our baggage.

At each transition point from positive to negative reality or vice versa, we are challenged to let go of our prior judgments or baggage in order to advance along our evolutionary path.

*"Chris Horvath told me he'd been taught by Leslie Fool Bull, a leader in the Native American Church, that the tipi is part of an image of sacred above and sacred below. They are reflections of each other. He made this Drawing."*

**X**

*"Sacred above grandfather and sacred below grandmother represent the two cosmic principles which together form a unity, sectoring a oneness to the One, the always and only One—Wakan Tanka."*

*~ Ronald Goodman,
Lakota Star Knowledge ~*

As a rule, these judgments have been created through the systematic programming to which we have been subjected during socialization, resulting in "soul loss" or disconnection from our natural expression. This programming effectively puts a ceiling on how far we can evolve, unless we clear the programming and release our judgments. For the most part, this requires aid in the form of a spiritual healing modality known as soul retrieval (more on soul retrieval in "Shamanism and Quantum Physics,"). It is through limiting our level of evolution that the current system keeps us subject to it. If we are allowed to evolve beyond the current reality, we become aware of the lies contained therein—not a good situation for the powers that be.

This symbol is not restricted to the Mayan Calendar. It shows up many other places, including the Lakota tradition.

As mentioned, Taurus is the most extremely masculine polarized age, and Scorpio is the age of greatest feminine polarization. At the end of each of these ages, we find ourselves at the apex of a pendulum swing, *i.e.*, at the most polarized position of either expression before it changes direction. We currently are moving through the "fall" of a patriarchal age when the pendulum has left its most polarized point in the masculine and is returning to center or balance. Through this process we will pass through numerous spiritual polarity shifts (eyes of the needle). These eyes of the needle, or "days" and "nights," are not the same as the ages of the zodiac. In fact, each age contains numerous "days" and "nights" whereby we end up passing through multiple realities, each seemingly inside out and backwards from the last.

Now let's take a closer look at the smaller polarity switchover points —the "days" and "nights" or eyes of the needle. While the symbol **X** may appear static, it is actually two vortices moving in opposite directions. The masculine (at the top) moves clockwise (as viewed from above) and the feminine (at the bottom) moves counterclockwise, collectively creating a torus. Each time we pass from one set of "days" and "nights" to the next set, we are actually passing from one toroidal field to another. Each field has its

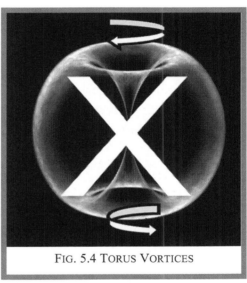

FIG. 5.4 TORUS VORTICES

own unique frequency and movement. Each "day" and "night" in a set is an equal but opposite reflection of each other, with each set being unique. Mind boggling? Yes! But hold onto that thought, as it is a major key to evolution and will increasingly become important in the following chapters.

## MASCULINE AND FEMININE PRINCIPLES

As demonstrated in "The End of Days," the power of positive and negative, (light and dark, masculine and feminine, respectively) fluctuate in influence over the ages. They are also the driving forces behind natural law and the formation of toroidal fields. From Jesus and Mary to Buddha and Quan yin, every tradition has archetypical representations of male and female, or god and goddess.

## THE LIGHT WORKER AND THE SHAMAN

The Leonean age was over, and two figures stood silhouetted on the edge of the cliff, robes blowing in the wind. It was both sunrise and sunset. The crescent moon hung in the sky. The tall blond man was dressed in white robes, his wings folded behind him. The diminutive woman's robes were a luminescent black, with her long blue-black hair lifting in the wind. Her black panther stood ever patient at her side, an owl on her shoulder. For a seemingly endless span of time they stood thus, unmoving, the light never growing or fading.

"The light will soon leave the darkness, and we must once again part ways," the woman softly spoke to the man in a voice of velvet, like water running over stones, tears flowing down the flawless curve of her cheek.

"It is the way of things, my beloved one, though it grieves me to be parted from you. The cycles will run their course, and we shall be reunited," he said in a voice like chiming thunder.

"But our children suffer so in the time of two, separated from us and each other," she lamented.

"With the suffering comes strength and knowledge, and, if they choose to embrace it, wisdom. It is their birthright, beloved," he responded. "What grieves me most is that this is the Dark Age when you, my beloved wife, will be denied, the patriarchy will rule, the mind will be worshipped, while the heart languishes."

"As you say, dearest husband, the cycles ultimately bring balance. The last long dark the matriarchy ruled, and you were denied and emotions were worshipped, while the mind languished. Hold me one last time, husband mine, before we are parted. Let the memory of our unity and love carry us through the long dark until we can reunite our sacred marriage in the Age of Aquarius."

As the couple embraced and the man wrapped his wings around his beloved, the Earth rose on the horizon. Then they stood back from one another and reached out together, making the planet spin, suspended between them. The spinning increased in speed until the planet split in two. One half became a perfect diamond, the other a black opal. He took the black opal into his left hand, she the diamond into her right—darkness within the light and light within the darkness. With pain-filled eyes, they looked at each other one last time and then turned. He unfurled his wings and flew into the heavens to greet the sunrise, while she walked into the Earth, where the sun set. Both were divine spirits, each a perfect half of the whole, the Light worker and the Shaman.

## THE EAGLE AND THE CONDOR

There is an Inca prophecy that says, and I paraphrase, "Now, in this Age of Aquarius, when the eagle of the North and the condor of the South fly together, the Earth will awaken." It goes on to state that the eagles of the North cannot be free without the condors of the South. In many interpretations, this is taken to mean that the industrialized nations are the eagle of the North and the indigenous, Earth-based peoples are the condor of the South. The eagle will have almost driven the condor to extinction. I have no argument with that interpretation, but, like all truth, it also applies at multiple levels, not just the societal one. Because we can only effect true change from within, let's look at this as it applies to us as individuals, rather than as nations. The condor can also represent heart and intuition, while the eagle stands for mind and logic. The condor is intrinsically feminine, while the eagle is the masculine principle. The eagle and the condor fly together during times of unity, creating male and female balance, where heart and mind counterbalance each other. When we are equally driven by heart and mind, logic is tempered by compassion, and passion is tempered by logic—we become sovereign and less likely to be pulled out of center and exploited by either logical argument or impassioned campaigns.

The prophecy of the eagle and the condor carries another important message—in times of imbalance, regardless of whether it is the heart or mind that dominates, attempting to achieve spiritual enlightenment through either the mind or the heart alone can create delusion, madness, and spiritual illness. We have but to look back in history to witch burnings or genocide to see the truth of this statement.

## THE DIRECTIONS

The Earth creates her own toroidal field as she spins on her axis at a tilt and with a wobble. Her North and South Magnetic poles are also called Magnetic Dip Poles, referring to the vertical "dip" of the magnetic field lines. East and West are established as points perpendicular

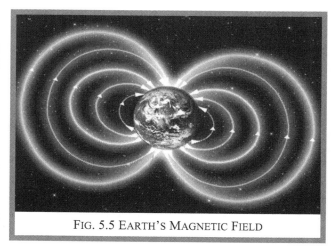

FIG. 5.5 EARTH'S MAGNETIC FIELD

lar to North and South. It is through relationship to these four directions that Center, or neutral, is established for ceremonial purposes. When performing ceremony, many traditions draw on Magnetic North instead of True North (the direction along the Earth's surface towards the geographic North Pole). This is because Magnetic North is directly related to the Earth's toroidal field and therefore is a source of great power. While the directions are traditionally established by the position of the sun rather than a compass, it is the magnetic toroidal field of the Earth that is accessed through ceremonies relating to the directions. The sun's position is more relevant when working ceremonially with the seasons.

## THE SEASONS

Due to the motion of the Earth's toroidal field (drawing inward at the North and flowing outward at the South), the direction in which the North Pole points at any given time influences the frequency of the flow. As we discussed in "The End of Days," the Earth's tilt and wobble create our days, nights, and seasons, as she travels around the sun, also creating the precession of equinoxes, which have been charted by shamanic cultures for numerous reasons. One purpose for this is to track the ages and the differing influences they bring. Another reason to track the equinoxes and solstices is that they are points of extreme influence and therefore extreme power.

The quality of this power is very distinct, whether it is a time of balance, such as during the equinoxes, or a time of light or darkness, as in the solstices. Working with the Earth's toroidal field at these times supports differing actions. For example, on a personal level, the winter solstice is a time that supports delving into the shadows of our lives—the subconscious or unconscious mind. The summer solstice brings greater light or understanding. The equinoxes can point out any imbalance in our lives. Bear in mind that this is a very simplistic example, but the principles hold true from the personal to the universal and can be drawn upon in amazing, if almost forgotten, ways.

> [1] *To every thing there is a season, and a time to every purpose under the heaven;*
> [2] *A time to be born, and a time to die; a time to plant, and a time to pluck up that which is planted;*
> [3] *A time to kill, and a time to heal; a time to break down, and a time to build up;*
> [4] *A time to weep, and a time to laugh; a time to mourn, and a time to dance;*
> [5] *A time to cast away stones, and a time to gather stones together; a time to embrace, and a time to refrain from embracing;*
> [6] *A time to get, and a time to lose; a time to keep, and a time to cast away;*
> [7] *A time to rend, and a time to sew; a time to keep silence, and a time to speak;*
> [8] *A time to love, and a time to hate; a time of war, and a time of peace.*
>
> *~ Ecclesiastes 3: 1-8 King James ~*

As we chart the seasons that result from the Earth's annual dance through the equinoxes and solstices, we see yet more influences or tendencies.

Spring supports new beginnings and the planting of ideas or intent.

Summer is a time of growth and co-creation.

Fall supports harvest, bringing things to fruition as well as discernment and sorting.

Winter is a time of rest and transmutation.

While it may seem as if I am simply describing the growing seasons, bear in mind that the growing seasons follow the natural order, or laws of the Earth, and her cyclic movements. The seasons therefore serve as great guidelines as to what is being supported at any given time. We may believe we are separate from these cycles, but the shamanic cultures knew we were not.

## PHASES OF THE MOON

The phases of the moon (see Fig. 5.6) are also created by the changing angles or relative positions of the Earth, the moon, and the sun, as the moon orbits the Earth. Exactly one half of the moon is always illuminated by the sun. At any time a portion of its sunlit side and a portion of the shadowed side are visible from Earth, creating the various moon-phase shapes. At the full moon and new moon, the Earth, moon, and sun are in approximate alignment. These alignments take place on the opposite side of the Earth, respectively. During the full moon, the entire sunlit part of the moon is facing Earth, while during the new moon the shadow side is exposed. The first-quarter and last-quarter moons (half-moons) occur when the moon is at a 90° angle with respect to the Earth and sun, which results in exactly half of the moon being illuminated and half being in shadow, from Earth's perspective.

FIG. 5.6 LUNAR PHASES

If we consider that tides are caused by the gravitational interaction between the Earth and the moon, we also have to consider that the portion of the Sun's radiation being reflected back at the Earth from the moon has substantial influence on the symphony of frequencies to which we are subject on the Earth's surface. The science of astrology delves deeply into moon phases and their influence as they relate to the positions of other heavenly bodies at any given time. The following are examples of some of the different characteristics that are associated with the four major phases of the Moon.

THE NEW MOON

Reincarnation and rebirth

The seeding of new thoughts, ideas, and actions

The strengthening of intuition

The support of action

The release of what doesn't serve; new growth

FIRST QUARTER

Balance between light and dark

Exploration of extreme experiences

Youth and vitality

Aggression and courage

Clarity of motivations

## Full Moon

The time of greatest illumination

An increase in consciousness

The unveiling of former hidden truths

Looking into truth of self and others

Avoidance of truth, which brings pressure to bear

## Last Quarter

Balance of light and dark

Time to seek harmony

Introspection

Reaching of crossroads and making decisions

Many a master gardener still observes that crops can be enhanced by planting in accordance with the phases of the moon. By performing ceremony or setting intent during the corresponding phases of the moon, one can be supported by the natural tendencies each brings to bear.

## Astrology

Diverse cultures, such as Indians, Chinese, Mayans, and other Native Americans recognized the importance of astronomical events and studied the positions and aspects of the celestial bodies and the influence the resulting frequencies had on their lives. There are many examples of elaborate systems developed to predict earthly events from celestial movements and relationships. Indo-European astrology has been dated as far back as the third millennium BCE. These ancient forms of the art have their roots in calendrical systems used to predict seasonal shifts and celestial cycles. As we have seen, one of the most elaborate and accurate of these calendars is the Mayan Calendar.

This knowledge is still used today in our modern version of Astrology. Like all arts and sciences, modern-day astrology has lost much of its original knowledge as we moved through the long dark, so it is laced with misinterpretations and erroneous assumptions. If we bear this limitation in mind, astrology can still serve as a very useful guidepost for individuals wishing to track the influences of the celestial bodies in their lives at any given time. Like any science or art form, it is only as good as the practitioner. One of the main mistakes you can make when seeking the guidance of an astrologer is to hand over your power to make your own decisions to the astrologer.

*~ ASTROLOGY IS NOT A PREDICTION*
*OF WHAT IS GOING TO HAPPEN TO YOU,*
*BUT RATHER A MAP OF THE CURRENTS RUNNING THROUGH YOUR LIFE. ~*

How you choose to surf those currents is entirely up to you. As always, the buck stops here. To see your sign as something to identify with is very limiting. It is so easy to say, "I am a Virgo, therefore I am like thus and so." Through my own healing process, I have gained increased mobility in my life, and now find that it is quite easy to draw on the traits of *all* of the signs as needed. I recognize that my default or strong suit may be Scorpio, but that is not who I am, nor does it restrict me.

## EXPANSION AND CONTRACTION

One of those powerful moments of enlightenment transpired when, in science class, I was watching time-lapse photography of a rose blooming. I had always thought the darn things just opened up, bloomed, and then dropped their leaves. To my surprise, they actually pulse into bloom with a series of expansions and contractions. Upon giving birth to my daughter, I found the birthing process is much the same, as my uterus worked in a series of contractions causing my cervix to expand. When my mother died, I witnessed the process in reverse. Her spirit slowly left her body in pulsations— expansion and contraction—before finally flying free.

These rhythmic pulsations can be found in all life from the pounding surf and your beating heart, to the pulsating expansion of our galaxy. Even the Earth's orbit around the sun is elliptical, rather than round, creating a boomerang-like effect. Drumming is used in many shamanic practices to align with this power. The pulsation of expansion and contraction is a power that can be found at all levels of nature.

## PUSHING THE ENVELOPE

The Vikings had gone a Viking. They had left behind their rich lands and lodges filled with stored food, beautiful wives, healthy children, as well as all the treasures and slaves from their previous raids. They took most of the men from their village to help procure more riches. While they were gone acquiring more booty, an enemy attacked their village, freeing their slaves, stealing their stores of food and treasures, and enslaving their wives and children. Months later, the victorious Vikings came home with their new treasures to an abandoned, burnt village and nowhere to rest their heads or to stash their plunder.

What the Viking's lifestyle demonstrates is that in the presence of expansion, without the counterbalance of contraction, an imbalance ensues, which results in not having enough substance to hold together. Urban sprawl, economic recession, and emotional burnout are all results of this state of overexpansion.

So many of our cities expanded outward with huge shopping malls until the heart of the city died. Inner cities became unkempt, corrupt, and desolate. Consumerism, over-borrowing, and irresponsible lending practices have repeatedly resulted in recession.

Our society supports high production and personal achievement, yet very little time is spent focusing on the inner landscape of the family or the individual. This is weakening our family units as well as creating burnout in the overstressed family members. Even our children are pressured to achieve in school, sports, and social arenas, leaving them very little time for introspection or personal growth.

## Waves of Creation; Waves of Destruction

Creation can be found at either end of the expansion/contraction cycle, as can destruction. Things are literally compressed or expanded into and out of being. It is at the extreme of these principles that things change form. Coal is compressed into diamond, while water expands into steam. Ocean waves crash to shore and then are drawn back to the ocean by the undertow in order to be able to crash again. While balance is vital to life, so are the extremes—all three are necessary for life. Positive (in the form of expansion) and negative (in the form of contraction) circle around the neutrality of balance to generate the toroidal fields of life. This is the very breath of Mother/Father God.

## Burning Up

In our modern-day culture, much value is attached to creation, but destruction, on the other hand, has a bad name. The masculine expression of creation and the feminine expression of destruction, or of taking things back down into their constituent parts, are necessary in equal measure for life. In our current culture we love to build or obtain things, but we fear dismantling or letting go of our creations, viewing it as loss.

> ### Right-Hand Man
>
> *Never an eyelash falls*
> *but an entire universe changes.*
> *Thinking ourselves powerless,*
> *we're stumbling around blindly*
> *destroying what took eons to create.*
> *Yet who is destruction*
> *but Creator's right hand?*

What has resulted from this bias is an unwieldy over-bloated system that can no longer sustain itself. The stress on the planet caused by our expansion and consumerism has reached critical mass in many areas. For years now, in my home state of Colorado, people have been building homes and communities in the much-coveted wooded foothills and mountains. This has necessitated controlling forest fires in order to protect these homes, rather than letting the forest burn periodically, as nature sees fit. This practice has weakened our forests—depriving them of their natural destruction and renewal cycle. Pine beetles move into our weakened forests, creating mile after mile of dead standing trees, forming fire hazards.

I have often looked at the hillsides of dead trees, thinking to myself, "When this puppy finally goes, there will be no stopping it."

In the summer of 2012 Colorado caught fire. Most days the air was nearly unbreathable. Hundreds of homes were lost. I live in the center of a small town in the plains several miles from the wooded foothills, yet hawks began perching on my roof, and owls rested on my light post at night. Deer and elk walked the streets, having been driven out of their habitat by the fires. Yet, this was not a tragedy, but a correction. Nature will have her way. The longer we delay it, the more impressive will be the display.

> ~ *NATURE IS A CLOSED SYSTEM.*
> *NOTHING IS EVER DESTROYED,*
> *WITHOUT SOMETHING NEW BEING CREATED.*
> *NOTHING NEW IS EVER CREATED*
> *WITHOUT SOMETHING ELSE BEING DESTROYED.* ~

## THE EVIL FOMORIANS

In Irish-Celtic mythology, the Fomorians were believed to be the Gods of chaos and wild nature, who inhabited Ireland in ancient times and took on the status of a semi-divine race. Fomorians were also portrayed as a race of demonic prehistoric giants, who raided and pillaged Ireland.

Tom Cowan, my favorite Celtic shamanic teacher, shares the myth of the Evil Fomorians from a shamanic perspective as demons created from our half-formed dreams, wishes, and intents. These unprocessed wishes, if left to their own devices, tie up our creative power, leaving us vulnerable to plague and misfortune. Every All Hallows' Evening it is the sacred duty of every good Celtic shaman to battle the "evil" Fomorians in order to protect their communities from plague and misfortune the following year. The Battle of the Evil Fomorians is a ceremony that Tom shares, whereby some trained shamanic practitioners comes together, and, through their combined intent, dismantles this tied-up energy, freeing it to be used by their community to manifest for the future.

If we only see ourselves as victims, it is easy to idly wish and dream for things, totally unaware that we are actually using our personal power on the quantum level to set our intent into motion. Believing ourselves powerless, we don't follow up on our creations. We don't recognize the things that start showing up in our lives as raw material that has drawn our intent to us. We don't see that these raw materials are there to create our manifestations, nor do we go back and free up our energy, should we decide the original wish is not really something we want to pursue.

We end up with the proverbial too many irons in the fire, with none getting hot. Our passing fancies tie up our energy and resources when the spiritual aspect of our intent is not managed. This situation eloquently demonstrates how unconscious we are in our use of personal power. It shows what happens when we fail to honor the expansion and contraction of life—breathe in and release, creation and destruction, "a time to get, and a time to lose; a time to keep, and a time to cast away." We are so programmed to forever seek more that we actually insure our inability to manifest.

In the following chapters I will go deeper into this concept as well as offer tools you can use to consciously manage your personal power.

**Broken Dreams**

*So often*
*Our dreams are short stopped*
*By shoulds,*
*By shouldn'ts*
*And by can'ts*

*That we are unable*
*To dream them*
*To their natural conclusions*

*Never forming them*
*Completely enough*
*To discern*

*Whether or not*
*They are a true desire*
*Or just a passing fancy*

*They remain in the back*
*Of our consciousness*
*As unfulfilled wants*

*Where they build resentment*
*That more often than not*
*We project on to those*
*Closest to us*

*Our boss*
*Our mate*
*Our children*

*Thereby sabotaging*
*Our relationships*
*And polarizing us*
*Into the victim stance*

*YOU CAN NOT MANIFIST*
*FROM A VICTIM STANCE.*

## HIGHER AND HIGHER

In our society seeking more and moving up higher is revered, yet, when we judge against the "dark" or moving downward and only seek the "light," upward movement, we compromise balance and integrity. In the new-age as well as the Christian cultures, there is much talk of the light as being good or holy. Light is seen as good and dark as bad. Heaven is seen as movement upward but to go to the fiery pits of hell is a downward journey to the bowels of the dreaded Earth. This carefully programmed bias has effectively put a ceiling on evolution. If we judge against the "dark" or moving downward and only seek the "light," upward movement, we compromise balance and integrity.

*~ ONE MAY NOT REACH THE DAWN SAVE BY THE PATH OF THE NIGHT. ~*
*~ KAHLIL GIBRAN ~*

## THE TREE WHO GREW TALL

Deep in the forests of the land we now call Alaska, there once was a new seedling spruce tree named Whisper. It had been a good year for seedlings, and there were eight of them all arranged in a nice, open park not far from the mother and father trees. They were all nearly the same height, with Whisper being slightly shorter than his brothers and sisters. Spring had finally arrived and with it the end of the long night. As the longer days arrived, Whisper asked his mother, "Why do you and father put all that effort growing your roots as deep into the earth as your branches reach the sky?"

"Because it is the way it is done." His mother replied. Whisper pondered this answer that was no answer at all, and he decided that his mother had never given it any thought. Being a tree with greater-than-average intelligence, Whisper decided he knew a better way. Why waste half of your growing season and energy growing roots under the ground where no one ever sees them? He was not pleased being shorter than his siblings, so he decided to take advantage of the coming summer. That year he put all of his efforts into his branches, and, by fall, he proudly towered over his brothers and sisters.

"Whisper, why have you not grown more roots this year?" His father enquired. "Your mother and I were careful to teach you the Way; why do you go against it?"

"I thought about it, and the Way makes no sense. I want to stand above all the rest, where I will be noticed, so I grew up, not down. Let my dumb brothers and sisters follow the stupid Way; soon I will reach the stars."

"Son," his father responded in dismay, "You can only move against the Way for so long, and then it will rebalance itself." Whisper, deciding his father didn't know much either, ignored his advice and continued his chosen path.

Winter came, and with it the howling winds of the north. Whisper, towering above all the others, had no wind break, and the storm buffeted him until his fragile root system could not maintain his towering height. During one particularly strong gust, his roots gave way, and he blew down onto the forest floor.

Over time, the Earth reabsorbed the rotting carcass of he-who-shunned-her-way, providing rich loam for the rest of the trees who grew steadily taller. Whisper's brothers and sisters stood strong for many years to come, while his spirit danced unseen among the stars.

## GOING TO GROUND

As we approach the unity point of the Mayan Calendar, passing through the extreme intensity of the Photon Band, the shifts from day to night, light to dark, positive to negative, and masculine to feminine, accelerate until they become a more unified reality—"oneness with God." This unity requires not only that our progression goes higher and higher, but also, as with the tree, that our roots sink as deeply as our branches climb, or we will fall. Grounding-in-the-dark feminine is absolutely necessary for evolution. Ungrounded conceptual advances lead to madness and cruelty, in the absence of heart.

Furthermore, exactly one half of our chakric system is feminine, or dark, in nature. To judge against and deny the dark is to disconnect from half of our power, which is only generated when both positive *and* negative poles circle around neutral.

## THE CIRCLE OF LIFE

My daughter Laura is a master falconer. One summer she and I were teaching a Wilderness Program in the Colorado Rockies. She had brought her red-tailed hawk, Tokaya, who was convalescing from West Nile Disease. Laura had also brought her young golden retriever, Gleskah. I had my 14-year-old golden retriever, Nagi, along as well.

One early morning Laura and I were in the cook tent setting up breakfast for the students. Tokaya was seated on her perch happily preening, and my old retriever was vole hunting. I didn't pay Nagi much mind, as she was old, slow, and virtually toothless. The chances of her actually catching anything were slim to none, and the hunting activity entertained her. Laura's golden, never far from her mistress, was asleep under the portable table we had set up for breakfast.

Suddenly there was a flurry of activity. Against all odds, old Nagi had caught a vole. Gleskah ran over to investigate. Nagi proudly shook the vole to show off her prowess.

"Drop!" I commanded. Nagi complied, dropping the hapless rodent.

"Fetch," Laura instructed Gleskah, who promptly picked up the vole and gently carried it to her mistress. Laura inspected the vole and upon finding it still twitching, but damaged beyond repair, gave it a blessing then tossed it to the red tail. Tokaya leaped from her perch, pounced on the vole, dispatched it with her sharp talons, and proceeded to enjoy her unexpected breakfast. Nagi went back to hunting, Gleskah curled up under the table, Laura added raisins to the oatmeal, and I continued making coffee.

Suddenly we heard a whimper from the side of the tent. One of my younger female students stood there, mess kit in hand, pale and wan, eyes wide. Laura, Gleskah, and I all looked at her like: "What?" The student swallowed loudly, blinked rapidly, and then bravely said, "I guess I still have to get used to the circle of life."

Process is inherent in life. It can be found at every level of existence. Every living thing is in the process of doing something.

On the physical level, it is through process that we break down our food to extract the nutrients that sustain our physical lives, which is what I find so humorous about "processed food"— it is a done deal, nothing left to be had. It is also the folly behind preventatives; they prevent process and therefore render our food indigestible. When we die, the same process that has sustained us—the process of decay—breaks down our bodies to be reabsorbed by the Earth and recycled as nutrients for other living things, which is what the concept of the "circle of life" referred to in many Native American teachings—to "become as grass." We eat to survive, and when we die, we feed the very things that fed us during our lifetimes.

Mentally, we process the information coming in through our other senses in order to chart our way through the world and find safe passage through life.

On the emotional level, we have to constantly process our feelings, examining, accepting, and responsibly moving them, which is essential for emotional balance and health. It also is necessary to keep abreast of the valuable information that is constantly flowing through our emotional realm. Applying this information, along with the mental information available to us, enables us to choose our actions from a balanced, informed stance.

Spiritually, we are always processing light or frequencies through our chakra system into the world. It is through this process that we manage the quantum level of our lives.

## IT'S NOT NICE TO FOOL MOTHER NATURE

There is this ever-so-arrogant assumption that things are not OK the way they present themselves in nature. The belief is that we can improve on the natural order by altering it.

If we see the "ungodly" as those who are not aligned with natural law, and the "sinners" as those who work against the natural law, Psalms 1 and 2 take on a whole new meaning.

> *1 Blessed is the man that walketh not in the counsel of the ungodly, nor standeth in the way of sinners, nor sitteth in the seat of the scornful.*

> *2 But his delight is in the law of the LORD; and in his law doth he meditate day and night.*

Basically it would be saying that if you work with the law of nature instead of against it, you will be able to manifest and prosper.

Also note in verse three the reference to bringing "forth his fruit in his season."

> *3 And he shall be like a tree planted by the rivers of water, that bringeth forth his fruit in his season; his leaf also shall not wither; and whatsoever he doeth shall prosper.*

Here we see reference to claiming what is ours in its appropriate time or season within the cycles of natural law.

The wisdom of cooperating with nature rather than trying to conquer her is proven over and over. If we just become observant and reexamine our assumptions about life, it is as simple as getting in the river with a canoe and choosing whether to go up stream or down. It is as obvious as deciding whether to plant a kernel of corn in the winter or the spring. Consciousness is the key. In order to realign with natural law we must first become conscious of our own nature, for within our beings we truly carry the blueprint of All-That-Is, which requires deprogramming from the concepts, beliefs, and limitations that have been artificially imposed on us.

## NATURE'S CHILD

As I have undergone my personal healing (or deprogramming) process, I have increasingly experienced promptings that direct me. Through following these promptings, I end up doing exactly the right thing at the right time in order to achieve what I have been intending. Increasingly, this pattern has become quite organic. It is only in hindsight that I see the eloquent choreography of the natural law as it works in my life.

At first, I had to engage in shamanic healing to free up my personal power and get back on line. This helped me come back more fully into the way I was designed. Then I had to dogmatically learn the laws and employ various methods of charting them in order to move with them. Soon, however, I built subroutines, which are a stepwise series of actions that when repeatedly applied form a unified routine. By building subroutines that were in alignment with the natural law, my actions became supported by the same. Now, for the most part, I don't have to think about it any more than I have to plan my next breath. I just let the spirit move me, so to speak. By following my promptings set in place through these subroutines, I find the flow of natural law, and I work within it, which is our birthright.

Everything in us is designed to work with the law. Our breath is the element air, our bodies are mostly water, our bones are minerals of the Earth, and the mitochondria of our cells create our energy, which is the power or fire of life. Our heart and lungs expand and contract, and our bodies create and destroy themselves in their cycle of renewal and decay. It is only our programming that makes it otherwise.

*~ THERE IS BUT ONE LAW THAT FLOWS THROUGH ALL THINGS—
THE LAW OF NATURE. IT IS THE BREATH OF THE CREATOR;
THE LAWS OF MAN—AN ABOMINATION. ~*

## SUFFERING OVER OUR SUFFERING

He was lost in the wilderness! It was a terrifying revelation as night fell and darkness settled around him, chilling him to the bone. Soon panic set in. He dropped his backpack containing his matches and emergency blanket, and he began to run. He ran and ran, as if pursued by demons. In ever-tightening circles he ran until he fell to the moist earth. Lying on his back, succumbing to the cold and his own self-induced exhaustion, he looked up into the night sky. The brightly shining North Star was his last sight before he died.

Through becoming conscious and observing our natural world, we can once again find our North Star. It has truly been there all along, looking down from a higher perspective as we blindly run ourselves in ever-tightening circles. Like Polaris, all of nature is patiently and silently waiting for us to look up from the illusion and seek its guidance.

We have lost our way; we have lost ourselves to our programming, compensations and defenses, thereby stepping out of our true nature. The more disconnected from our natural expression we become, the less mobility we have and the more drag we encounter, rendering us unable to move with natural law, which results in extreme suffering as we are slowly ground to dust by our resistance to the perpetual movement of life.

Much of our suffering comes from resistance to nature—resistance to what is. Lack of acceptance of death compromises the quality of life. It is only through yielding to the way life works that we find peace, harmony, and ultimately personal power.

> *~ THE MASTER OBSERVES THE WORLD BUT TRUSTS HIS INNER VISION.*
> *HE ALLOWS THINGS TO COME AND GO.*
> *HIS HEART IS OPEN AS THE SKY. ~*
> *~ LAO TZU ~*

## A QUESTION OF BALANCE

Balance is not static, it is in constant motion. Imbalance creates friction, which eventually leads to destruction of whatever created the imbalance. Through this creation and destruction process, nature renews itself.

Imbalances result from our repeated attempts to harness power by hacking into the toroidal fields of life.

It can be no other way.

Ultimately all of our manipulations, aspirations, and acquisitions are ground to dust through the friction caused by our own imbalances as they collide with natural law.

Soon this dust is lifted in the wind and carried out to sea. The rains come, washing it into the ocean, where it sinks to the bottom, becoming sediment, which is subjected to the colossal pressure of miles of water pressing down on the ocean floor.

Time passes, and the dust is pressed into rock.

Ages change, new influences are brought to bear, and plates shift, pushing the rock to the surface.

Land masses rise.

A mountain is born.

Ultimately, we are the mountain and the dust, the alpha and the omega, the beginning and the end, as we ride the cycles of life carried aloft by the winds of time.

The Eagles said it so well in their song...

### Dust in the Wind

*I close my eyes only for a moment*
*and the moment is gone*
*All my dreams pass before my eyes a curiosity*

*Dust in the wind*
*All they are is dust in the wind*

*Same old song just a drop of water in an endless sea*
*All we do crumbles to the ground*
*though we refuse to see*

*Dust in the wind*
*All we are is dust in the wind*

*Don't hang on nothing lasts forever*
*not the Earth or sky*
*It slips away*
*all your money won't another minute buy*

*Dust in the wind*
*All we are is dust in the wind*

*~ The Eagles ~*

# 6

# A Magic Temple

The human body is an exquisitely refined organism that is designed to anchor spirit to the physical. It has many mysteries, from its ability to transmute organic matter into energy and form, generate electric current, and translate and store information, to its ability to reproduce itself. As the temple that houses our souls, it can prism light-light and dark-light into a rainbow of colors, and move spiritual energy into the world.

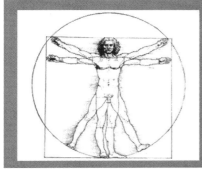

*In 1490, Leonardo daVinci, through his famous drawing—The Vitruvian Man—was exploring the human body as it relates to nature through sacred geometry. Through his anatomical drawings, daVinci presented the human body as a cosmography of the microcosm. He established the workings of the human body as an analogy for the workings of the universe.*

DANCE OF THE SPHERES

In addition to its amazing physical attributes, the body has a chakra system. The word Chakra comes from the Sanskrit word for "wheel" or "turning." The chakra system is very complex and far reaching, therefore, I can't hope to cover it in depth here, but for our purposes, a brief overview will suffice.

The chakras work together to manage the spirit body, and with it our interaction with the quantum level of life. It is through the chakra system that we draw to us the circumstances we need, and repel what would be harmful. It is also through the chakra system that we draw to us the raw materials needed to manifest.

Each physical chakra (we will discuss the esoteric chakras later in this chapter) is anchored into the physical body through governing organs or glands. For now we will focus on ones that work through the endocrine glands, including the heart. Endocrine glands work together in perfect consort to run the functioning of the physical body.

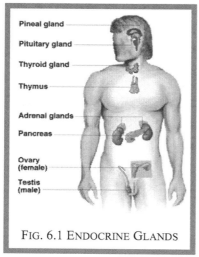

Pineal gland
Pituitary gland
Thyroid gland
Thymus
Adrenal glands
Pancreas
Ovary (female)
Testis (male)

FIG. 6.1 ENDOCRINE GLANDS

Light-light (masculine) is drawn in through the crown chakra, which is anchored in the pineal gland and dark-light (feminine) is drawn in through the root chakra, which is anchored in the reproductive endocrine glands—ovaries or testes, depending upon gender. This light is then run through the prism of each chakra, creating individualized frequencies that correspond with the "color" and individualized function of each chakra.

Each chakra has a masculine (positive) and a feminine (negative) expression. The light that is directed in through the crown and root chakras provides a constant flow of energy, supplying movement. The center of each chakra is a neutral vacuum, which creates the perfect environment for... you've got it... a torus. Each chakra expresses in the form of a differentiated toroidal field.

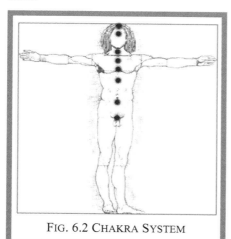

FIG. 6.2 CHAKRA SYSTEM

These toroidal fields shift and flex according to our conscious (and unconscious) intent. This constant fluctuation and movement adjusts itself to our intent and our environment, maintaining balance while effecting change in accordance with desired outcome. This is where expressions such as, "my heart goes out to her" originate. All life expresses in varying combinations of toroidal fields. The human body is no exception. When we feel a heart connection with someone, the toroidal field of our heart chakra is actually connecting to that of the other person.

Up until now I have been discussing the portion of the chakra system that is anchored to a physical gland. It needs to be noted that the chakra system is not restricted to the physical. Each chakra, physical or esoteric, has its own toroidal field containing a positive, negative, and neutral, therefore, each chakra presents a crossover place—an eye of the needle. This progression of eyes of the needle moves both above and below the physical body into infinity. In this way our souls do reach to the edges of the universe and beyond as we approach unity with All-That-Is.

> ~ *Matter is Energy. Energy is Light. We are all Light Beings.* ~
> ~ *Albert Einstein* ~

The body's ability to do all its work is totally dependent upon a delicate balance of minerals, nutrients, light, temperature, water, air, pH, hormones, frequency, its physical location on the planet, and the planet's location in the universe, to name just a few. The body can shift this magical balance with the seasons and even the ages, as it translates the astrological frequencies from the light it draws in and responds accordingly.

## Nothing if Not Adaptable

The human body is a true opportunist. That is to say, it is a master of using what is at hand. During times of lower frequency or energy, such as the long dark, it subsists on the physical, which requires us to kill in order to live. During times of greater frequency/energy/light, the body can sustain itself mostly on light. It is of times of increased frequency/light that the biblical prophecy found in Isaiah 11:6 speaks:

> *6 The wolf also shall dwell with the lamb, and the leopard shall lie down with the kid; and the calf and the young lion and the fatling together; and a little child shall lead them.*

A time when predator and prey coexist in harmony as sustenance is increasingly drawn from light rather than the consumption of other life forms.

During the long dark, when the Earth was traveling through a time of reduced frequency, the body had much less light available to sustain it. This necessitated obtaining its sustenance predominantly from the earth or the physical. This had us living a caveman status—a whole lot of animal and very little spirit. Each age has its lessons and purpose for our souls, so this is not a quality judgment, but just an example.

As the ages change, so do our bodies, enabling us to make use of the frequency, light, and nutrients present during our particular lifetimes. In this way, the human body alters and adjusts itself, not just within one lifetime, but also across generations, in accordance with the ages. And we profess to understand the mysteries of the human body—a laughable concept.

*~ HUMANITY IS A RIVER OF LIGHT RUNNING*
*FROM ETERNITY TO ETERNITY. ~*
*~ KAHLIL GIBRAN ~*

## ENTER STAGE LEFT: MODERN HUMAN

Somewhere during the age of too much brain and not enough animal, we decided we could improve on our environment. Instead of letting our bodies adjust to the length of day, we adjusted the length of day by adding artificial light and daylight savings time. Instead of letting our bodies adjust to the seasons, we now keep our dwellings at 70° F or so year in and year out. Instead of eating what we grow locally, in season, which is, by the way, balanced to our longitude and latitude, we ship our genetically modified, irradiated, chemical-preservative-ridden food across the globe. Or better yet, we ship our bodies across the globe to enjoy the foods along with the ambiance. This snatches our bodies, which are precariously balanced to exactly where we are, to somewhere they are not. We stay there just long enough for the poor body to almost adjust, then we snatch it up again and take it back. Jet lag begins to make more sense. When we arrive back home, some of our cells are comprised of things balanced to Denver, while others think they belong in Hong Kong.

Suffice it to say that even before we add pollutants and chemicals, the delicate balance of our body is grossly compromised, which translates as illness and eventually disease, which we then treat by adding chemicals (drugs), which are taken out of their natural order and synthesized, creating further imbalance (side effects). We treat these side effects with further chemicals until we are walking cocktails of God only knows what and humans don't want to.

Our bodies' ability to prism light diminishes as the resulting hormonal imbalances compromise the attunement of our chakras to our endocrine glands. We become less spiritual (light) beings and more imbalanced physical ones. Eventually, this imbalance makes us incapable of maintaining not only spiritual consciousness, but also physical life. Individuals who lose their spiritual connection are subject to "the system" for guidance and thus become exploitable. In trying to live better lives, we are killing ourselves. I like my comforts as much as the next person, but there has to be a better way.

Now we have another complication.

## ENTER STAGE RIGHT: THE AQUARIAN AGE

While modern-day lifestyles compromise our balance and therefore our frequency, our sun—therefore our solar system—is moving into the high-frequency band of light particles called the Photon Band. Not only does the Photon Band make high frequency/light available for our bodies to work with, but the increasing frequency also demands exacting balance.

The higher frequency demands more refinement, while our lifestyles have created more coarseness in the form of the imbalances mentioned above. In effect we are running against the wind. This leaves us with several choices:

❖ Stay as we are and get shaken apart

❖ Go deeper into denial—stick our head in the sand where the higher frequency passes through unnoticed (like radio waves through a brick wall)

❖ Obtain greater refinement and evolve.

Gee, let me think.... As Winston Churchill said, "When you are going through hell—keep going."

The first two choices have predictable results. The third is more involved than it first appears. As in the case of bi-planes trying to go super-sonic, just recessing the rivets is not enough. We will need to obtain greater balance on all four levels of our being.

## FOUR LEVELS

There are four levels to this magic temple that comprises our expression as human beings—physical, emotional, mental, and spiritual. Starting to sound familiar? These four levels are a continuum of frequency from the lowest frequency—the physical—to the highest—the spiritual. While they seem quite different upon first glance, they all hold to the same principles, but at different frequencies. In addition, just like the endocrine glands, they are designed to work together in harmony with each other. These harmonics are not static—they change, in consort, with each situation, expression, and intent, while ideally remaining in harmony. One of the greatest contributors to restrictions in our overall frequency is toxic overload, which can be found in all four levels.

## THE PHYSICAL LEVEL

We have already gone over much of the imbalances that compromise our physical bodies in "Smoke and Mirrors," From the artificial hormones that leach out of our handy-dandy plastic containers, to the ones injected in the animals that we eat, and the pesticides and chemical fertilizers that we ingest with everything else we eat, our physical bodies can't help but be compromised by our diet. Exposure to artificial lighting and living out of rhythm with the seasons also compromises our balance. In our attempts to conquer nature we have outsmarted ourselves into a stupor.

How we choose to minimize the physical compromises to our bodies is a personal choice. It's not necessary to address all of the compromises to effect notable improvement. The following are suggestions of simple things that can make a large difference.

## PURE WATER

The single most important thing you can do for your physical health is to stop drinking artificial beverages and consume copious amounts of purified (not distilled) water. So often, I hear people say, "I drink coffee or pop or—you fill in the blank—I get plenty of liquid." *NOT!* Water is the universal solvent. It is the major contributor to the detoxification of our bodies. If the water is already mixed with something, that something is in suspension, binding the water so it can't pick up the toxins. By drinking soft drinks or coffee *instead* of pure water you are actually *adding* to your toxic load, not diminishing it. I am not saying that the only thing you can drink is water, but your health will be greatly enhanced if most of the liquid you consume is purified water. You also need to drink much more than you may think. In dryer climates a gallon a day is not overkill. The kidneys need pure water in order to efficiently detox. Our bodies are 70% water. You do the math.

## LOSE THE WAVE

We previously covered the negative effects of microwaving our food, but it can't be emphasized enough. I had a student who ate mostly organic food but still carried a lot of extra weight in his belly. After our discussion in class about microwaves, he lost 30 pounds in two months. The only thing he changed was to quit microwaving his food.

## GO ORGANIC

One of the best ways to minimize toxic overload and enhance frequency is to eat organic, non-GMO food. Not only does this help our bodies, but it also encourages the responsible growing methods practiced by organic farmers, thus minimizing our impact on the planet at large. The counter argument I often hear is: "But organic is so expensive."

Non-organic food is full of chemicals, which not only add to the toxic load, but also bind up the nutrients in the food, making our bodies expend much more energy in order to assimilate them. It takes much more non-organic food to gain the same amount of sustenance that one can get from organically produced products. So, it can actually take more energy to process non-organic food than what you get out of it. Between reduced nutrient value and increased toxicity of non-organic food, you are dealing with diminishing returns. In addition, the body's method of dealing with the toxins is often to store them as fat. There is growing evidence that toxic overload may be responsible for many diseases such as obesity and cancer, which is not cheap to deal with on any level.

Natural skin-care products are also advisable. Our skin absorbs whatever we put on it. It doesn't make any sense to eat organic and then put chemicals of uncertain effect on our skin.

## AVOID PLASTIC

Every chance you get, choose food and drinks in glass containers. Plastics leach artificial hormones like BPA into our food.

## EAT LOCAL

Food grown locally is balanced with the frequency of the part of the planet where you are. Local food takes less energy from your system to be converted into what you need. It also reduces the pollutants that are added to our environment by transporting food over great distances. Plus it is fresher.

## EAT WITH THE SEASONS

Our bodies function best when aligned with the natural order. This alignment is greatly aided by eating what is naturally available in the seasons—fresh fruit and vegetables in the summer, mainly root crops and seasonal greens in the winter, and so on.

## NATURAL LIGHT

As much as possible, expose yourself to natural light. The natural-light rhythms of sunrise and sunset are what regulate melatonin production by the endocrine gland known as the pineal gland. Melatonin in turn regulates our sleep and sweeps up disease-causing free radicals while we are asleep. Some scientists in Europe have discovered that the pineal gland confuses radio-frequency radiation from cell phones and cell phone towers for visible light, thus suppressing melatonin production, leading to disease as the free radicals build up. You can check with your health care practitioner, but with this latest information, you may find that it is a good idea to supplement, especially since its production also declines with age. The pineal is also the seat of the crown chakra, where we channel light-light into our entire chakra system.

I love to sit in my west-facing living room with the lights off and watch the sun set. By watching the light shift and finally fade to indigo, then darkness, I expose myself to the frequencies of the changing light. I wait until it is finally fully dark outside before turning on my lights. I use a full spectrum bulb in the lamp next to my chair to read by.

I built my house so that my bedroom faces east, and I have a top-down shade on my window. I leave the blind open at the top at all times. This allows me privacy, while at the same time allowing me to enjoy natural light. The sunrise shines into my room every morning, enabling me to wake to the progressing light frequencies of dawn.

## MOVE

While using the gym is better than not moving at all, there is no substitute for fresh air and exercise. Our heart is a one-way sort of guy. It pumps blood out to the body. The return trip of our blood to the heart is totally dependent upon the expansion and contraction of our muscles. Exercise increases breathing, which helps detoxify our bodies through our lungs. There isn't much of that going on when we are planted on our back side.

The sun is the absolute best source of Vitamin D, deficiency of which is almost epidemic in our culture. Sunlight also helps detoxify our skin.

Our houses emit gases. Almost everything in them is at least partially made of chemical-laden artificial materials. Even on a day of poor air quality, the outside air is better for us than the air inside of our homes. I sleep with my window cracked year round.

## THE EMOTIONAL LEVEL

Our emotions are also in one big modern mess. From childhood we are taught to stuff our emotions rather than to process them. For instance, few of us have ever been taught how to responsibly move anger. Instead, we are so emotionally backed up that we tend to dump toxic rage upon the hapless sole who is unfortunate enough to put the proverbial straw on our camel's back.

We so avoid our sorrow that we can no longer access our joy. Joy and sorrow are interrelated—a sine wave requiring balance between the two expressions to maintain movement. Life by its

> ### Bathe Deeply
> *Joy and sorrow form a sine wave*
> *When we run from our sorrow we cannot truly enter our joy*
> *Suffering is the result.*
> *When we try to cling to our joy the flow of life is restricted*
> *We experience an emotional death*
> *If we do not bathe deeply in our sorrow, We are not sufficiently cleansed to fully enter our joy.*

very nature is in constant motion and process. Shutting down any natural process has negative ramifications and limits our mobility and therefore our life. Rather than having responsible ways of processing emotions in the moment, we stuff them until we either flat line or become volatile. The answer we have for such issues is drugs and more drugs!

Because we are emotionally unprocessed, it is difficult to discern what deserves our zeal. Few of us realize that much of what we may be feeling in the moment is actually backed-up, unexpressed emotion from our past. It is very difficult to be "in the now" when we carry around baggage from the past that is constantly being triggered by present events. In the rapid acceleration of our times, there is no room for extra baggage, or drag.

## IT'S ABOUT...

As we move through these times of rapid acceleration, it is important to recognize that extreme emotion (particularly above and beyond what the situation warrants) is not about the people and situations around us. It is really all about us and our unprocessed baggage. This is an inside job.

When I am in doubt about how to responsibly manage my emotions, I look to nature. The mother bear uses her anger to protect her cubs. When her young are threatened, she lets it rip until the danger is past—then goes on with life. She doesn't hold a grudge or seek revenge. In all animals, even humans, anger is natural and necessary for setting boundaries. Only toxic, unexpressed rage seeks to blame, hold grudges, or indulge in revenge. To be rage-full is really to be full of *unprocessed* rage.

## STORAGE SHEDS

Emotions are energy—never created or destroyed—and if they are not moved, they need to take up residence somewhere, thus the saying "venting your spleen." Anger often takes up residence in the liver or spleen, while fear often resides in the kidneys. Love, unexpressed or not returned, tends to reside in the heart. Grief sets up camp in the lungs. These unwanted guests create restrictions in the organs, which impinge on our toroidal fields, in turn limiting our mobility, compromising our longevity and quality of life. When our toroidal fields are not impinged upon, they are virtually self-generating power sources that naturally result in longevity.

## TOXIC DUMP

As our toroidal fields are being challenged with increased frequencies, the stuffed emotions tend to rattle loose. Road rage is an illness particular to our times.

*~ ANY EMOTION WE JUDGE AGAINST AND RESIST, PERSISTS. ~*

Every thought or feeling is energy. When we direct it at another, it does have an effect, whether positive or negative. Even romantic love can be burdensome if it is directed at a person who cannot receive or return it. The responsible management of our emotions requires that we move it into one of the elements to transmute it rather than to direct it at anyone. The following are several simple rituals that can help you responsibly manage your emotions without stuffing them and causing yourself damage.

## WATER

The safe movement of emotion can be facilitated by the element of water. Stand in a stream facing downstream. Ask the water to transmute your words and feelings to do no harm, then tell the river your woes. A shower works well for this as well, if you are not close to a moving body of water.

## AIR

For those dwelling in a windy area, go out to a windy, private hillside, address the wind and ask it to transmute your emotions to do no harm, then send your words on the wind to spirit rather than to the people involved in your life.

## EARTH

One of my personal favorites that can be done anywhere is to get some natural clay from a pottery store. Kneed it, and as you do, pass all your angst through your hands into the clay. When you are done, take it out and bury it, asking the Earth to transmute your feelings to do no harm.

## FIRE

If you have a real fireplace or fire pit, build a fire in it. If not, go to a remote campground and build one. In a pinch, a candle will do. When you get the fire raging, ask it to take the words you have to say and transmute them to do no harm. Proceed to tell the fire, yelling and cursing if necessary, how angry you are, at whom and why. You can express grief, unwelcomed love or deep discouragement, as well as rage. Any emotion you need to move can be handled in this way. Do not try to be fair or reasonable. The fire will take care of that for you. It also works well to write a letter expressing the unwelcomed love or anger and then burn it.

These suggestions may seem trite until you consider the power of our intent, conscious and unconscious. By using the transmutative properties of the elements, combined with the power of our intent, not only can we move our backed-up emotions consciously and harmlessly, but we can also free ourselves of restrictions as well. Try it, you'll like it.

## THE MENTAL LEVEL

During the long dark, when we had lost direct access to spiritual information, it became necessary to store all information in our physical mind and to use our mental capacity to figure out how to apply it. This was the time of the oral traditions, and it was a vital use of the brain, appropriate to the times. Later, as we developed the written word, we also developed ways to study our environment, dissect it and try to understand the workings of the world around us with our minds (a laughable concept). What we decided to be true, based on our study, became "irrefutable truth" (aka dogma) and was applied with religious zeal and taught in our schools, at least until the latest, greatest study disproved it, if the powers in control at the time allowed the "irrefutable truth" to be refuted.

Now, as we enter higher-frequency times, direct, personal access to spiritual information is becoming increasingly available, so how we use our minds also needs to change configuration. Soon it will no longer be necessary or desirable to clog up our brains with dubious facts, as our minds will need to become translators from spirit to the physical. At higher frequencies we will have access to the Akashic Records. Akasha comes from a Sanskrit word meaning "sky, space, or ether." These records are often described as a library or collection of all existence. They are frequency-encoded information from the unity of All That Is, or spirit.

*~ THE MORE WE CONNECT WITH OUR TOROIDAL FIELDS, THE GREATER OUR REACH ON ALL LEVELS; GENIUS IS THE NATURAL RESULT. ~*

All things express according to frequency. Information is therefore frequency, and frequency is energy. Remember, energy is never created nor destroyed, so it makes sense that the frequency signature of everything that has ever taken place is available somewhere. Accessing the Akashic Records follows the same principles used by forensic investigators at crime scenes. Forensic psychics read the frequency traces left in the environment after a crime.

Having access to the Akashic Records instead of mentally storing information is much like accessing what you need on the web when you need it, rather than storing it all on your PC.

We all have experienced access to this "field" of information in the form of intuitive or instant insights. It is important to bear in mind, however, that to fully access and translate the information found in the Akashic Records is a skill set that must be learned and perfected. There are many among us that already have this access, but in the absence of the skill set required for translation, some really wild and equally erroneous assumptions are being made and passed off as truth.

*~ Only a trained occultist can distinguish between actual experience and those astral pictures created by imagination and keen desire. ~*
*~ C.W. Leadbeater (1910) On the Akashic Records ~*

## Tree of Knowledge of Good and Evil

When we were in polarized times, the brain had to judge what was good or bad and respond accordingly. In an extremely polarized environment, judgment was a necessary part of our reasoning and responding in order to survive. The problem arose when we applied that same judgment to all situations. While it was necessary to apply discernment, it was crippling to "sit in judgment." Rarely is the same response appropriate for every situation, which has become the major failing of our judicial system.

## Unlock Your Head

The first step in evolving mentally is the simple acceptance that our current reality is extremely limited and primitive, if not completely erroneous. The willingness to let go of our attachment to what we think we know is paramount in order to evolve. While this sounds simple, the almighty brain and our formidable ego involvement in knowledge will not give up easily. In "Shamanism 101," I offer techniques that will help you to access universal knowledge and decode it. Employing these techniques on a regular basis will start to retrain the brain in its proper place in the scheme of things.

## Spiritual Level

Our body is the gateway through which spiritual power is moved from the ethers into the physical. In short, it is the channel for true manifestation. The physical body is a finely tuned instrument that prisms light and frequencies, which are, in turn, used to influence the energetic matrix that surrounds us. This matrix (or auric field) is what is responsible for drawing to us what we need for any particular project or manifestation and for repelling what is harmful or not needed. Our auric field is also a toroidal field that expresses our spirit or interaction at the quantum level of life. Just as the Earth's electromagnetic field protects her from the galactic winds, our toroidal field naturally protects our energy body from harmful energy in our environment.

Each of our four levels is represented as a layer in our auric field (Fig. 6.3). The physical level has an energetic emanation running from the physical surface of the body to about two feet out. At two feet from the physical body, the physical auric field gives way to the emotional auric body. Two feet from the onset of the emotional comes the mental and then, two feet beyond that, the spiritual. These distances are approximate, as they are constantly shifting and flexing, depending upon what we are doing at any given time.

FIG. 6.3 AURIC FIELD LEVELS

Likewise, there is also a lot more going on in our auric fields than just the representation or resonance of the physical, emotional, mental, and spiritual bodies. This example is just the basic anatomy and is by no means the totality of the auric field.

In Celtic shamanism, it is believed that our spirits extend from the body to encompass the entire universe. This is a great way to view the complexity of our systems and our ability to merge with All-That-Is. We are a system of wheels within wheels, tori[1] within tori that intermingle and interrelate from the quantum level to the intergalactic one.

There is really no separation between us and spirit. It is simply a matter of there being enough frequency or light for us to perceive it. Our chakras, as well as our auras, extend well beyond the physical body, traveling out into infinity. How much access we have to our chakric and auric fields is determined not only by the light present but also by our level of processing. This is the deciding factor in our gifts. Can we align with the physical auric fields of another and

*For to one is given by the Spirit the word of wisdom; to another the word of knowledge by the same Spirit;*

*To another faith by the same Spirit; to another the gifts of healing by the same Spirit;*

*To another the working of miracles; to another prophecy; to another discerning of spirits; to another divers kinds of tongues; to another the interpretation of tongues;*

*But all these worketh that one and the selfsame Spirit, dividing to every man severally as he will.*

*~ Corinthians 12, 8-11 ~*

---

1. tori is plural of torus.

feel his/her pain? Can we feel the emotional trauma left in a room after a violent act? Can we align with the mental auric field of others? Can we access the Akashic Records and download the light into information to translate with our brain? All of these abilities are very real; how proficient we are is dependent upon the presence of light, the level of personal processing, our aptitude, training, and mastery.

## LIVING PRISMS

Humans have been portrayed by many shamanic cultures as the link between Heaven and Earth—this is to say that they are the link between spirit and the physical. In order to better understand how this works, it is necessary to first address frequency as it pertains to the human body.

*~ ALL THINGS EXPRESS ACCORDING TO FREQUENCY. ~*

There is a scale of frequencies that runs from the denseness of matter to the invisibility of radiation and beyond. The frequency of sound is produced by repetitive disturbances of the air, causing waves to travel at the speed of sound, at a frequency determined by the number of disturbances per unit of time. These waves are picked up by our eardrums and translated in the brain. Some intense sounds—drumming for instance—can be felt through the body as vibration.

Some frequencies are created by the transmutation of one form into another. An example of this is the light from our sun, which is created by the element of fire as it burns and transmutes gases, which produces waves that travel through time and space at the speed of light. Light is picked up by the cones and rods in our eyes and translated by our brains into vision. Each frequency within the scale of light gives us a different color. White reflects all colors and black absorbs them all. It is necessary to have black as well as white to create contrast. Without contrast there would be no vision as we know it. Some frequencies of light can also be felt by the body. Infra-red, for instance, is perceived as heat.

Other frequencies cannot normally be perceived by the human body. Among these are radio waves, which are of such a high frequency that they can pass virtually unnoticed through lower, denser ones, like the walls of buildings or the human body. There is increasing evidence that constant bombardment from radio waves (RF) does have long-term effects such as causing cancer in humans or causing bees to lose their ability to navigate. Earlier we discussed how radio waves confuse the pineal gland into suppressing melatonin production, thus potentially causing disease.

Sound, light, radio waves, and nuclear radiation form a range of frequencies in the scale. Just as you can dial different radio stations, the scale of frequencies is actually a continuum of harmonies, like a musical scale that repeats harmonically at higher or lower frequencies, like chords on a piano keyboard.

## EXPRESSIONS OF LIGHT

The human body not only receives and perceives a certain range of frequencies, but it also produces its own unique range. Every individual has a set of harmonics particular to their expression. The frequency of a person varies according to their level of processing, as well as what they are doing at any given time.

Every thought, intent, belief, emotion, and denial alters our frequency. This alteration of harmonics has a marked effect on our environment, and it leaves a trace. It is through these alterations that sensitives, such as natural psychics, can "read" the scene of a crime and "see" what happened there.

These alterations in frequency also dictate the law of attraction and repulsion in our lives, which is how what we believe, think, or intend affects our experience, including our abundance (the observer effect). Frequency interacts in our world with an electromagnetic push and pull that is generated consciously or unconsciously by our intent.

The range of frequencies each of us produces has a home base, if you will, where a person is in balance and at rest, which is the true form of being here now, and it is also each person's base-line signature. Because of our polluted food, water, environment, and technical manipulation of frequencies causing energetic pollution such as massive amounts of radio waves, microwaves, nuclear radiation, *etc.*, it is increasingly difficult to find our natural home base. Plus, the use of carbon fuels has produced a yellow filter in the Earth's atmosphere that distorts the light spectrum from the sun.

Many of us have never been at home base, as our mothers and fathers have been subject to this distortion altering their DNA, which in itself is a light-and-frequency code dictating how matter (frequencies) come together to form our bodies. The way our bodies are comprised, to some degree, dictates our harmonics. Oh, what a tangled web we weave.

The farther we are from our true home base, the less able we are to perceive subtle frequencies and, the less psychic we are. The less psychic or privy to the subtle energies at the quantum level we are, the more unconscious our intent and therefore our manifestations are. Most of the population doesn't even believe psychics exist because the distortion and lack of mobility within our expression has reduced us to the five senses and even limited those. Yet, being psychic *is* our birthright.

Now, here is the clincher: our bodies, being mostly water, are natural prisms of frequency. Remember, our chakra systems express divinations of light, both (dark/feminine and light/masculine) by taking in light-light through the crown chakra and dark-light through the root and expressing a rainbow of colors or frequencies.

Most people cannot see the chakras because their "colors" are of a more expansive frequency than the visual spectrum. We call them colors because they harmonize with the colors we use to describe them (remember the continuum of harmonics, much like a piano keyboard). They also harmonize with a sound, a smell, and an action or quality of expression. As we discussed earlier, each chakra is anchored in an endocrine gland, which in turn produces hormones particular to the frequency to align the body with it. In this way, we align our physical being to our spiritual one, and our intent becomes manifestation. Much as our DNA, through frequency codes, draws together the matter needed to form our bodies, the frequency signature put out through our chakras, as they respond to our intent, interacts with the physical world in order to manifest.

If we do not perceive subtle frequencies or understand our effect in the world, we are basically shooting in the dark, yet we are indeed shooting. The results are much like a blindfolded skeet shooter, and we are randomly putting holes in things. Through our unconscious use of power, we become victims of our own creations while, at the same time, we are unable to consciously manifest what we want and need.

Becoming conscious and deliberate in the use of our bodies as living prisms is a complicated process. As stated above, much of our imbalance is from our environment and history. For some conditions, such as the polluted atmosphere, we personally have little to no control, but others, such as what food and liquids we consume, we do. We all sustain spiritual damage and are subject to cultural conditioning that separates us from our true expression, or our home base. To complicate matters, no two roads home are the same. There is no canned answer for everyone.

The process of finding home base is actually an evolutionary one. Where we currently are in the ages has put us in a position to regain our birthright as conscious prisms of light and dark—the true balance points between Heaven and Earth.

*~ THERE IS NO STRUGGLE OF SOUL AND BODY SAVE IN THE MIND OF THOSE WHOSE SOULS ARE ASLEEP AND WHOSE BODIES ARE OUT OF TUNE. ~*
*~ KAHLIL GIBRAN ~*

٠

## SAULES MEITA

Saules was the Sun Goddess, and Saules Meita was her beautiful, golden daughter. Mother and daughter were inseparable, as Meita worshiped her mother and Saules's pride and joy was her daughter. The sky was bright with the innocence of Meita and the flaming beauty of Saules. Their shared laughter and love brightened the dawn and set the sun in glories of reds.

Alas, all things change. Seasons came and went, and Meita grew into womanhood. Then came the fateful day that night fell hard. During that long dark night Meita decided it was not safe to grow into a beautiful woman. What good was it if it brought about lust and rape? What good was it if it turned her mother's love into searing jealousy? No, it was not safe. In fact, her life depended upon her not becoming beautiful and sexy. Decision made, she set her powerful will into motion. Her intent to stop becoming womanly was translated to her body. Like the dutiful servant it was, her body responded to her will. The sex hormone levels altered so her body could never reach its full potential.

It was also not safe to let down her guard. This had happened, she decided, because she did not notice the way her father was looking at her that eve when she kissed him and her mother goodnight and went to bed. Again, she set her will into motion, and again her body made the hormonal adjustments. Adrenalin levels climbed, synapses got scrambled, and melatonin production dropped, as she had also decided that she needed to know all that was going on around her, and it was not safe to go to sleep. Now her senses were extended far out from her body. She would be able to feel lust directed at her. She could feel jealousy and plotting for revenge. Never mind that it created a state much like autism or that she would never truly rest. Never mind that she felt the world's trauma as if it were her own. It was not safe to not know.

Years went by, and Meita grew ill. Her bones became weak without adequate estrogen to help absorb calcium. Exhaustion claimed her as her overtaxed adrenal glands failed. She gained weight and lost muscle tone without adequate thyroid to sustain her. Her brilliant mind became foggy and sluggish. The daughter of the Sun was dying, having never really lived.

## PERSONAL POWER

Our auric fields are the physical container for our spiritual or light bodies while we are incarnate. They are generated by our chakras, and their strength or quality is dependent upon the balance between the chakras. Many chakras are centered in endocrine glands, which create our hormones, which in turn regulate all bodily functions. The entire system is subject to our conscious and unconscious will and intent.

We have so much more power and control in our lives than we know. Every decision or strong intent we make impacts our physical bodies. This is the complication behind hormone replacement. Unless we access and heal changes we have set into motion in the past in an attempt to protect ourselves, our ever-faithful bodies will compensate for everything we put in them in order to maintain the imbalance we unconsciously believe will save our lives.

As in the example of Saules Meita, many women in our culture live in the paradox: "I must be young, slender, sexy, and beautiful to be worthwhile," and "If I am young, slender, sexy, and beautiful, I will be hated by women and raped by men." So we diet or develop eating disorders, starving our bodies. At the same time, we unconsciously create a thyroid imbalance that in turn causes weight gain in order to keep us safe.

Many young men growing up are taught they have to be manly to make their fathers proud of them. Yet they dare not become so virile as to threaten their father's dominant position in the family. It is also secretly believed that by being too macho, they will scàre women who will see them as testosterone-driven pillaging beasts. After all, modern women want the sensitive new-age kind of guy. This results in testosterone deficiencies and sex hormone-related problems.

## PRISMS OF LIGHT, PRISMS OF DARK

Since our physical bodies work as prisms, we take in masculine light-light through our crown chakra and isolate different ranges of frequency or light with each chakra below, giving them their individualized color or frequency. Likewise, we take in feminine dark-light through our root chakra and the same procedure operates upward through the chakra system. The same is true of sound. Although it is out of the range perceived by the human auditory system, every chakra indeed has a set of tones. When we are in balance, harmony is created by the tones. If you are a person who understands sound, you know that each added sound wave also builds volume.

Two of the ways in which energy is transported in the world around us are through mechanical and electromagnetic (EMF) waves. Our bodies move our intent into the world through a combination of these waves that are generated through our chakra/endocrine systems. Our endocrine system, through the frequency delivered by hormones, creates mechanical waves, while our chakras create electromagnetic waves.

Mechanical waves require a medium in which to propagate, but the energy is transferred without transporting matter through the medium. For example, the energy of a wave in water travels through the water, while leaving the water molecules in place. Sound is a mechanical wave.

Electromagnetic waves are formed by the interaction between a magnetic field and an electric field. Charged particles, such as electrons and protons, create electromagnetic fields when they move. These fields transport the energy of electromagnetic radiation, or light, much of which is beyond the human visual spectrum.

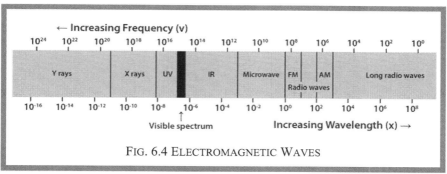

FIG. 6.4 ELECTROMAGNETIC WAVES

Electromagnetic waves differ from mechanical waves in that they require no medium to propagate. Because of this, electromagnetic waves can travel not only through air and solid materials, but also through the vacuum of space.

Electromagnetic waves are the medium through which the shaman's consciousness is carried across time and space, while mechanical waves are the means by which he or she effects change on the physical level. All of this is achieved through conscious control of the toroidal fields found in our chakras. This is not restricted to shaman, however, because the same principles operate in every individual.

Our chakras are not static. Our personal power is directed into the world through our chakra system. Every shift in our intent creates a different interplay of the chakras, much like a symphony as opposed to solid, unchanging harmonious tones. In our natural state, we have amazing flexibility of movement. Living in the world, however, subjects us to various traumas that cause us to leave our natural expression.

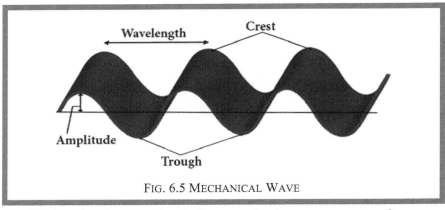

FIG. 6.5 MECHANICAL WAVE

We then develop complex defense mechanisms to prevent us from repeating whatever action we may judge caused the trauma in the first place, as in the example of Saules Meita judging against becoming a woman because of her misperceptions, which resulted in her entire hormonal balance being compromised. The power generated by our chakras is limited by damage, programming, and defense mechanisms. In addition, it takes power to run the defense mechanisms. Avoidance of any natural expression reduces mobility, which then restricts movement, further reducing power.

~ *PERSONAL POWER IS COMPROMISED*
*PROPORTIONATE TO THE RESTRICTIONS*
*IN THE TOROIDAL FIELDS OF OUR CHAKRA SYSTEM.* ~

Each chakra expresses on all four levels of our auric field—physical, emotional, mental, and spiritual. This is a continuum—rather than compartmentalized segments—with a translation point or transducer between each of them where information from one is stepped up or down to the next. The conversion of frequency from one level to the next creates a band of turbulence that can be detected by a sensitive person. Any time we shut down on any level, there is a disconnection at the transducers, resulting in an interruption in the continuum that restricts full access and mobility.

It is fascinating how much power we have over our physical bodies, yet we use it unconsciously. I would hazard to guess that it is through reclaiming the conscious use of personal power that the masters are able to bilocate, produce manna, exhibit stigmata, live five hundred years, regulate their body temperatures, or shape shift, if the existence of those things is to be believed. Personally, I don't find them hard to believe in the least.

Through a spiritual illness, known to shaman all over the planet as "soul loss"—the imposed disconnection from our natural expression and resulting compensatory systems—we have systematically lost consciousness as individuals and as a people. As we have discussed, other things are involved in our slide into unconsciousness, such as where we are in the ages and the lack or presence of the high-frequency spiritual light of the Photon Band / Sagittarius Galaxy and so on. In brief, we can come a long way towards consciousness and the conscious use of power if we come back into balance within our bodies. A balanced body is better able to align with our place in the larger scheme of things.

## How Do I Work This?

If you treat one level of an illness or imbalance without also treating the other three, the correction will not hold. We therefore need to work with all four levels of our expression—physical, emotional, mental, and spiritual in order to establish true and lasting change.

Balance can be achieved through a personalized combination of modalities designed to treat all four levels.

On the spiritual level, trauma results in the spiritual illness of "soul loss." This damage causes compensatory alterations in one's natural expression—such as adjustments in the hormonal balance of the body. In order to return to one's natural expression, this soul loss needs to be corrected through a shamanic healing technique known as "soul retrieval" and requires a well-trained shamanic practitioner to perform it.

I am often asked, "If I learn to journey, can I do my own soul retrieval?" And I answer, "If you learn to sew, can you do your own surgery?"

Spiritual healing is never imposed, but requires a well-trained healer and the participation of the one being healed. It is not like getting a tooth pulled—pop, out-of-there... problem solved. The frequency shift of the healing needs to be stepped down or transduced into the other three levels. This stepping-down process is called "integration" and can take some time.

On the mental level, spiritual illness causes a reframing of the way one views life. What was once viewed as a neutral event is now seen as a dangerous circumstance to be avoided at all cost, which creates restriction and impinges upon mobility. This restriction needs to be uncovered and understood by the mind in order to reevaluate the altered life view and return to natural expression.

There is almost always intense emotion involved in any spiritual illness or trauma. One does not let go of a natural expression easily. They have to be convinced that they are going to die if they do not relinquish part of themselves. When one is convinced of impending death, whether real or imagined, emotional trauma results and the resulting emotions are then suppressed in an attempt to forget the traumatic event. These emotions must be accessed and processed. Often, in our overmedicated culture, they are instead, judged to be neuroses, and, as the cause of them is not evident, they are forcefully suppressed through the use of psychotropic drugs.

Stepping out of avoidance can be an interesting process, as there are usually neuropathways burned in the brain due to the repeated avoidance. These pathways result in a knee-jerk reaction of stimulus and response that will need to be corrected in order to regain mobility. This correction is achieved by when the individual consciously and repeatedly chooses to live his/her life in a different way after the healing—again, active participation in one's own healing process.

On the physical level, we are looking at imbalances that can take up residence in any part of the body. Where the symptoms take up residence is dependent upon a myriad of factors such as genetic predisposition, environmental toxins, diet, *etc.*, whatever is the weak link. Due to the chakra/hormonal involvement, there is a profound correlation between illness and cause, if one knows how to track the evidence. In our current compartmentalized medical framework, however, we often find ourselves chasing symptoms around with no lasting results.

Often the body needs support to regain its balance. The form of that support is dependent upon how gross the imbalance is. I am a great advocate of homeopathic remedies, but they are a very refined adjustment. I was once working with a medical doctor who was on a massive amount of prescription drugs (live by the sword, die by the sword). He mentioned that he had observed that homeopathic remedies didn't seem to have any effect when he took them. I responded, "It is hard to shovel poop with a feather."

*~ THERE IS NO RIGHT OR WRONG CORRECTION,*
*JUST WHAT IS APPROPRIATE TO TIME AND FREQUENCY. ~*

It is important is to meet people where they are, then step them up through a series of increasingly refined corrections, rather than a lifetime of coarse medications. It may very well be that a powerful correction is needed at first to get the ball rolling, but in most cases, all that is needed is a reset, not a lifetime of taking pharmaceuticals. The body needs to remember where it belongs. Yet, if any level is left untreated, it will continue to pull the rest out of balance, resulting in a lifetime of required correction, which is what we now see as we develop resistance to drugs or find ourselves on life-long hormonal replacement.

Light and sound therapies provide a powerful adjunct to assist integration, as does biofeedback. While many of these modalities are being used individually, the best use is a combination, carefully calibrated to each individual, so that the impact is true and lasting.

Please bear in mind that this has just been an overview to help you get the big picture of where we are headed. Furthermore, it is not a process that a person runs through just once. A series of processes is required to see change. Healing is like peeling an onion. We need to repeat the process with each disconnect to unravel the illness and its resulting limitations.

I mentioned that spiritual healing requires the participation of the individual. If that individual is under undue emotional distress, he/she may not have the wherewithal to participate, in which case it would be appropriate to work with him/her through psychotherapy and possible medication to stabilize the person before implementing spiritual-healing modalities. The beauty of this holistic approach is that any and all corrections can be a temporary support, rather than a lifetime of dependence.

*~ THE LIGHT IS ONLY AS CLEAR*
*AS THE WINDOW THROUGH WHICH IT SHINES. ~*

The quality, accuracy, and validity of anything we do is totally dependent upon the clarity of our bodies—physical, emotional, mental, and spiritual—as well as upon the balance we maintain between them. Any place we are not in integrity compromises our power in the world.

For those of us who chose to come at this time to provide support and guidance through these powerful times of change and evolution, the effectiveness of our work is directly related to how effective we are in anchoring to life here on this planet, which is the stepping down or transducing from spirit to the physical. This process is achieved through moving light (both light-light and dark-light) in to the chakras, then into the endocrine glands, and from there into the physical body.

Spiritual power is wielded on the physical plane in the reverse manner by moving from our intent through our hormonal systems to the endocrine glands, and then to the chakras, through our auric fields, and finally into the world. Any restriction or residual damage in any of these areas distorts and limits both the accuracy of our expression and our effectiveness in the world.

We are Earth angels of light who have lost our wings and fallen into unconsciousness. This very unconsciousness is the "dark" we all judge against, not the beautiful darkness of the night or the feminine, and certainly not the dark-light we draw from the root and prism through our chakras. The dark-light is the Goddess returning, bringing with her balance, wholeness, and our key to spiritual evolution.

# 7

# Shamanism and Quantum Physics

Shamanism is an ancient healing practice that is at least 40,000, perhaps even 50,000, years old. It has been practiced in Siberia, Asia, Europe, Australia, Africa, Indonesia, and North and South America, to name just a few, and it contains elements that are remarkably similar across cultures.

*~ IF YOU GO BACK FAR ENOUGH IN HISTORY,
EARTH-CENTERED SHAMANIC SOCIETIES CAN BE FOUND
AT THE BASE OF ALL OF OUR MODERN-DAY CULTURES. ~*

The nature of shamanism has evolved and devolved along with everything else through the ages. During the long dark it too was reduced to a dogmatic adherence to rituals. While shamanism is often seen as an Earth-based modality, the shamanism practiced by ancient Egyptians and Mayans the last time we were in the Photon Band, was actually a galactic form of shamanism, which was used to engineer the pyramids and create the remarkably accurate Mayan Calendar. As we reenter the high frequency of the Photon Band in the Aquarian Age, this more expansive shamanic form is once again becoming available. It is this ancient galactic-oriented shamanism, dating back to the age of Leo, that can enable us to manage matter at the quantum level and aid us in these evolutionary times.

When observed from the outside by the novice, shamanism can indeed be seen as its more classical definition of "a magical-religious practice whereby a practitioner reaches altered states of consciousness in order to interact with the spirit world." On one level of reality, that is exactly what it is. Yet, as we delve deeper into the practice, we find that it is anchored in a much more significant and powerful, if less esoteric, form.

Shamanic skills are wide and varied, including, but not restricted to, the practices of astral projection, mediumship, divination, dowsing, clairvoyance, psychic surgery, herbology, spiritual healing, depossession, channeling, animal communication, and medical intuition.

There are several factors that have led to the misleading and limiting view of shamanism as a religious or magical-superstitious practice.

Many shamanic practices are attached at the hip to the religions of the local culture. For instance, Celtic shamanism is associated with Catholic practices, Tibetan Shamanism with Buddhism, and Native American shamanism with Native American religions. While crossover exists between the religious and shamanic practices of many cultures, shamanism is not a religion and can operate quite effectively outside of any religious practice.

Another major factor contributing to people seeing shamanism as magical superstition is interpreting metaphoric information literally. The spirit world is often seen as another level of reality, full of spirits and animals that perform magic. When taken literally, this has a strong tendency to become a superstition.

Earlier we discussed how our understanding of our world is more polarized at lower frequencies and more unified at higher frequencies. Having come out of a lower-frequency time, our language and understanding of life is polarized and mono-dimensional. Matter at the quantum level, being the behavior and interactions of energy and matter, is much more unified and multidimensional. In order to obtain information and power from the quantum level to use in everyday life, we need a translation point. In shamanism, this translation point is known as the shamanic journey, or the journey trance.

The journey trance is a measurable, altered state of consciousness, much like an interactive dream, whereby the principles operating at the quantum level of life are represented by the imagination in a metaphorical form that then can then be translated by the polarized mind. The journey trance is achieved through various ritualistic ceremonies, usually employing some form of repetitive sound. It was for this purpose that, among many other instruments, ceremonial drums, rattles, and didgeridoos were built. Dancing, chanting, or gazing into one of the four elements such as a fire, a crystal, or water is sometimes involved.

The shamanic practitioner uses some form of journey trance to access information from, and to direct their intent through, the quantum level of life. Basic instruction on entering the shamanic journey trance is included in "Shamanism 101."

## THE LONG ARM OF THE LAW

We've established that everything is subject to the natural laws that are found in nature. Quantum physics is the study of the behavior and interactions of energy and matter, or nature, at the quantum level.

*~ SHAMANISM IS A NATURE-BASED MODALITY;*
*MODERN-DAY MEDICINE IS BASED IN THE MIND. ~*

Shamanic rituals are designed to help the practitioner work within, and be supported by, the laws of nature as observed by Doug Boyd in his book "Rolling Thunder":

> *I knew Rolling Thunder was not breaking laws of body and mind, of chemistry and energy, rather, he was somehow making use of them. The entire ritual was an application of laws.*

To move with the natural laws is to embrace life; to move against them creates friction or drag, eventually leading to distortion and death. The true mastery of shamanism is working within and wielding power according to the laws of nature. To harness nature for one's own purposes— purposes that originate from our patterns rather than our true nature—is sorcery. While sorcery may carry power for a while, it tends to have a nasty backlash. You can only bend the laws of nature to a distorted purpose for so long before nature corrects itself with some very interesting results.

Shamanism in all of its forms is a practice designed to work with the natural laws in order to restore and maintain homeostasis through the balances held and found in nature. All illness is a result of being separated from this balance.

All shamanic cultures refer to the "spirits" of things. Most cultures have archetypal representations for the powers found in nature. The Native American Thunder Bird, the Roman God Thor, and the Greek God Zeus are all represented as deities. From a quantum perspective, the "spirit" of a thing is a metaphoric representation of the energy brought to bear by that particular thing's individualized toroidal field. By working with, rather than against, these toroidal fields, we can obtain universal power to back our intent. This is true mastery.

## TORUS AS THE SHAMANIC VEHICLE

Shamanism is a subject so wide and varied that I could easily write several books on the form and hardly scratch the surface. What is important for us to understand for the purpose of this particular book is how spiritual healing through shamanism can correct restrictions in our personal toroidal fields, enhance mobility, and free up our personal power.

As we explore shamanism and its effect at the quantum level, we find that managing toroidal fields is the heart of all shamanic practices. Through the use of ritual, the masters align with the toroidal fields found in nature, then using this balance, direct their personal toroidal fields to realign and correct imbalances in their client's toroidal fields. The practitioner's ability to align with nature powers this process.

This alignment with nature requires the practitioner to be as free of personal restrictions as possible. The less processed a person is, the less mobility they are afforded and the less effective their work. Every time the practitioner aligns with the toroidal fields of nature in order to perform shamanic healing, pressure is brought to bear on their personal restrictions. This requires the practitioner's first and foremost responsibility to be the constant evolution of their personal processing through the very healing modality they wield.

In addition, the entire process is directed by the practitioner's conscious and unconscious intent, as well as the client's. The more conscious the practitioner, the cleaner and more effective the work. The more shamanic healing the practitioner and client undergo, the more conscious and mobile they become, resulting in spiritual evolution and increased personal power for both parties.

## NO ONE OWNS THE WIND

There are many views on shamanism, varying greatly in accuracy and levels of understanding. The "traditionalists" view shamanism as a set of sacred rituals practiced and owned by particular tribes. What can be entertaining about the "traditionalist" view is exactly *when* they choose to take "tradition" from. Many practices in North America hold to "traditions" that started well after the "long robes" or missionaries came to the continent and polluted the originally matriarchal Earth-based system with patriarchal Christian-based practices.

All shamanic practices operate through rituals designed to focus the practitioner's natural ability to manage matter at the quantum level. During the long dark we lost sight of the underlying purpose of ritual and began to worship the rituals themselves, seeing them as the source of the power rather than the tool to access it.

When we view the ritual as the source of the power, it is easy to believe that by owning the ritual we can own the power. We also overlook the fact that any ritual is only as effective and clear as the practitioner wielding it. Again, the light is only as clear as the window through which it shines.

*~ WHILE FIRE CAN KEEP US ALIVE IN INCLEMENT WEATHER, IT IS NEVER WISE TO PUT IT INTO THE HANDS OF A CHILD. ~*

Natural law has these wonderful checks and balances built in:

- ❖ Our ability to access power is limited by our level of processing and integrity.

- ❖ The more processed we are, the less likely we are to misuse power.

- ❖ We can only misuse power for so long before nature corrects itself.

Many rituals employ the elements (water, air, earth and fire) to access and align with the laws of nature. One of the most beautiful of these is the Lakota Inipi ceremony, or sweat lodge. In this ceremony a domelike structure is built out of, most commonly, Red Willow in a very specific formation that is positioned in accordance with the cardinal directions and in specific relationship to the constellations. It was traditionally covered with hides. A hole is dug in the center, and the dirt from the hole is placed outside the door of the lodge to create the mound or altar. Further away and also in front of the door, a large fire pit is dug, in which volcanic rocks are heated. The ceremony usually consists of four rounds—each one representing and drawing on the differentiated power of one of the four directions. At the beginning of each round a specific number of heated rocks are taken from the fire and placed in the hole in the center of the lodge. Water (often containing sacred herbs) is then poured over the rocks, creating steam.

This ancient Inipi practice combines the elements of water, air, earth, and fire, along with the masculine/positive, feminine/negative and neutral principles. These are combined with sacred geometry and archetypal forces by a well-trained spiritual leader, who constructs and initiates the lodge. The ceremony is run by a consecrated "lodge pourer" and is most often accompanied by drumming and chanting, which when done properly, creates mechanical waves that produce movement that can create and direct toroidal fields.

When the ceremony is activated, it creates its own toroidal field that amplifies the intent of all the participants of the ceremony. It is important to note that the toroidal field simply amplifies intent. If this intent is distorted or imbalanced, that is what gets amplified. The lodge pourer is responsible for managing the toroidal field and maintaining the clarity of the overall intent of the participants.

## Ain't Nothing Like the Real Thing

Once I was participating in a sweat-lodge ceremony in Wyoming. The people there didn't know that I was trained in shamanism, which suited me well enough. Realizing there are as many ways to pour a lodge as there are pourers, I prefer simply enjoying the healing ceremony without getting into a lengthy discussion about procedure.

As we entered the lodge, the lodge pourer, who appeared to be mostly Caucasian, informed me that women were to be seated on one side well away from the men. I was dressed "traditionally" with a long, loose, cotton lodge dress that covered my shoulders and arms while he (also in accordance with "tradition") wore nothing but shorts. I lowered to my knees, uttered the customary Lakota phrase that loosely translates as "all of my relations," then I crawled clockwise around the interior of the lodge to my assigned position. Several young Caucasian women and a few men followed me into the lodge. From their nervous behavior I could tell it was probably their first time participating in the ceremony.

The lodge pourer stopped a particularly attractive young blonde woman as she was about to enter and informed her that she would be the exception to the rule. She was to sit by his side and "hold the feminine" for him. This was a new one on me.

*After* we were all seated in the lodge, the lodge pourer demanded in a loud, authoritative voice to know if there were any women present that were on their moon time. In my experience, this question is normally and quietly addressed by a mature woman before the young girls enter the lodge, but then it wasn't my lodge.

"What is a moon time?" the young woman next to me whispered. I was whispering back an explanation when the lodge pourer reprimanded me, saying women were not to speak in the lodge. I shrugged at the young woman apologetically.

The pourer demanded that any women on their menses leave the lodge post haste. Two young women, blazing red with embarrassment, started to crawl toward the door. The pourer then took them to task for going the wrong direction, further humiliating them.

At this point, I was struggling not to get my dander up at the unnecessarily insensitive treatment of these poor young women.

Next he pulled out a pipe. While of the traditional design, it looked to be quite new.

"Women, cover your heads in the presence of the pipe," he demanded. I was incredulous. "Wasn't it White Buffalo Calf *Woman* who brought the pipe in the first place?" I uncharitably thought to myself, as I threw my towel over my entire head, covering my face, not trusting my expression.

"Just your hair, not your entire head," he snidely reprimanded me again.

At this point I knew I could not hold a proper attitude to participate further in his brand of lodge, so I uttered the proper phrase and started to crawl clockwise for the door.

"Aren't you a little old to be on your moon?" he sneered at me. Having already been told not to speak, I elected not to honor him with an insult and continued toward the door.

As I stood up outside the door flap, very grateful to be in the cool evening air, an old pickup pulled up and three Lakota men got out. I recognized one as a respected pipe carrier and lodge pourer, having sat in one of his lodges before. After warmly greeting me, he looked at the lodge already in process then looked back in my direction raising one eyebrow.

"Who is pouring?" he asked me. I told him the name of the man.

"You are joking, right?" one of his companions asked me. I assured him I was quite serious.

"He is no lodge pourer!" the younger Lakota man stated in disgust, looking at the first man.

"This should be interesting. Let's watch for a while," the Lakota lodge pourer suggested, with a knowing smile. He put down his old Samsonite suitcase containing his sacred herbs and pipe and leaned up against a tree.

Not wanting to intrude, I turned to leave, but he stopped me, asking why I had come out of the lodge before it started. I politely and very briefly enlightened him.

"That apple is no pipe carrier!" his companion heatedly exclaimed, while looking at the actual pourer in outrage. "We should stop this now."

"Spirit has a way of taking care of things," the pourer mysteriously responded, with a twinkle in his eye as heated rocks were delivered to the lodge and the door flap pulled shut.

Again I turned to leave, but he called me by name and asked me to stay. I looked up at him in surprise.

"I know who you are. This won't take long, when the lodge is cleared out, I would like to have you sit in the west if you are willing," he said indicating the lodge with his chin.

I gratefully accepted his kind offer and rejoined the three men.

A chant began, accompanied by offbeat drumming.

"What *is* that song?" one of the men asked the lodge pourer.

"I think it is supposed to be the healing song," he replied, lips twitching.

"Someone should shoot him and put us all out of misery," the first man declared, rolling his eyes.

Finally the terrible sounds thankfully quit emitting from the lodge, followed by some bellowed instructions from the man holding court within, and muttered prayers began.

Suddenly a loud shriek came from the lodge, followed by the sound of a slap.

"Get your hand out from under my dress, you jerk!" an indignant woman's voice shrilly demanded.

"What are you doing to my wife over there?" an enraged bellow followed.

Soon the lodge shook and shuddered as a fight broke out and people began to squirt out of the door amongst billows of steam. My Lakota companion stood casually leaning against a tree with his arms folded over his chest, watching the uprising.

Eventually the self-appointed "lodge pourer" emerged. One side of his face bore a clear red handprint and he was sporting a split lip and the beginnings of a black eye. Still on his hands and knees in front of the lodge door, pipe stem in hand: minus the bowl, he looked up to see the real lodge pourer calmly looking down at him from his position by the tree. The charlatan's face lost all color as he looked up at the silent man, clearly recognizing him.

"I thought you were out of town," the imposter stammered. The pourer slowly shook his head from side to side, saying nothing. The small smile never left his face; his black eyes glistened in the firelight as he silently watched the charlatan slither off in shame. Then, pushing away from the tree, he lifted his Samsonite, hefting it as if to test the weight.

"I hope I brought enough sage; it is going to take a lot to clean up this mess," he said, as he approached the now vacant lodge.

## WANNA-BE

Often self-appointed, untrained, want-to-be leaders often appropriate ceremonies, going through motions they really know nothing about. And, unfortunately, "new age" movements often view shamanism as something to dabble in, taking only what suits them and discarding the rest. Then, often naming it after themselves, they claim it as a new form and market it as a cure all. These ungrounded, ego-centered approaches often have disastrous results, as it is the imbalanced identification with ego that is amplified by the toroidal field of the ceremony rather than the balance of nature.

## NOTHING NEW UNDER THE SUN

All shamanic practices lead back to the original or universal "way." All spiritual healing practices and ceremonies were originally built by drawing on principles firmly anchored in the laws of nature at the quantum level, be they Aboriginal, Siberian, Tibetan or Celtic.

While referring to principles that are common to various traditions, it is necessary that we be mindful not to appropriate specific ceremonies. These ceremonies were built by the medicine men and women of a particular tribe or nation, for their people at that time, and are sacred to them.

Many of the native peoples on our planet who have preserved and practice the ancient methods understandably object to societies who first tried to destroy their ways and now borrow freely and arbitrarily from these same sacred ceremonies.

On the other hand, just because we may be of one race or another doesn't give us carte blanche to practice ceremony. When individuals attempt to perform ceremony without the lifetime of training and personal processing that has gone with them for generations, they often lack the deeper understanding necessary to perform them safely and accurately. This results in distortion and often undesirable outcomes. Make no mistake —shamanism is as complicated as modern-day medicine, if not more so, and should not be taken lightly. Just as natural talent can greatly aid one in becoming an exceptional medical doctor, genetic predisposition to the shamanic gift can be very helpful, but in and of itself, it does not a shaman make. Attempting to perform shamanism without proper training can be disastrous. Just because my father may have been a famous brain surgeon doesn't mean you would want me operating on your head.

## THIS STUFF REALLY WORKS

One common mistake made by the novice is playing with ritual while never really believing in it. It is never wise to underestimate the true power behind the shamanic form. The good news about properly performed shamanic ritual is that it really works; the bad news is—it really works, and if you don't know what you are doing, it will kick you in the back side.

In ancient times, shaman were set apart from the rest of the tribe by their ability to easily move at will between states of consciousness, which is influenced by various things.

I can teach almost anyone to perform and decipher the shamanic journey in order to obtain information and to help focus their intent. This information can guide our use of personal and universal power. Through shamanic journey information, we can discern how to manifest in a harmonious and responsible manner.

Becoming a competent shamanic practitioner who is well-versed in wielding the powers of nature in order to effect change in the material world requires a much deeper aptitude, training and skill set. A well-trained and highly processed shamanic practitioner can perform physical, emotional, mental, or spiritual healing, as well as gain information and guidance. A shamanic practitioner can become the conduit through which spirits, or the natural laws, interact with every-day life to reestablish balance and effect healing, which can be of a person, place, thing, or even circumstance, as there is a shamanic or quantum-level component to everything.

Shamanism is like any other complex skill—some are naturally better at it than others. Really exceptional basketball players tend not to be old, short, mostly Caucasian females, such as myself. Trust me, Michael Jordan I am not. The only thing I can dribble is tea out of my overfilled cup on my way to the breakfast table.

Shamanic skill requires a certain amount of genetic predisposition. Lower resistance to higher frequency, is such a genetic trait. This is much like using gold wire for speakers as opposed to copper as the increased conductivity of gold produces a more pure sound. Some people are just naturally wired to more easily conduct spiritual information. As I studied the life of Christ, it occurred to me that he had to have been one of the greatest shaman to have ever walked the planet. Einstein was another stunning example—highly intelligent, thinking with his entire being rather than just his brain, and able to accurately interpret the information he had access to. In Einstein's case, much of the interpretations came in the form of mathematical proofs. At the same time, it was reputed that the poor man couldn't match his own socks, if he remembered to wear them at all.

If you aspire to learn shamanic skills, don't despair—you don't need to walk on water or be an Einstein. Many other things contribute as well. Traumatic childhoods, near-death experiences and head injuries have also been shown to enhance shamanic skills—trust me, I know about those. But, in my experience, the largest contributing factors are training, personal healing, processing, and motivation.

The purpose of this book, however, is not to train you as a shamanic practitioner. It is to demonstrate how the average individual can evolve with the new era through the application of physical, emotional, mental, and spiritual healing, and the acquisition of basic shamanic journey skills. This evolution results in increased personal power, and, with it, the ability to manifest.

One of the main things standing between us and much of our personal power is the spiritual illness known as soul loss.

## SOUL LOSS

In "A Magic Temple." we introduced the spiritual illness known as soul loss. The story of Saules Meita demonstrated how soul loss affects the physical, emotional, mental, and spiritual bodies.

When we are exposed to trauma or extreme stress, parts of us may be forced offline, so to speak. A clear example of this is "post-traumatic-stress disorder." Any time you hear "he or she has not been the same since..." you are probably hearing about someone who has suffered soul loss. There are innumerable things that can cause soul loss—from the death of a loved one, an accident, physical, emotional or sexual abuse, to basic socialization.

The symptoms of soul loss are as varied as the causes. Symptoms include depression, feeling spaced out, having recurring abusive patterns show up in our relationships, not remembering parts of our past, feeling disconnected from our feelings, not being present in our bodies, having ill health or poor boundaries, feeling depleted, or having obsessive attachment to person, place, or thing.

## OUR PROTECTIVE FIELDS

Recall that we come into the world surrounded by a semi-permeable membrane or auric field. This field is generated by our chakra system and operates much like a cell wall, in that, through simple electromagnetic charges of positive, negative, and neutral, combined with motion, they draw in what is needed and repel what is not. Like each individual cell, the auric field operates as a torus.

This ever-moving and changing toroidal field manages our lives at the quantum level, providing protection and driving manifestation through its interaction with our chakras, our conscious and unconscious intent, and the outside world. The effectiveness of our auric field depends on freedom of mobility, which enables us to adapt to the ever-changing circumstances of life.

From the moment of birth, and probably before, we are vulnerable to all the energies around us in the world, which can impinge on our energy field. From electromagnetic pollution and chemicals, to the intent and judgments of others, we are constantly being bombarded with things that compromise our freedom of toroidal movement.

We are also subjected to all sorts of physical, emotional, mental, and spiritual traumas and shocks that cause an aspect of us to disconnect from the whole, in an effort to avoid the pain or repetition of the trauma.

In order to disconnect from a natural response, we must impose a polarity against it and freeze that polarity in place. This becomes avoidance, which by its very nature, impinges on mobility.

## OUCH! I'LL NEVER DO *THAT* AGAIN

I was cleaning my kitchen one day. Forgetting I had just used one burner of the gas stove. I picked up the still-hot grate with my bare wet hand and burned myself quite severely. Deciding I had no interest in repeating the experience, I judged against ever picking up a grate without something covering my hand. Now the stove could be stone cold, but I will still pause and find a hot pad before lifting the grate. This adds an extra step to my cleaning process, marginally slowing me down. The act of always using a hot pad has become a defense mechanism.

This might seem overly simplistic, but you would be amazed how much of our behavior is dictated by pattern, avoidance, and defense mechanisms rather than natural, spontaneous response.

Once I started receiving soul-retrieval healing, I was amazed at the increase in efficiency in every part of my life. I have already explained my grate behavior, but when I was working in the kitchen, I would also hover over a pot filling with water. Every time a crumb would hit the counter I would stop, get a rag, and wipe the surface three times to make sure I had gotten all the crumbs into it before carrying the rag to the trash to carefully deposit the crumbs into the can.

My mother, a depression baby, used to be paranoid about letting the water run, and she nagged incessantly about it. She also suffered from OCD and had a real thing with crumbs. This stilted my kitchen activities, making them robotic and stressful as I tried to maneuver around all the rules and regulations imposed upon me from childhood, just to cook a simple meal.

Now I turn on the water to fill the pot, accomplish three other things while it is filling, and then arrive back at the sink to shut off the water at the exact moment it is full. I wipe the crumbs off onto the floor and when completely done cooking, I sweep the floor on my way out of the kitchen. My movements are fluid and efficient, no water is wasted, and my kitchen ends up neat and clean when I am done. Cooking is now a joy, and it takes less time than it used to.

I did not engage in soul-retrieval healing in order to improve my competence in the kitchen. I started noticing my increased proficiency as a by-product of my healing other, much more debilitating patterns.

This same level of efficiency has become present in most aspects of my life. Everything flows—I seem to always be where I need to be, doing exactly what I need to be doing, and when I need to be doing it. People are always commenting on how much I accomplish in a short time with seemingly little effort. With everything so much more natural and fluid, I am able to dance through my life with less stress and more energy.

Every arbitrary rule I had to follow growing up became a restriction in my toroidal fields that restricted my natural expression. These restrictions showed up in my behavior as I have described. This is not to say that rules are bad. I still use a hot pad to pick up something hot, but I am free to discern appropriate response rather than always or never doing something.

When we suffer soul loss, we judge against the behavior we think caused the trauma, setting up always-and-never scenarios. "Always" and "never" are frozen polarities.

When polarities become frozen, they tend to attract into a person's life incidents similar to those that caused the damage in the first place. Once a "soul part" leaves, an electromagnetic charge reversal occurs. Instead of drawing in what you need, you repel what you need and attract what you don't. Note that this reversal in your energy field only pertains to that area of your life in which the soul loss occurred. For instance, if your trauma was related to being physically abused, then your energy field would tend to attract other physically abusive situations.

## LITTLE JOHNNY

There is a story I have devised to help explain the concept of soul loss to my students and clients. The story of little Johnny helps us delve deeper into this spiritual illness and its long term effect upon our lives. First, however, I would offer a reminder for the parents among us (myself included):

1) Everything is perfect given where we have been and where we are going,

2) We are all doing the best we can given our own limitations inherent in these times,

3) If we brought up totally undamaged children they would not be able to relate nor would they be tolerated in our current society,

4) This is a hypothetical story designed to demonstrate a point, not put parents into the damaging frequency of guilt and shame.

With that said: one day, Johnny is sitting on the floor, playing with his ball, when he loses his grip on it. It rolls in front of the door just as his mother and father come in. After a long day at work, a stop off at the bar, and an argument on the way home, his parents enter to find the baby sitter asleep on the couch and Johnny still up way past his bedtime. His mother trips over the ball, gets mad, and yells at Johnny. His father orders him to bed, telling him he is a bad boy. Johnny, instead of being greeted and loved upon his parents' long-awaited return, is rejected and ostracized.

At the age of two, Johnny can't tell his parents that they don't have a right to take their bad day and the baby-sitter's negligence out on a child.

Aside from being unable to communicate at that level, doing so might also bring on further painful rejection.

He also depends on his parents to be "right." If they are not, Johnny believes he won't be fed, safe, cared for, or provided for. Feeling that the continuance of his life is totally dependent upon his parents, Johnny judges against himself in order to make his parents right and preserve his security. He now believes that he must assume blame so he can be cared for.

While he used to think of himself as a good boy who deserved to be protected and provided for, he now believes he's a bad boy, and he accepts blame for the incident. He disconnects from his right not to be taken to task for other people's issues.

Johnny's auric field undergoes a polarity reversal in order to accommodate his new view, that of *always* being bad and to blame. In the future, instead of repelling blame, the now-frozen polarity reversal actually causes his field to draw it in. In this area of his life, he now draws in the things that are harmful and repelling the very things that he needs.

If this frozen-polarity reversal goes uncorrected, Johnny will be the guy at work who will take responsibility for the copier breaking, even though he was in the bathroom four doors away when it happened.

## THE RIPPLE EFFECT

This soul loss and resulting frozen polarity restricts Johnny's toroidal field, causing his spiritual frequency level to drop, which sets up an energetic disharmony among the four levels of his being.

If Johnny were a four-cylinder car with a fouled spark plug, he'd run roughly until the spark plug was replaced. However, he's an organism, not a machine, so all the other levels of his being will compensate by dropping their frequencies, thereby reestablishing harmony and homeostasis. Johnny will function at a slightly lower overall output, reducing his options and personal power. In this way, the spiritual illness of soul loss ripples through his auric field, impacting Johnny at all four levels of his being as each level must leave its optimal frequency in order to compensate.

Because Johnny is not sure exactly what he did wrong, he may think about the incident and try to eliminate any behavior that may have caused his punishment. On the physical level there are activities he no longer deems safe, such as handling a ball or sitting next to the front door. On the emotional level, he now experiences fear, guilt and shame, which cause emotional stress that also impacts the body by creating heightened levels of adrenalin. On the mental level, he has to reframe how he views himself and life in general, which changes his overall reality.

Johnny becomes further traumatized by all the blame now directed his way due to his frozen auric field polarity. He compensates by putting up a labyrinth of defense mechanisms. He may scream and hide any time he sees a ball, avoid going close to the front door, or hide under the bed when he expects his parents to come home. These defenses further affect his behavior, causing more restrictions.

By the time Johnny is 25, he may have identified with this defensive behavior, believing it is just who he is. He may believe that he is just not a ball-playing kind of guy. He has most likely forgotten the initial incident that caused the frozen polarity in the first place.

It is common with soul loss to have compensatory behaviors that we don't even recognize or remember putting in place. We just know we don't do certain things, although we usually don't remember why. Yet at some level we believe that doing those things could cost us our life.

Johnny might eventually seek psychotherapy. He may be able to make some behavioral changes, such as watching hockey games instead of baseball, or using a relaxation technique to quell his desire to hide when he fears his parents or some authority figure might come around. He may also come to understand that his fears and self-blame were a result of his parents' alcoholic behavior, and he may be able to rebuild some of his self-esteem and grieve his losses.

These changes may help to relieve some of his emotional distress and rearrange his defense mechanisms, so he is less crippled, but as long as the frozen polarity remains, he will continue to draw in blame. He will continue to be re-injured because he is still drawing in the very things that harm him.

Soul loss can cause the same undesirable things to recur again and again in our lives. The faces may change, but the situations are similar, and we are the common denominator. It's like the person who grows up with an alcoholic often ends up marrying one, causing yet more soul loss. In this way, soul loss begets soul loss.

We all have been subjected to soul loss for generations. It is the basic technique used in socialization. It is also the tool used to program the masses. Some people have suffered more soul loss than others, leaving them with obvious symptoms that stand out against the backdrop of society. Through soul retrieval these individuals can return to a more "normal" level of functioning. Soul retrieval can also help us heal beyond the limitations of our current society and propel us along the evolutionary scale towards spiritual enlightenment and personal empowerment.

## THE MIGHTY MIASM

Miasms are restrictions in the physical, emotional, mental or spiritual body and can show up physically as localized pain and illness. Emotionally, they may appear as shut-down or over-active emotions that are not appropriate to the present situation. Mentally, they express as locked-down judgments about reality that are then erroneously applied to all situations. Spiritually, they are restrictions in our toroidal field that limit our mobility and ability to effect change at the quantum level of our lives.

Every time we suffer soul loss, it impacts us at all four levels of our being, which creates miasms in our toroidal fields that prevent us from being able to cross through the eyes of the needle we discussed in "The Natural Law."

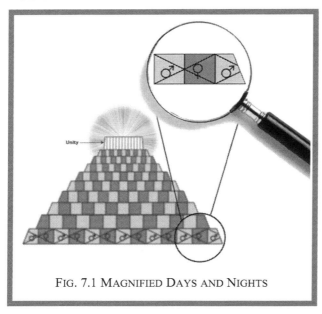

FIG. 7.1 MAGNIFIED DAYS AND NIGHTS

Miasms created by frozen-polarity reversals prevent us from advancing on our evolutionary path as the sun moves into the higher frequency of the Photon Band. In fact, compounded soul loss actually causes us to devolve down the scale of enlightenment by restricting our mobility and frequency, and reframing our reality. Miasms cause failure to thrive, illness, and eventually death.

While the overall frequency of the Earth is rising due to the new era and our placement relative to the Photon Band, an individual must heal their miasms in order to move with the evolutionary times. The more miasms, the more pressure a person feels every time the planet moves from "day" to "night" or "night" to "day" on the Mayan calendar.

There are miasms frozen in negative polarity that are under pressure in the "day" (positive polarity), and there are miasms frozen in the positive that are under pressure in the "night" (negative polarity). The faster we move from one polarity to the next, the greater the pressure.

Has anyone noticed how crazy it is getting out in the human world? The general populace is literally being shaken apart at the seams by the rapid shifts in polarity that their miasms cannot accommodate.

## IN IT FOR THE LONG HAUL

This phenomenon of increased frequencies imposing pressure on our miasms didn't magically stop after December of 2012. We can expect to dance with it for the next 2000 plus years. Talk about a cat on a hot tin roof!

Once we have suffered soul loss and the resulting compensatory behaviors are in place, another interesting mechanism comes into play—triggering, which is an event that ignites unconscious emotions and precipitates actions that aren't necessarily beneficial to anyone involved. It can look something like this: I had a summer job at a car-rental booth in the airport. Nancy had been working in the rental booth next to mine for quite some time, and she had seemed perfectly normal. Then one day a blonde woman walked up to her counter, dressed to kill in a short skirt, low cut top, and spike heels. She was draped in expensive jewelry and reeked of high-end perfume. Nancy looked up at her, and all the color drained from her face. Then she looked back down at the counter in front of her, completely ignoring the woman.

"Excuse me, what does a person have to do to get some service around here?" the customer demanded, tapping her acrylic nails on the counter for some time while Nancy continued to ignore her.

"Miss! Are you deaf or what?" the irate woman demanded. "I need a car sometime today."

"We don't have any." Nancy mumbled, never looking up.

I couldn't believe my ears! I knew for a fact that they had an entire fleet, just like my company did. Finally the woman flounced over to my counter in exasperation. I was in the middle of setting her up with a sporty little number from our fleet when Nancy called my phone from her booth.

"Don't rent to that woman." She whispered into the phone.

"Why not?" I inquired.

"She is evil." Nancy informed me in no uncertain terms.

"You know her?" I asked confused.

"No."

"Then how do you know?"

"Look at her, she is here to steal our husbands," Nancy enlightened me.

"But we don't have husbands," I reminded the distraught woman.

"That witch will cast them under her spell and take them from us, and we will starve." Nancy's voice wailed, rising in hysteria, drawing the woman's attention.

"That woman is nuts," the customer whispered to me behind her hand. I had to agree. Nancy appeared to have gone around the bend.

I hung up the phone and completed leasing the car to the lady. After she left I looked over at Nancy to find her glaring at me as if I were a traitor to my country.

"What?" I wanted to know.

"Now you've done it. She will get our men, and our kids will starve. Just you wait and see," Nancy persisted, as she grabbed her purse and abandoned her booth, running as if the devil were on her tail. Her booth remained unattended until the next shift arrived.

"Where is Nancy?" The night attendant wanted to know.

"She seemed not to be well," I honestly responded, without elaborating.

The next day Nancy was back at work as if nothing had happened. Whatever had come over her never recurred. Over the next months we developed a friendship of sorts. Finally one day she happened to mention that her father had run off with a younger woman, leaving her mother with five children. She shared that their mother had no way to support them beyond a minimum-wage job. Eventually they had been evicted from their home, her family having fallen from upper-middle class to what she described as trailer-court trash. After her father deserted them, Nancy and her siblings didn't have enough to eat most of the time.

"Was the woman your father ran off with a flashy blonde, per chance?" I asked.

"Why yes, how did you know?" Nancy asked surprised.

"Just a lucky guess," I responded.

Nancy had been triggered into her past damage by seeing the blonde customer. She reminded Nancy of the woman for whom her father had abandoned his family. In that moment it was as if Nancy were four years old again, fearing for her life, and she responded accordingly. We can expect that level of fear, judgment, and loathing from a four-year-old child being abandoned, but it was grossly inappropriate from an adult toward a customer trying to rent a car.

*~ TRIGGERING IS A SET OF STIMULUS RESPONSES THAT CAN BE USED*
*TO PROGRAM AND MANIPULATE BEHAVIOR. ~*

Triggering is extremely common. We all experience it to one degree or another on a daily basis. When we are triggered, we tend to take the events of the past and superimpose them on the present. When we are triggered into past trauma, we are no longer responding appropriately in the moment. My feeling of needing a hot pad to pick up a cold grate was not appropriate to the circumstances at hand. Any time we are triggered out of the natural time flow our toroidal fields destabilize and our personal power is compromised, making it available for redirection and exploitation.

On the day-to-day interpersonal level, people also are easily manipulated by their triggers. A mother who has almost lost a child due to an illness becomes hyper-vigilant of their children's health. Later, that child can (and usually will) use that to their advantage. They soon discover that all they have to do is sniffle, and Mom will hold them out of school, which can be very convenient on a day they are to take a test for which they are not prepared for. One sniffle—problem solved.

## HOMELAND SECURITY

The system we live in has intentionally created triggers through group soul loss that it then uses to control and exploit the masses. Before 9-11, there was no way the average individual would have tolerated the invasive searching techniques now employed at every airport security check point. Now just the thought of what can happen if a terrorist gets on board with a weapon of any kind has us docilely taking off our shoes and walking through X-rays like cattle, being frisked, and having our personal belongings examined.

After the masses are programmed into accepting one level of invasion, the intrusion can then be generalized into other areas of our lives. We remember when people were traumatized into wearing arm bands bearing a Star of David and the next thing they know, they are herded up and loaded on a train to Auschwitz. It has happened.

## INTUITION OR TRIGGER

We are all intuitive by nature, yet it is a skill few of us openly acknowledge or employ. The more triggers we have, the more difficult it is to tell if what we are feeling and perceiving is clear and present danger or something triggered from our past. We may be feeling fear because something dangerous is about to happen, or we may be triggered into fear by an event that subconsciously reminds us of a past trauma. The triggered emotion feels as real as the first instance of it.

Nancy was absolutely sure that she was in the presence of dangerous, unspeakable evil. The blonde customer might as well have been holding a gun to Nancy's head. After a lifetime of false alarms, overreaction, and having people look at us strangely, we tend to lose faith in what we feel. We learn to ignore our intuition, which makes us yet more exploitable. While her intuition may be telling her that something is not right, Nancy would tend to be looking for evil blondes rather than noticing a customer with a gun.

This is not to say that intuition is invalid or without value—quite the contrary. During these times of rapid change, when every day is unprecedented, it is absolutely necessary to intuit what choices and actions are appropriate rather than going on past experience. As we heal soul loss and have fewer issues to trigger us, it becomes even easier to know when we are being triggered and when we are getting valuable intuitive input.

## SHRINKING HABITAT

Upon suffering soul loss and judging against some aspect of ourselves, we tend to set up defense mechanisms to prevent repeating what we have judged to be the cause of the trauma, which establishes areas in our natural expression where we will not go, creating a void between us and our consciousness—a place where the left hand doesn't know what the right hand is doing.

### ~ NATURE HATES A VACUUM ~

Something else can and will move into every place we no longer occupy due to soul loss and the resulting avoidance or denial. Sometimes this "something else" will be programmed avoidance behavior, like my hot-pad fetish. In more severe cases it can show up as something much more sinister, which is how damage is passed down through family lines.

When children who have been extremely abused become parents, seeing their children behave in the ways that drew the original abuse will actually trigger them. Unfortunately, when damaged parents witness their children behaving in ways that they previously judged against in themselves, they will often respond with the same abusive behavior they received as children.

## SPILT MILK

My son and daughter were horsing around at the breakfast table, and I could feel myself becoming agitated, so I told them to stop. They would behave for a while, then take up the game when they thought I wasn't watching. Soon my son predictably spilled his milk.

"You weren't going to be happy until you made a mess," I raged at him, fighting an unfamiliar urge to backhand him off of his booster seat. I was horrified by the urge. I also recognized the phrase as something my mother repeatedly screamed at my brother and me just before knocking us off our chairs. It was as if I were channeling my mother. The next day I did soul retrieval, after which the trigger phrase and related urge to strike my child never returned.

Some months later, my uncle came to visit. He shared what he considered to be a funny anecdote from his and my mother's childhood. It involved my grandmother saying the same thing and knocking my mother off of her high chair. These are the patterns that unconsciously get passed down from generation to generation until we choose to heal them.

## THINGS THAT GO BUMP

Behaviors are not the only things that can move into a place vacated due to soul loss. There are parasitical energetic forces that can move through us any time we are triggered. The gap where we are no longer in the present becomes an access point for other energies to interface with the physical world. Concepts such as energy vampires, possessing spirits, and demons have a real basis in truth.

Individuals can also be programmed to respond in a particular way when triggered, then activated at a time and place of the programmer's choosing. We have all seen movies where a person receives a phone call, hears a particular phrase and then leaves his respectable home, job, and family to assassinate a dignitary. Subliminal advertising works in a similar way.

We sit in front of a television and hear phrases that prompt all sorts of behaviors on a daily basis, doubt it not.

*~ AS ABOVE, SO BELOW;*
*WE ARE ALL SUBJECT TO ENERGETIC PARASITES ~*

The pyramidal food chain, mentioned in "Smoke and Mirrors." extends into the non-physical realms of the quantum level. As you can probably tell, all of this is a deep and disturbing topic that I will address more deeply in Book 2 of the Map Home series, *These and Greater Things*, when we have developed a more solid knowledge base on these concepts.

## A HEART'S SECOND CHANCE

One spring day some years ago, I received a call from a medical doctor and longtime colleague, Dr. Joe Swartz. We had been referring patients back and forth for years, so I assumed his call was about a mutual patient. I was surprised to learn this time that he was calling for himself. He had received a heart-valve transplant and was failing miserably. He was experiencing dangerous arrhythmias, and his body was rejecting the new valve.

He did not need my work as a medical intuitive, which was how we often interfaced in the past. He already knew what the problem was. What he needed was for me to talk his body into accepting another person's heart valve as its own. He also knew that what he was asking me to do was medically impossible.

As a shamanic practitioner, I specialize in the seemingly impossible. Dr. Swartz had seen me crash through the "medically impossible barrier" often enough to know that there was a chance I could help him.

By entering into a shamanic trance and asking for guidance, I was directed to go back in time to the operating room where the transplant took place. While I (in spirit) watched Dr. Swartz's surgeon remove his defective valve and set it aside, I was guided to remove the energy frequency from the valve. After doing so, I sensed a deep sadness and a sense of failure coming from the defective valve.

As the valve from the donor was presented to the surgeon, I was directed to clear the donor's essence from the tissue. As I did, I suddenly became overcome by terror. A vision of a truck hurtling toward me washed over me like a tsunami. Feeling certain that I was about to die, I pulled my spirit back from the donor's experience and rose above the vision to see a semi-trailer truck broadside the car that a young man was driving.

I was told to take the essence of the donated heart valve to the "other side." This is a technique known as psychopomping, or helping the dead to cross. I had performed this technique many times in my practice for people and animals, but never for a body part. Fortunately, the method was the same, and I was able to successfully clear the donated valve of the trauma and frequency signature the donor held at the time of his death. I then took the frequency I had obtained from Dr. Swartz's original valve and imprinted it into the donated valve.

Then, while still in journey, I asked if there was anything else I could do to help, and I was instructed to retrieve the valve's "right" to function without failing.

In a discussion immediately following my shamanic journey for Dr. Swartz, he told me that I had perfectly described the procedure, the operating room, and all the equipment in it. Within one week of the shamanic session with Dr. Swartz, his arrhythmia and all signs of organ rejection were gone. He also reported that the anxiety and fear he had been experiencing since the transplant surgery had completely cleared after our work together.

Twelve years have passed since the shamanic healing I performed for Dr. Swartz. He and his wife Yvonne have since moved to Hawaii Yvonne emailed me to tell me that they were on the mainland for a visit and wondered if we could meet for lunch. As we shared Indian food in a quaint little Colorado restaurant, Dr. Swartz thanked me once again for the healing. He said he had no doubt that it had saved his life and continued to do so. At my puzzled look, he told me valve transplants don't last. His surgeon had told him to expect needing another replacement valve in eight or ten years. Dr. Swartz has had his donated valve for over 12 years, with no sign of valve dysfunction, failure, or rejection.

While Dr. Swartz's story is an example of how soul retrieval can effect a change on the physical and emotional level, it can effect change at the mental and spiritual levels as well.

Shamanism is not limited to living beings. Everything forms itself around the information present at the quantum level. The implications here are as vast as they are amazing. If we can affect the quantum level, we can affect manifestation—this is the art of co-creation.

*~ ALL THINGS HAVE SPIRIT AND THEREFORE CAN BE MANAGED*
*AND HEALED BY SHAMANISM ~*

The trauma still held in the donated heart valve was creating miasms in the toroidal field of Dr. Swartz's heart. The clash in frequency between the harmonics of the donor and that of Dr. Swartz created more restrictions. On the spiritual/quantum level, this was causing the body to reject the new valve and the heart to fail.

Was I really in the operating room? Yes and no. It is one of the many mysteries of the shamanic form. I have related actual incidents and environments seen in journey that I had absolutely no way of knowing, for example, the procedure, the operating room, and all the equipment in it.

When I enter the journey trance to perform soul-retrieval healing, I am actually entering into my client's unconscious. My job is to find where the client disconnected, align with his/her frequency before the disconnect happened, and bring it back to correct the current imbalance in his/her toroidal field.

The journey itself is a metaphor created by my imagination to represent to my mind what needs to happen on the quantum level. It can also be a literal representation of events that is stored in the client's unconscious. It is usually a combination of both literal and metaphorical information.

The story created by the journey also serves to help the client integrate the soul retrieval. As the client listens to the story, emotions may come up that have been buried and now need to be dealt with to complete the healing. Old beliefs about life may be brought to light to be reframed. Physical frequencies can be altered by increased processing and understanding.

## WHAT DOES THIS MEAN FOR YOU?

Every place you have disconnected from your natural expression a miasm is created that causes restrictions in your toroidal fields. You then develop defense mechanisms to protect you from repeated damage. Defense mechanisms require taking more of your natural expression offline to use in running them, further compromising your toroidal fields and therefore your frequency. The residual trauma creates triggers that take you out of the present moment. The only place you have real power is in the present moment—it is the only place you can align with natural law. When you are not present, you are not acting in alignment with natural law. Working against natural law creates drag, which further compromises your frequency. Low frequency enslaves you to the system, or your past as it renders you incapable of manifesting for yourself. At this point the real question is: Where, in this nasty little lineup, *isn't* there meaning for you?

## DECISIONS, DECISIONS

Now let me refer you back to "Wheels Within Wheels." and the concept of our future being a multidimensional series of personal choices rather than a predestined set of linear events. You will remember that I stated that in a perfect world, we would have access to all of our options. In the real world, we take a bit of a beating, and, as a result, we disconnect from many of our options, resulting in the spiritual illness of soul loss. We all have numerous incidents of soul loss and innumerable places where we have disconnected from our options. This being the case, how do I, as a shamanic practitioner, or you, as a client, have any idea which soul loss to heal and when?

Shamanic work is run through intent. As a practitioner, I set my intent that the session is dictated by the intent of my client, which is, in turn, set by what the client wants for his/her life. The session then naturally focuses on the soul loss standing between the client and what he/she wants.

## CONSCIOUS OR UNCONSCIOUS?

Shamanic work can only be as accurate as the intent of the client. It is important to recognize that much of our intent is unconscious—directed by soul loss, defense mechanisms, triggers, avoidance, and hidden agendas. This may appear to be a double bind with no solution in sight unless we recognize that healing is a process. Every time we receive and integrate soul retrieval healing, we become more conscious. As we become more conscious, we can modify our intent to better represent our true desire rather than our damage. Methods for achieving this will be offered in "Stairway to Heaven."

## THE SORCERER'S APPRENTICE

There is a fine line between shamanism and sorcery. In order to walk that line with integrity and stay out of the sorcery arena, I have five rules that I follow religiously:

- ❖ Always work in cooperation with natural law
- ❖ Don't put energy onto someone that doesn't belong to them.
- ❖ Don't take energy from someone that does belong to them.
- ❖ Don't work without permission.
- ❖ Do no harm

I make sure my clients are well versed in this concept. Even so, I will often have to remind them when they indicate that their intent is to change another person's behavior. We are all very conditioned to take the stance of victim. It is often hard to remember that we, and we alone, are responsible for our experience. The same is true of every other person in our lives, eventually even our children. Ultimately, we have to heal ourselves and let the chips fall where they may. Those around us will adapt, adjust, heal, or distance themselves when their patterns can no longer work their way with ours. We simply have to trust another's path and stay out of the way. No matter how good our intent, any attempt to intervene through shamanism becomes sorcery— the use of supernatural power over others and their affairs without permission.

## DO IT YOURSELF?

I mentioned that one of the questions I most frequently hear after teaching people how to journey is, "Now that I can journey, can I do my own soul retrieval?"

In order to do soul retrieval, the practitioner needs to be able to align their toroidal fields with the frequency the client disconnected from due to soul loss. If you are disconnected from a frequency, it is not present for you to align with. This is why a practitioner's processing level is vitally important to their effectiveness as a shamanic healer. It is also why you can't do your own soul retrieval.

*~ THE DOCTOR THAT TREATS HIMSELF HAS A FOOL FOR A PATIENT ~*
*~ SIR WILLIAM OSLER ~*

## BUYER BEWARE

I would be quite remiss if I did not mention that there is no regulation of shamanic healers. I am not saying that that is a bad thing, as there is much regulation of medical doctors, yet there are a lot of lousy ones in practice, while really good ones are sometimes crippled by regulations.

Anyone that has had a one-day shamanic workshop can claim to be a shaman, with no one the wiser. For that matter, in some cases, one doesn't even need a workshop. So how do you find someone you can trust to provide you with soul-retrieval healing?

If you don't have a reputable practitioner in your area, you will be happy to know that shamanic healing can be performed quite effectively over long distances. In the back of this book I have included a resources section where you can find contact information for the Path Home Long Distance Shamanism Program. All Path Home practitioners have graduated from a rigorous 380+ hour, two-year shamanic-practitioner certification program from Path Home Shamanic Arts School, which is a Colorado-State-certified occupational school.

This is not to say that the only excellent practitioners are those who have gone through Path Home's program. People tend to be known by their works, so look to the person's reputation for clues. Also remember the things I listed above—training, personal healing, processing, and motivation. Interview your potential practitioner; ask about their training and experience in the field. Have them describe soul-retrieval healing to you. While you are speaking with them, listen carefully to what they say, and ask yourself the following questions:

❖ Is this person coming from ego or a place of service?

❖ Can this person accurately describe the form, or is the description full of woo woo and vague generalities?

❖ Is this person aware of the underlying principles behind the form, or are they just aping rituals and going through the motions?

❖ Does this person appear to be grounded and processed?

❖ How do I feel when listening to this person?

Don't be afraid to pay well for good shamanic services. There is an old school of thought that says spiritual workers should work for free or donations. This originated from indigenous tribes, where money was not a form of exchange and the shaman was totally cared for. His or her food and lodging were provided by the community. In exchange, the shaman would see to the society's ceremonial and divination needs. Should an individual need personal healing, they would gift the shaman with a large portion of their household in exchange for the additional service.

If a modern-day shamanic practitioner doesn't charge a fair price for their services, they have to do something else for a living, leaving much less time to dedicate to the perfection and performance of the form. Do you want a competent experienced healer or a weekend warrior? When shopping for a shamanic healer, *do* look a gift horse in the mouth.

Expect a session to run between an hour and an hour and a half. If it is evolution of consciousness and personal empowerment you are interested in rather than elimination of a particular symptom, expect to do a series. Be mindful to take enough time between sessions because shamanic healing requires integration on the part of the client, which is the process of unifying or bringing all parts together on all four levels: physical, emotional, mental and spiritual.

If you have suffered extensive trauma, it may be advisable to seek out other practitioners to support your integration process. I have made a point of developing a strong network of healers to support my clients on the physical, emotional, and mental levels of their healing process. Some of us have been referring clients and patients back and forth for over 20 years, and the benefit to everyone concerned has been amazing.

If you don't click with a shamanic practitioner, trust your instincts. This work is very intimate, and you need to feel comfortable with your healer. Shop until you find one that is a good fit, someone you feel you can trust. Remember that we are trying to come out of denial through shamanic healing. If we don't trust our practitioner, our tendency to doubt them—rather than face our denials—will be very strong.

## SHAMANISM AS AN EVOLUTIONARY TOOL

We have looked at evolution as a process of spiraling up the tiers of the Mayan pyramid, whereby each tier holds to the same principles at an ever-increasing rate of polarity shift. These accelerating shifts result in higher frequency as we approach unity consciousness. Every time we move from one level of reality to another, we pass through an eye of a needle or a "day/night"– "night/day" transition. Each of these transitions is a polarity reversal that progresses in frequency as we move up the scale. Any time we undergo a polarity reversal, pressure is brought to bear on our miasms. If we do not clear them, our defense mechanisms, or our triggers, we soon hit a frequency beyond which we can no longer evolve and maintain integrity.

Shamanic healing can clear these structures, allowing us to be in the present moment, facilitating a continuation of our evolutionary process. It can also correct the damage that makes us subject to the programming of the exploitative system, thus freeing up our personal power for our own use.

Note: this is a *process,* not a one-time deal. Every time we transcend from one reality to the next we have to address the restrictions and programming on all four levels—physical, emotional, mental, and spiritual—before moving to the next shift.

## NO DEAD CHICKENS

There are many ways to perform shamanic healing. Each shamanic tradition was designed for the people of a particular culture at a specific time. The appropriateness of any tradition being applied to the people of today depends upon where, and more importantly, *when* those traditions originated.

## OH EEEUW

I was discussing extraction and depossession with my Tibetan teacher one day, which is a shamanic-healing technique whereby practitioners remove incompatible frequencies from their clients that may be causing pain and illness. My teacher informed me that in order to do extraction, I first needed to swallow a bowl of worms. He explained that this was so I would have something to vomit up to prove to my clients that I had actually sucked something out of their body.

"But what I am removing is energetic, not physical," I responded in confusion.

"We know that, but the client needs physical proof," he sagely replied.

He then proceeded to inform me that to do a depossession, or cast out the possessing spirits, I had to have a live chicken on hand. When I asked what I needed the chicken for, he told me that I was to remove the possessing spirit from my client, put it into the chicken then kill the chicken in front of my client in order to prove that I had destroyed the possessing spirit.

I decided right then and there that I would find a way to convince my clients of the validity of shamanic work that didn't involve swallowing worms or killing chickens. While these traditions had been very appropriate to the Tibetan peasant of old, I was relatively sure that they would not be well received by modern-day Americans.

Thus began a lifetime quest. I have spent the last three decades delving into the solid principles behind shamanic techniques in order to make them user friendly for my clients and students today. The key is to not throw out the baby with the bathwater. There are vital checks and balances inherent with every tradition that must be maintained to preserve the quality and integrity of the work. A practitioner needs to totally master and understand the form before modifying it in any way.

I would like to honor the work of anthropologist Michael Harner for his profound contribution to modern-day shamanic practices. Michael spent his career collecting shamanic traditions from all over the world (submitting himself to heaven only knows what in the process). By compiling the principles they all have in common, Michael filtered out the cultural and religious aspects to create the form he calls core shamanism.

Through the deepening knowledge of quantum physics, science is evolving to the point where it can understand shamanic principles. Hence, through the modern understanding of shamanic principles as they relate to natural law at the quantum level, shamanism is becoming a science.

It is important to honor where the traditions have come from, and be thankful that our brothers and sisters had the foresight to preserve the old ways. Ultimately, it is also necessary to honor where it is all going, which is back to center and to that which we all share. It's time for us to come back together—the future of the Earth and all who live upon her depends upon it.

# 8

# Shamanism 101

During the long dark when frequency was less expansive, we had less light to see by, which is like being in a large, windowless auditorium with only one small candle for illumination. While we may suspect that there is more out there, we all huddle around the one small circle of light in which we can actually perceive what is going on. After generations of a reduced perceptual field, the totality of the auditorium becomes a distant myth, and our reality has become our small visible portion of it. Those who possess good distance vision learn to ignore it, as it is not useful in their current reality. What good is distance vision if you can't see at a distance?

Like this example, we have been trained to register and interpret information that comes in through our five senses from a very limited portion of physical reality. We have also been taught to ignore more subtle information that is available to all of us in varying degrees.

For generations a tribe that lived deep in the jungle had their vision restricted to several feet by the deep foliage. When a member of this tribe was taken to the open plains and shown water buffalo at a distance, he informed the anthropologist that, it was not a herd of water buffalo. After all, anyone could see they were much too small. They had to be a colony of ants. The anthropologist took the man to see the buffalo up close in order to prove to him that they were not ants. The man patiently explained to the anthropologist that they had been ants but magically shape-shifted into water buffalo when approached.

~ *WE HAVE BECOME MULTIDIMENSIONAL BEINGS REDUCED TO A MONODIMENSIONAL WORLD.* ~

Just like the man from the jungle, we have come to perceive reality based on incomplete information. Like the individual in the auditorium who possessed great distance vision and learned to ignore the information he could obtain that others could not, we have come to ignore information coming to us from nonphysical sources.

As educated individuals, we pride ourselves in the awareness that perceivable physical reality is only a small portion of All That Is. In the study of particle physics, we discover that there are things smaller than we can see, such as the atom. In exploring cosmology, we have also learned that there are things much larger than we can see, such as galaxies. Though most of us have never actually seen either an atom or a distant galaxy, most of us can conjure up fairly accurate pictures of each in our imagination. We take information provided to us in physics class, for instance, and build a representation in our imagination to help grasp the concept with our mind. This is a simple process that most of us take for granted, yet within this lies the secret to obtaining much more information. Hold that thought.

## ENTER STAGE LEFT: THE LIGHT BULB

Meanwhile, back in the dark auditorium, someone starts to turn up the light. Most of the people huddled around the candle will do what they have always done and pay attention to their agreed-upon reality. The guy with great distance vision, however, will start to notice that things are expanding around him, yet he may not know how to interpret the new visual information. After a while, he will become intrigued, and his imagination will become engaged.

"I wonder," he may think, "what if there is more out there than we have always believed?" Soon, he will start to play with the new data. He will design possible explanations to incorporate the information in his imagination and try them on to see if they fit with what he already knows. Once he has a plausible theory or two, he may tap the guy next to him on the shoulder and say, "Look over there, do you see that? Do you suppose it may be..." or "What if...?" Soon the second fellow's imagination is also piqued.

We can actually take information coming in through subtle frequencies and design a representation in our imaginations that expands our understanding of reality, which is the foundation of true genius and the basis of the shamanic journey. In this very way, Einstein, and others, changed our entire reality.

## THE SHAMANIC JOURNEY

As you have come to understand, a shamanic practitioner must master skills every bit as complex and involved as those of a medical doctor. On the other hand, like physical medicine, there are shamanic skills that every individual would do well to possess. Most of us have made it our business to know basic first aid or how to treat a common cold, yet we have no idea how to obtain and decode spiritual information for guidance in our daily lives.

At the same time, we no longer have the information base of how life operates at the quantum level in order to discern our place within it. We don't have any way of figuring out with our minds the effect that our thoughts and intentions have on the whole. Our minds operate on a polarized binary system, while the whole is a unified reality. Yet, our intentions, both conscious and unconscious, interface at the quantum level and interact with reality, impacting our environment in seemingly unpredictable ways.

A personal shamanic journey practice is vital to the evolving individual. While not everyone has the skill set or interest to be a physician or a shamanic practitioner, most people can master the simple divination journey and learn the skills necessary to interpret their results. Even if you ultimately decide to have a trained practitioner perform your divination journeys for you, experience with the interpretation of the shamanic metaphor will greatly aid your understanding and implementation of the information that the journey makes available.

*~ THE ART OF THE SHAMANIC JOURNEY IS THE SINGLE MOST PERSONAL*
*EMPOWERING SKILL ONE CAN ACQUIRE. ~*

Ideally, I recommend taking a journey class from a certified shamanic instructor who is well versed in creating and holding sacred space and guiding the beginning student through their first journey attempts, but I recognize that this is not always possible. For this reason I have included instructions on the basic lower-world shamanic journey in this work, in the hope of making this powerful tool available to those who are not able to attend a formal class.

*The following material is derived from the Path Home Shamanic Arts School's classes and workbooks. Path Home and its classes are certified by the Colorado State Department of Higher Education Division of Private Occupational Schools.*

## THE JOURNEY STATE OF CONSCIOUSNESS

As I have mentioned, one of the basic elements common to all shamanic practices is the altered state of consciousness known as the journey trance. An indispensable tool for anyone engaging in spiritual evolution is the ability to travel into other realms and realities to meet with spirit guides, power animals, ancestors, and spiritual teachers to receive guidance and information upon which to base one's decisions.

> ### *A Drumbeat Away*
>
> *Eyes close, drums sound*
> *Animals come*
> *My spirit leaves my body*
>
> *Not awake nor sleeping*
> *Visions, dreams*
>
> *That rewrites the past*
> *That tells the future*
>
> *Untold freedom*
> *Natural laws bend*
> *Time is not*
>
> *I am all*
> *And yet nothing*
>
> *What mystery is this?*
> *Just a drumbeat away*
> *Across the veil*
>
> *Across the galaxy*
> *Yet contained*
> *Inside my being*

The majority of the ancients used some form of rhythmic sound—the beating of a drum, the shake of a rattle, or a repetitive chant in order to enter the journey trance. For a beginning journey practice, I recommend using a drumming recording specifically designed for the journey trance, such as "On Wings of Spirit" or "Betwixt and Between."[1]

## WHAT IS JOURNEYING?

When we go into a journey state, research has shown that our brainwave frequency drops down to closely match that of the Earth's surface at 7.8 Hz.[2] Journey is literally a measurable altered state of consciousness.

All of us actually already journey on a regular basis. We experience spontaneous journeys all the time. For instance, have you ever thought of a friend just before receiving a phone call from that same person? When your friend set their intent to go to the phone and call you, they literally journeyed to you with their intent. They popped into your mind because you unconsciously sensed their famil-

---

1. *These are available at: tinyurl.com/WiyakaDrumming or tinyurl.com/WiyakaMusic.*
2. *In 1952, Dr. Winfried Otto Schumann discovered the "Schumann Resonance" which he calculated to be 7.8 Hz. (Cycles per second), which some refer to as the heartbeat of Earth. We also resonate at 7.8 Hz.*

iar field as it entered your personal space, setting up a resonance much like when they are actually in the room with you.

### The Watcher

*Upon the request of her mother, and with the young daughter's permission, I journeyed long distance to aid a very gifted child.*

*She was suffering with the whooping cough.*

*After I transferred the appropriate frequency information to her immune system, I hung out for a while in spirit to support her. Throughout the day I would "check in" on her in spirit form.*

*Later that day I received the following email from her mother:*

*Dear Gwilda,*
*My daughter tells me that she cannot rest because she feels as though you are "watching her," or as though there "is company."*

*She knows that you are trying to help her.*

*I personally am glad you are trying to help her. However, I'm writing to see if there is another tack you can take. Thank you!*

*Warmly, Sandy*

In ancient times when shamanism was more common and journeying more controlled and intentional, people likely had a lot more communication at the non-verbal level, as well as across distances. I expect we will all see much more of this in the future as well.

Daydreams that you've had that later come to pass are also a form of journeying. When we drop into our imagination, we are more likely to receive spiritual information that is not bound by time or place because the imagination is the major channel through which spiritual information comes to us. Our sleeping dreams are yet another form of journey. In intentional, controlled journeywork we choose when we will journey—we enter into trance (or dream state) and return consciously rather than spontaneously.

While we all journey frequently, we have ceased to recognize what it is and when we do it. Some of us tend to be in journey space more, here less, and we are often seen as *spacey* or *out there*. Such individuals also tend to have uncanny intuition. Others tend to be here in ordinary reality more and *out there* less, having a firm grip on *linear reality*, and they tend to be well-grounded. Some of us will journey to get into journey space, while others journey to gather and ground ourselves back into ordinary reality. There is no right way, but the challenge for those of us who want to be able to access unified information and bring it into our more polarized world, is to be able to reliably walk both worlds at will.

In "The Watcher," above, the ill child is one that "lives" in journey space. She is able to tell when another's awareness is in her field. The child could sense my journeying to and from her space during the extended time I was working with her. Therefore, in order to accommodate her comfort level, I assigned a power animal to attend to her while she needed extra support, and I had her call upon it when she needed it.

For most of her life she has been traumatized by the metaphoric representation with which her perceptions express themselves in her imagination. Since undergoing shamanic training with me, she is much better able to receive and decode the information, reducing her fear through understanding.

This example of her ability to accurately perceive nonphysical energy in her environment shines a whole new light on imaginary playmates and monsters in the closet, which carries an implication that most parents may not find overly comforting. Just because it registers in the imagination, doesn't mean it is not real.

In "The End of Days," we discussed how we become more unified as we reenter into a time of greater frequency. We also discussed how our current reality is one of polarized concepts and the act of evolving is one of taking advantage of the more-unified reality now becoming available.

"Spirit" or unified, higher-frequency information, is by its very nature non-polarized. Things in spirit are seen as having equal value, while in ordinary reality even our language is polarized. In ordinary reality, events are perceived to be good or bad, right or wrong, and so on.

*~ THE VERY NATURE OF BEING INCARNATE ULTIMATELY RESTRICTS OUR RANGE OF FREQUENCIES. ~*

The restrictions of being incarnate necessitate that even the most evolved individual creates a bridge between the lower-frequency information available at the physical level to the higher-frequency, more expansive information of spirit.

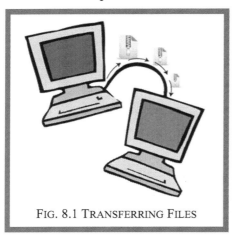

FIG. 8.1 TRANSFERRING FILES

Think of it as if spirit—or unified reality—is a Mac, and ordinary reality is a PC. They can't talk directly to each other. In order to transfer huge files from one to the other, they have to be "zipped" in one then transferred in zipped form to the other before being decoded. In order to pass information from unity to polarized reality, we use our imagination to translate the information into story or metaphoric form. This story is the zipped file. We then journal the story and decode it by interpreting the metaphor with our logical mind as we would a dream, which corresponds with transferring it to the PC, then unzipping the file.

Our imagination functions as a two-way street. One purpose of the imagination is to build and try out a proposed creation. By first constructing it in our imagination, we can decide if we really want to pursue creating it in our physical world and how it will look if we do. In this way, we dream or imagine what we wish to create, then we move it out into the physical world. Imagination also works as a receptor and translator of information from non-polarized reality. Through dreams and shamanic journeys we receive unified or spiritual information. We design a story or metaphor in our imagination to translate this information into ordinary reality. Through this shamanic metaphor, unified information can take the form of concepts more easily understood by the mind, which is operating in a polarized reality.

*Journey Where?*

*The only way*
*To truly understand*
*The journey process*
*Is to relinquish our ideas*
*Of the way life is.*

*Do I journey*
*Into my own subconscious*
*Or to another world?*

*Yes and yes,*
*For we ultimately*
*Are one*
*With All-That-Is.*

*Wake up*
*To the beauty and totality*
*Of that,*
*And breathe a breath*
*Of God.*

A journey is like an interactive or lucid dream during which you are awake and can direct the dream or journey to some extent. However, it is not like a scripted guided visualization in which you can pre-plan what will happen at each stage. In a journey you can choose your actions, unlike in most dreams, but when it comes to the landscape and what you will encounter, you are essentially along for the ride.

## No Bells and Whistles

When I first started to journey, I fully expected it to be like Hollywood—complete with full Technicolor, special effects, and sound track. I discounted my journeys for quite a while because they were such a familiar format. It was much like daydreaming.

Spiritual information tends to come to us through what we have available—our own personal wiring, if you will. If you are normally a visual person, the journey will tend to come through predominantly in the visual medium. Likewise, if you are mostly auditory, the information may be "heard," and if you are kinesthetic, it might feel like a knowing or feeling, or as if you are empathizing with what is going on.

Most of us receive such information through a combination of these channels, but one will predominate. As you gain more experience doing journeywork, you may be able to intentionally move the information through particular channels.

Each of us can experience in any one of the modes, and the more you do journeywork, the more you can refine them all. In the beginning of your practice, expect the information to mostly come into the channel that you already operate on, as things flow along the path of least resistance.

## IS THIS REAL?

One of the most harmful things we, as a culture, do to our children is to tell them that something from their experience is only their imagination and not real. It is actually through the channels of our imagination that *all* spiritual information comes to us, and it is also through our imagination that we move the things that we care to manifest out into the world. To discount our imaginations is to stifle our creativity, block the spiritual information that is our birthright, and cripple our ability to manifest the things we need or desire in our lives.

When you are on a journey, it may be hard to believe that you are not just making up the information. It can be confusing, because you are and you aren't. Any time you engage your imagination, you are either receiving or creating information. The received information can feel very much like something you have personally dreamed up. What is actually happening is that your imagination is receiving spiritual information, then creating a metaphor in order to translate the unified spiritual information into a polarized, ordinary-reality format.

Even if it feels as if you are making it up, continue the journey and simply note and remember your experiences. Often you will be validated when the information you received is confirmed by later events. These validating experiences tend to happen frequently, and, over time, they will help you gain confidence in your practice.

> When I was a fledgling journeyer just starting to get quite full of myself and my ability to access information from the other side, I was journeying for a friend who was considering breaking up with her boyfriend who, as she put it, had begun to "bore her to tears."
>
> With great confidence I journeyed to the lower world and asked what it was that my friend needed to know about her relationship.
>
> When I got there, suddenly I was riding my horse, flogging her with a crop, until she literally dropped dead.

I was mortified! I had killed my beautiful power animal! My lovely white mare was lying there, starting to look suspiciously like a mule with X's in her eyes.

I was so upset that it took me a good week to get the courage to show my face in journey space again. When I did, there was my horse, as right as rain.

"I thought I had killed you," I wailed. She just pranced around me, ready for our next adventure.

It took me another week to realize that my friend's answer to her question (what she needed to know about her relationship) was: She was flogging a dead mule.

## WHO IS THIS "SPIRIT" WE ARE CONSULTING?

This is a very difficult question with multiple answers. Because we are in the process of evolving, the answer depends upon what reality (or frequency) we are in when we address the question. Most indigenous peoples considered "Spirit" to be "The Great Spirit," or "The-Spirit-That-Moves-Through-All-Things," or "Creator," and ultimately it is.

For the sake of simplicity, let's consider total unity to be "Spirit." As we step down in frequency from absolute unity, where all things are one, we start to experience different divinations of spirit and more polarized, or binary, realities. These levels are still part of "Spirit," but just not the whole enchilada, so to speak.

Answers we receive at this level are truth, just not the whole truth. This may sound dicey, but remember that this is a truth that we can conceive of and process with our minds, which is what we are asking for. It provides a more complete picture than what we already have. This intermediary truth can serve as a bridge to the next step of our evolutionary path when we develop a greater capacity to encompass unified reality.

## THE METAPHORICAL NATURE OF THE SHAMANIC JOURNEY

One of the challenges of the shamanic journey as a source of information is our own polarized mind set and language. Spirit is not polarized. Also, we as individuals have a limited view and understanding of any subject, as compared to the ultimate overview.

~ *OUR ABILITY TO ACCESS ACCURATE INFORMATION IS LIMITED BY OUR BELIEF SYSTEMS, JUDGMENTS, AND LEVEL OF UNDERSTANDING.* ~

Much like the process of zipping a big file to pass information from a Mac to a PC, through the use of metaphor, it becomes possible to pass concepts across the veil between unity and polarization. In journeywork the information from spirit has to be translated into a form that is understandable by our polarized minds in ordinary reality. This is done by a series of steps. First, the spiritual information is presented to us via the imagination into the unpolarized or more circular portion of our minds, or our right brain. If we try to figure out the meaning at this point, more often than not, we miss the point. It is most effective if we just set the events in our memory, return from the journey, and then journal the story. This runs it through our "logical" or polarized, linear mind—the left brain—into ordinary reality via language. The journey story can then be translated into ordinary reality with meaning intact, sealed in the content of the story line and metaphor.

Information you receive on a journey can be metaphorical, literal, or, most commonly, a combination of the two. By journaling the information as soon as you return and then relating it back to the question at hand, we can glean the information we need. Oftentimes it is the very act of working with the information in this manner that brings enlightenment or an opening of some closed view we may have held. Often, the process is ultimately more valuable than the answer.

In my early journeying experience that involved the flogging mule, the metaphor may have had much more meaning than that the woman was simply wasting her time with the relationship. The simple image also contained the messages that she was trying to get more out of the horse than it could provide and that the situation was quite hurtful to both of them, which exemplifies how metaphor allows us to receive additional information in a gentle and non-threatening way. It also demonstrates how the meaning of shamanic metaphor can deepen over time with our expanding capacity to encompass unified reality. The mystery of the story opens us up to be receptive to deeper meanings by engaging our curiosity.

The instructions that follow are designed for your personal journey practice, not to use on behalf of others. Yet, I would be remiss if I did not point out several things pertaining to all shamanic journeywork:

1) It is important that we never journey on behalf of others without their permission.

2) We do not assume that we can interpret their journey.

3) When seeking guidance in dealing with another, we do not ask, "What does this person need?" To do so can result in acquiring information about another, which constitutes working without permission. Instead we can ask, "How can I best serve this person?" In this case, the question really relates to us and how to use our skills.

4) If, for instance, we ask, "Is my son involved with drugs?" We are violating another's space, no matter how well-meaning our concern.

5) Any information we obtain in reference to another is strictly confidential.

6) Journey information is to be used to help ourselves make more informed decisions—not to make those decisions for us. How we live our lives remains entirely up to us, and we are responsible for our actions.

## POWER ANIMALS AND HELPING SPIRITS

Who are these helping spirits and power animals that go with us on journeys, and provide us with information and guidance?

According to the ancient shaman, there are helping spirits and power animals that surround us at all times. Some of them come with us when we come into the world and leave when we leave. Others come and go depending on what energies we need to support us in our lives at any given time.

Often imaginary playmates and invisible animals that many of us had as children will show up during journeywork. They presented themselves in our imagination as metaphors for our spirit helpers and have likely been with us since we were born.

Power animals and helping spirits are our guides and consultants when we enter journey space. Once we learn to work with them, our power animals can inform us and protect us in ordinary reality as well. They serve to balance our energy fields, and they provide a particular energy frequency that enables us to operate proficiently in the spiritual realm.

The spiritual energies of any power animal are aligned with the universal energies of their species, and therefore, carry the particular gifts of that species. For instance, a skunk is known to help us with boundaries. You do not harass a skunk, because you are likely to be sprayed. So, if you were working with boundary issues, it wouldn't be a surprise to have skunk show up as a power animal.

Normally, we have more than one animal at a time. All power animals have equal power—a skunk is no greater or less than an eagle, other than that it would bring a different expression of power to you. What you get depends upon what you need in your life at that time.

If you have a strong affinity for certain animals, they may very likely be your power animals, although other animals may also come to you even though you've had no relationship with them before.

With all of that said, let's reframe the power animal/helping spirit concept at another level. As we step down from total unity into the binary system necessary for biological life, different expressions take up residence in various species. As humans, when we get out of balance, or find that we need particular strengths we may lack at any given time, attuning to different expressions of frequency can help us regain that balance. Through the metaphor of different animals or helping spirits entering our field, we draw on the appropriate expression to balance or strengthen us.

There is an amazing correlation between the behavior of animals in ordinary reality and the ones we encounter in spirit. You may find that you tend to see your power animal in the feather or fur showing up around you at auspicious times. While "spirit animals" may well be metaphors, they do relate to their animal nation in ordinary reality. We are, after all, one with All That Is, functioning as a giant organism in the larger scheme of things. At the cellular level, we draw in what we need from the rest of the body, and the same principles apply in spiritual and physical reality as well. Are we not the same as individual cells in the body of All That Is?

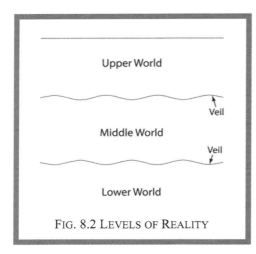

FIG. 8.2 LEVELS OF REALITY

## THE LANDSCAPE OF NON-ORDINARY REALITY

There are three levels to reality one encounters during journeys that seem universal across indigenous cultures—lower world, middle world, and upper world.

Middle world is the reality we live in, but it exists outside of time and space. Therefore, it can be used to travel to another location (astral projection), to our past (regression), or to our futures (divination). Depending upon where we set our intent to journey and the purpose of that journey, both upper and lower world may be landscapes of the unconscious mind of individuals or that of the collective. Lower world appears more grounded and

Earth-based, while upper world gives the impression of being more ethereal. For this reason, I will focus your journey instruction on lower world.

The journey landscape may not necessarily always look the same each time you go, although you may run across the same basic landmarks consistently. Sometimes it is totally new and different, and you are taken to a place you've not been before because it is the most expedient way to get the information. Also, when you change geographical locations in ordinary reality and do journeywork there, you may see some new landscapes based upon the differing longitudinal and latitudinal energies present in that particular location.

Both upper and lower world are beyond the veils bordering middle world, and both are places you can go to obtain accurate and consistent spiritual information and healings. When you know how to journey to both, simply ask your power animal or spirit guide where would be the best place to journey to get what you have requested, and they will direct you to the most efficient place to obtain it.

## MIDDLE WORLD

Middle world is the reality we are normally in, but outside of time and space. As in the prior example of spontaneous journeys, when we think about a friend, and they call us shortly after, they have performed a middle-world journey and entered our space with their intent to call.

Middle world is not restricted to time and space in the sense that you can take a journey in the middle of winter only to end up in a summertime scene. Trained shamanic practitioners can journey to a past event and collect part of a person's essence left there. This is a healing known as middle world soul retrieval. Interestingly, you can go into your future and meet yourself there. For instance, if you have a future event coming up, you can journey to the space where you will be and already start preparing that space to support your project even before you come into it.

We use middle world to journey to and from our entry point into lower or upper world. There is a veil between middle world and upper and lower worlds. We cross that veil during a lower world journey when we go down through the Earth and during an upper world journey when we go past the sky. Once you've crossed the veil, you can trust anyone you meet there as the information they have to offer is of a higher level of understanding than the one you currently hold.

Your power animals and spirit helpers are accessed and brought back from the other side of the veil, either from upper or lower world, and can be trusted even if you access them later in middle world.

However, in middle world there are a lot of disembodied spirits hanging around who may not know they're dead or are afraid to cross over. Individuals who believe they have not lived a good life and also believe that hell is the result of the life they have led, may be afraid to cross over. Other times people die a sudden death in an accident, or while under anesthesia, and don't even know that they are dead. Members of our culture often hold onto the dead because they don't know how to mourn. As a culture, we have moved away from the shamanic practices of our ancestors, and we find ourselves left with little provision to help the dead cross or for the survivors to consciously release them to do so.

In many Native American traditions, mourning was loud and intense, yet brief. Once the mourning was done, the person's name was never spoken again. Instead the deceased was referred to as "the brother of my wife" or "husband of my sister." They believed that to speak the name of the deceased too frequently would prevent them from crossing over completely. There is much wisdom in that.

Most indigenous cultures used some form of a practice to help souls cross to the other side. In our culture, for the most part, this procedure is no longer practiced. As a result, we may very well have many more misdirected, disembodied souls floating around in middle world than in times past.

When people cross over, they cross through the veil, shed all their baggage and become pure spirit. Another way of looking at that is that they reenter unity. Many indigenous cultures believe that there are individuals on the other side who have decided to stay in the "between worlds" to help us. They function as a translation point between unity and polarity. Because of this, your spirit guides may sometimes also be your ancestors or someone who was once incarnate.

If you come across a spirit in middle world, remember, as several of my teachers said, "Just because they're dead doesn't mean they're smart." We always journey with a power animal; don't leave home without one. If you have your power animal with you, and you run across something or someone who wants to talk with you, ask your power animal if they are a reliable source of information. Your power animals and helping spirits are all originally accessed from the other side of the veil, so even in middle world you can trust them. Make sure your power animal knows you *do not* want to have the spirit join you in your body. If your power animal indicates that it is in your best interest to converse with them, invite the spirit to meet you in upper or lower world. If they show up there, they are reliable; if they do not show up, conversing with them is an advanced shamanic technique known as mediumship. Understand that they are no more reliable as a source of information than any other person in ordinary reality. A good rule of thumb is to obtain proper training as a medium before engaging disembodied spirits in middle world.

## LOWER WORLD

Lower world is the level of reality we will use for your beginning journey practice. It is very Earth based, and is accessed through the earth by your memory or imagination of a place where things go underground. For instance, you could access it where water goes underground, or through the roots of a tree, or via a cave, a hole, or crack in the ground, an animal den, or even a tunnel or mine.

It is best to choose locations with which you have a connection, or to which you have actually been in the past—an actual place in ordinary reality that you have experienced. For instance, you may use the roots of a tree in the yard you grew up in, or one you leaned up against yesterday, when you had lunch at the park. You could use a cave you toured on your last vacation, and so on.

Because you will journey with your power animal, you can ask it whether you have arrived in lower world if you are unsure. As with all things, practice and familiarity will soon dispel doubt.

Finding a power animal to work with you once you arrive in lower world is rarely difficult. This is because Spirit is there waiting for us all the time, and it is there to help us as soon as we ask. We live in a free-will universe, so the power-animal divinations of Spirit cannot impose themselves on us, but they are always anxious to respond when asked.

## PREPARING YOUR SPACE

For now we will just address some basic elements that will enable you to experience your first journeys in comfort and safety.

It is important that you are comfortable. It is difficult to journey when you are distracted by physical discomfort, say, for instance, lying on a hard floor or having a full bladder. Too much comfort, however, can result in the journey being one into sleep, restful but not overly productive. Choosing a spot to journey where you do not normally sleep can work well. If you do choose to use your bed, lying in a novel position rather than in your normal sleep orientation can help your body understand that this is not naptime.

Choose a time and place where you will not be interrupted. Turn off the phone and let family members know you are not to be disturbed for the duration you have chosen for your journey.

Burn sage in the room, light a candle, and set up any sacred objects around you that remind you of your power animals or what represents Spirit to you—anything that helps you feel at ease.

## SAFE TRAVELING

The first step in any journeywork is to call in your power animals. The rules of safe travel are:

1) Never travel without your power animals.

2) Don't talk to strangers.

3) Be specific about coming and going.

You can use some form of percussion to call in your power animal, such as the first portion of the drumming recording, or a rattle. While listening to the drums or rattle, ask your power animal to come join you so you can journey. In your imagination, "see" your power animal enter the room and come to your side.

## HOW TO JOURNEY

You will need:

- ❖ Drumming CD or MP3[1]
- ❖ Personal CD player or iPod with headphones
- ❖ Rattle (optional)
- ❖ Bandana or eye shade to cover your eyes
- ❖ Throw pillows and blanket for comfort (optional)
- ❖ Sacred objects to help set space
- ❖ Journal and pen
- ❖ Dream-symbols interpretation book
- ❖ Power-animal book

I want to emphasize again how important it is to find a space in your house where you won't be interrupted. If you are interrupted while on journey, you may be left feeling scattered or spaced out. If you've ever been deep into thought, in a daydream, or absorbed in a good book, and have been interrupted, you may have experienced spaciness for quite a while afterward. What has happened in all of these cases is that you are stretched

---

1.  *tinyurl.com/PathHomeMusic*

between ordinary reality and imagination or journey space, and you are not totally present in either.

If you are interrupted, as soon as you get an opportunity, go back to your prepared sacred place and methodically journey back into where you were before the disruption occurred. There you can collect yourself, and either go on with the journey or come back out. You may also find yourself feeling scattered if you don't follow the usual, methodical way of entering or leaving journey space. You can always ask a power animal to help you, if you are feeling scattered. It will let you know if you have left a part of you behind during a journey and then can help you go regain it.

Losing a part of yourself in journey, is relatively easy to retrieve, compared to losing a soul part through some trauma where you need someone else to go get the pieces for you. The soul parts are usually in a guarded space that you cannot enter alone, and much personal processing is required to integrate the soul part back into the whole. Remember that this situation requires professional help from a well-trained shamanic practitioner.

Unknowingly, we hold off and field all sorts of energies all day long, and this takes up a fair amount of our energy. When you set up sacred space, it fields the energy for you. You can then relax, focus on leaving your body and go on the journey in safety. Another way of looking at it is that we operate at a particular frequency in our daily lives. Engaging in activities that raise or expand our frequency before entering the journey greatly aids the process.

To summarize the journey process, begin by getting aligned with the spirit world first. These few initial steps are important to make a space where you can start to move into an altered state before beginning the journey. Surrounding yourself with your sacred objects helps set your intention and enhances both the quality and clarity of your journey.

At this point you might softly beat a drum or shake a rattle and hum to yourself, which helps you to gently begin to enter an altered state of consciousness.

Once you have set up the space for a journey, use your drumming CD or MP3. Lie down and cover your eyes. Next, call in a power animal or spirit guide to accompany you. If you haven't had a power animal retrieved for you yet, ask for a power animal to accompany you and "see" who shows up in your "imagination."

State your intention for the journey to your animal. Once you have done so, follow your power animal to your entry point into lower world. Keep in mind that in journey space you travel in a way that is unlike how you would in ordinary reality, often going as the crow flies and moving very rapidly. It is best to travel a nice direct route that you know you can find later to travel back on. So be as specific as you need to be to accomplish this.

When on journey, a waking dream will unfold for you. Open up to all your senses, and learn how spirit best communicates with you. Everything that happens can have meaning—emotionally, physically and how you respond—are all important.

It may feel awkward and unnatural when you are first learning journey skills. With time and practice, it becomes easier and more fluid. To start out with, and in the interest of instruction, a generic method is being imposed on your natural ability to journey, which will set you off in the right direction. As you gain your journey legs, just do as your power animals and helping spirits instruct, and you will enjoy the best instruction available and have many wonderful adventures.

In order to perfect your skills, practice journeying as much as you can. It is best to start with a 15-minute journey. Later you can expand that to 30 minutes. Otherwise, it is hard to keep track of all the information that comes to you. As you become more advanced, journeys of 45 minutes to an hour might be useful.

INITIAL JOURNEY TO LOWER WORLD

15-minute Journey[1]

Choose an entry spot in ordinary reality that meets the before-mentioned criteria.

Call in your power animal, introduce yourself, and state that you are there to practice lower world journey and graciously ask for help. You will almost always get an affirmative answer.

Once you perceive that your power animal is with you, imagine yourself sitting up out of your body, and either ride, fly, walk, or even become your animal. Do whatever your animal shows you to do or whatever feels right.

"See" yourself go with your power animal cross-country to the spot in middle world that you've chosen as your entry point to lower world. Whether the spot is nearby or far away, it shouldn't take you more than a moment or two to get there.

---

1. *Track 4 on "On Wings of Spirit" or "Betwixt and Between" CDs/ MP3s. Available at: tinyurl.com/PathHomeMusic.*

Once you arrive at your spot, approach it respectfully, introduce yourself, and ask for help in making the passage to lower world.

Your chosen spot will show you how. Follow those instructions, while making sure that your power animal is with you.

If you are underground with roots and soil, you have not arrived yet. Just keep going until you break out into another landscape. This will be lower world. If you are in doubt that you have arrived, ask your power animal.

Once there, imagine yourself calling for a power animal that is willing to help you; it may be the same animal that accompanied you there or a different one. When your animal shows up, ask for a guided tour of lower world. If you have any questions or doubts along the way, ask your power animal for guidance.

At the end of your chosen track, the drumbeat will change. This is your call back. When the drum sounds the call to return, thank whomever you are talking to and journey back exactly the way you came. This can happen rather rapidly.

If you have not yet fully returned from your journey when the drumming stops, continue your methodical retracing of your path until you do.

When you have arrived back at your body, thank your power animal, say goodbye, and see yourself lie down into your body. Journal *everything* you remember from your journey as soon as you return.

Only after you have recorded the journey can you begin working on interpreting your experience. Trying to decipher your journey while you are still on it is counterproductive and will only result in getting your mind in the way. The mind's job while on journey is to document and remember the information coming through the imagination. We will go over effective journaling and how to decipher the journey information in the next few sections.

## The Divination Journey

Journeys can be used to answer any questions you might have. The clarity and accuracy of your interpretation of the answer will be greatly affected by how you word the question.

Because spirit is unity, it does not deal well with questions that require a yes-or-no (polarized) answer. Nor does spirit deal well with questions requiring value judgments such as whether you *should* or *should not* do something. What you might view as a horrible experience might be an incredible lesson in the eyes of spirit—grounds enough to answer yes to your question. Needless to say, that may not be what you had in mind.

Remember, when we consult spirit, we are seeking information to help us make more informed decisions, not seeking to have the decisions made for us. A wonderful story that relates this kind of attitude was an experience I had with my son during one of the school's outreach events.

### SPIRIT TELLS ME

My son, who is a general contractor, was helping me set up the Path Home Shamanic Arts School booth at a metaphysical fair in Denver one spring. He was up on a ladder, wearing his tool belt, hooking up the lighting when two middle-aged women draped in silk, feathers and crystals started setting up the booth they were sharing behind us. One side of the booth clearly had better exposure than the other.

Standing, hip cocked and delicately nibbling on the acrylic nail of her right forefinger, one woman looked from one side of the booth to the other. With a flourish of her arm indicating the side with the best exposure, she turned to the other woman and said, "I am *getting it* that I should set up my oils on this side."

Her partner looked from one side to the other, narrowed her eyes, then responded, "Actually, spirit tells me my jewelry should go there."

The first woman put her forefingers to her temples, closed her eyes briefly before countering, "No, spirit says it should be my oils."

"I don't know who you are talking to, but my spirit guides tell me that is clearly my side," the other woman heatedly stated. The two women were about to come to blows when my son had had enough.

With an exasperated exhalation he climbed down from the ladder, pulled a toothpick from the breast pocket of his flannel shirt and broke it in half. With deliberation he laid the two pieces down on the coveted table.

Raising back up to his impressive six-foot-four, he softly said, "Frankly ladies, *I'm getting it* that spirit doesn't give a damn. Why don't you two draw straws?"

For us to excuse our behavior or justify our actions by claiming spirit "told me to do it" is not only manipulative, it is also disempowering. To do so in one of my programs will most likely result in getting hit over the head with a drum stick (yes, that is how I really feel about that).

Answers will mostly come to you in metaphors, so if you ask more than one question per journey, you may not know which metaphor refers to which question. It is best to limit yourself to one question per journey when you are beginning your practice.

Sometimes you may just ask spirit what lessons a certain choice could bring for you and then decide if you want to experience those particular lessons or not.

You always have free will. Spirit doesn't have the same value system or think the same way as we do, nor does it have an investment in how we learn our lessons, so you need to be very specific about how you ask your questions in order not to be inadvertently misled.

Spirit can give you information to base your choices on, yet, there are no right-or-wrong choices. Ultimately, it is up to us to make the choice and glean the lessons along that particular path. Spirit is not attached to what lessons you have. You will get them one way or another.

Again, remember that if you are trying to help someone in your life when you pose your question to spirit, ask what *you* can do and not what that other person needs to do. While very similar, the first phraseology is asking about yourself, while the second would be journeying into the other person's personal space without permission, which is a boundary violation and therefore inappropriate.

Journeying is a way in which to reconnect with spirit so that we have a direct personal line to our own inner sanctuary and own inner knowing. In our culture, we flail around trying to find our way in the world. We go to different places and different people, hoping someone will tell us who we are and what we need to do. Ultimately, our own connection with unity consciousness is where we must go to find answers, and journeying can take us there.

## THE BOTTOM LINE

When asking a question of spirit, I always like to come from what I refer to as my bottom line. The bottom line is what *I am* and *am not* willing to experience at this time. This gives spirit a starting point and helps me refine my intention.

An example of a question asked with a bottom line is: *"Given that I want to live in health, joy, abundance, ease, and be present for my children...,"* (followed by the question) ...what would it look like if I take this new job?"

A bottom line may change from time to time and from question to question, but you will probably find that particular elements tend to consistently be included. These are the things that are the most important to you and need to be considered when making decisions and when asking questions to guide these decisions.

## TAKING A DIVINATION JOURNEY

Write your question and bottom line in your journal, being careful to avoid polarized questions or those requiring a value judgment.

Call in your power animal, say you have a question, and ask to be taken on a lower world journey to be given an answer.

Once you arrive in lower world, state your question and bottom line. Everything that happens after that is considered part of the answer, but remember that the answer will most likely come to you in metaphor.

Do not try to figure out the answer while you are on journey—just set your experiences to memory and accurately journal it upon your return.

## THE ART OF JOURNALING

The shamanic metaphor is sacred, spiritual information, and, like many spiritual works, such as the Tao Te Ching it can take on deeper meaning with every reading. Journey information, like the journey itself, is trans-temporal in nature and can serve as guidance in and for the future.

Sometimes on journeys we are also given symbols that warrant drawing out in our journals as well. The journaling of your shamanic journeys can be an entire art form in itself. The following are some things I have found most useful over the years of my practice.

I like to start out with a journal that I find esthetically pleasing and easy to write in. I also have on hand colored pens. Before going on my journey, I write down the date, my bottom line, and question or reason for the journey in my journal. When I return from the journey I transcribe it, writing on every other line in my journal, to leave room for later interpretations.

After writing the journey, I will go through it and with one of my colored pens, I will underline the words I want to examine metaphorically. Once I look up the words in a dream journal, or come up with possible meanings, I jot them down in the extra space between the lines in another color.

I study the information and possible meanings of the words and symbols, and try to understand them from the perspective of my bottom line and question. Once I think I have a fairly accurate understanding of the material, I journal my interpretation below the original journey.

I keep my journals and go over them at special times, such as the New Year or my birthday, when I find it useful to contemplate my process and give gratitude to spirit for my many lessons and blessings.

## INTERPRETING JOURNEYS

Again, spiritual information is by its very nature unified. It doesn't convert well into our polarized world. In spirit, there is no light/dark, good/bad or right/wrong. When we seek spiritual guidance, there is a lot of room for misinterpretation, based on our limited polarized view—like trying to get a PC to talk to a Mac. The language doesn't cross over well, therefore the language of metaphor is used to help translate things into our polarized format.

Some of the information received on journey is metaphorical, while other information may be quite literal. When you are distinguishing between what is the two, ultimately it is your call. You can use a book of dream symbols to get ideas of possible meanings, but realize that since what you access on journey is translated from the contents of your unconscious mind, the choice of metaphors is very personal. The more universal dream interpretations found in books can be helpful, but you are the ultimate authority.

This is the time to recall everything that you experience on journey, including your thoughts, physical sensations, emotions, what went through your mind and how you responded to what you were shown.

In the process of translating your received metaphors, the journey becomes a living thing. This is why it is very important not to judge your journey while it is unfolding in unified reality. Only after returning from the journey and carefully writing down everything you can remember, is it time to work with the images.

Sometimes journeys pose more questions than they answer. In that case, keep a list of the questions and plan follow-up journeys to find deeper answers.

## JOURNEY ASSIGNMENTS

Because, next to soul-retrieval healing, the shamanic journey is such a powerful evolutionary tool, I recommend performing a journey every other day for a month to build a solid foundation for your practice.

The following are some assignments that can absolutely empower you to change your life, and which will help develop and perfect your journey practice for future use.

## Lower-World Journey Assignment #1:

### Journey to Clarify a Dream

15-minute Journey[1]

Write down the dream in your journal. Use your dream books to interpret the dream and write that down as well.

Choose an entry spot in ordinary reality that meets the before-mentioned criteria.

Call in your power animal. Let it know that you'd like to obtain an interpretation of your dream, and if needed, specify what aspect of the dream you want clarification on.

Travel to lower world with your power animal, according to the instructions in this chapter.

When you arrive, state (based on your bottom line) that you are here on your own behalf to obtain an interpretation of your dream about (give a brief description *i.e.,* the cat on the roof).

Everything that happens after that will be in reference to the dream.

Don't try to interpret the information spirit is giving you while it is unfolding. Just note everything that you experience, then journal it when you return.

When you hear the call-back beat, journey back the exact way you went and record the journey in your journal as soon as you are back.

Use your books and interpret the journey by translating metaphors. Then refer the journey back to your bottom line. Cross-reference all three. This is akin to looking at the dream with two eyes versus one, so you get a better view or greater depth perception.

If you are still unsure about the meaning of the dream, you can repeat the exercise, asking for further clarification.

---

1. *ibid.*

## Lower World Journey Assignment # 2:

### Journey on a Personal Question

15-minute Journey[1]

Work with wording the question as you were instructed to do in this chapter. Remember, an answer can only be as good as the question. Also decide on your bottom line, as it applies to the question you are asking.

Write both your bottom line and question down in your journal.

Call in your power animal. Ask it to take you to lower world to obtain the answer to a question.

Journey to lower world as you have been taught. When you get there, state your bottom line and question.

From the point you pose your question forward, everything that happens will apply to the answer. Don't try to interpret the information; just commit the journey to memory.

When you hear the call-back beat, journey back the exact way you came, and record the journey in your journal as soon as you are back.

Use your books and interpret the journey by translating metaphors, and then refer the journey back to your original question and bottom line.

---

1. *ibid.*

# 9

# Stairway to Heaven

## TEARS OF THE PHOENIX

He lies face down on the battlefield of his life, all of his hopes and dreams dashed, all his accomplishments hollow, all his aspirations and labor for naught. There is nothing left him but his courage and determination, and even those had failed him. He has been deceived and exploited, then cast off by the very system that he had given his life to serve. His heart and spirit are broken, and all hope is gone. He rolls over to look to the stars—a prayer on his lips that they have mercy on him and just take him home.

Suddenly, bright unearthly plumage comes into view. The mythological phoenix drops from the sky and lands on the blood-soaked battleground beside him. As the warrior's life passes before his eyes. Phoenix cries tears of compassion for his pain, then she bursts into flame. Together they burn up, only to rise from the ashes, reborn.

> **Tears of the Phoenix**
>
> *Fly high, sweet phoenix*
> *Even though you are free*
> *Soar above my broken life*
> *Bring your healing tears to me*
> *Fly high, sweet phoenix*
> *Let your flame burn ever bright*
> *Come lead this fallen warrior*
> *Through his darkest night*
>
> *~ StarFaihre ~*

The wheels turn, ages shift, and the warrior's life is transformed through his willingness to release it. Through sacrificing all he is to the fire of transmutation, he becomes much more than he ever believed possible. He stands, lays down his rusty sword, and walks off the battlefield. Boldly he steps into the new world emerging—this powerful warrior reborn—this warrior of the heart.

So here we stand at the precipice of this remarkable adventure, the adventure of human evolution. We have the opportunity to be among the chosen ones to steward an entirely new way of being.

We indeed do have the chance to move beyond the current system. We can *now* become the co-creators of our experience.

As we have seen, there is a price of entry. That price is nothing more and nothing less than undergoing a shamanic death. Yet, what must die is the illusion; through its death we are truly reborn.

## THE CHAINS THAT BIND US

We have been enslaved by a system that no longer serves us. This system has outlived its time, and, like anything that hangs on beyond its shelf life, it has become distorted and rotten, fouling the environment and all it touches. This system is no more evil than anything else that is cornered and fighting for its life, and, at the same time, it is no less dangerous.

To participate in this system we must remain chained. Those chains have names—addiction, ill health, denial, guilt, shame, judgment, projection, defense mechanisms, victim mentality, and ego. To continue in the system, we must remain fragmented, polarized and mind-centered, continuing to invalidate our hearts and dreams.

## UNPLUGGING THE MACHINE

The current system—"the machine"—has no power in and of itself. It must take it from us. In order to leach power from us, the machine must hack into our toroidal fields. The more whole or healed we become, the more sovereign we are and the less vulnerable we are to the system.

*~ DOING BATTLE WITH THE MACHINE OR POLARIZING AGAINST IT
IS TO DO BATTLE WITH OUR OWN ENERGY. ~*

The process of disengaging from the system is not one of doing battle with it. In fact, fighting it only feeds it. In order to battle a thing, one must polarize against it, which results in denying that very thing in ourselves. When we are polarized against anything, we are frozen in polarization and have lost our mobility, which weakens our toroidal fields, rendering them more vulnerable to exploitation.

In order to unplug from the machine, we must choose to remain neutral in heart and to not participate in frozen polarizations. From this stance of neutrality or non-judgment, we can accept who and what we are, thus embracing our own shadow. Willingness to embrace our denials empowers us to heal and evolve. The more we evolve, the more sovereign and unavailable to exploitation we become.

## RUNNING AGAINST THE WIND

Nature deals in win-win scenarios. Plants exhale the oxygen that mammals need for life, while mammals exhale the carbon dioxide needed by the plants. Everything in nature is symbiotic; this is the circle of life.

The current system is not symbiotic—it is parasitic—totally self-serving. The machine works against the laws of nature, which is to practice sorcery. As you recall, sorcery has a nasty back lash, as nature *will* correct itself.

We have the dubious honor of living in one of those times when nature is in the process of making a monstrous correction. The degree to which this correction will impact you is directly proportionate to the degree with which you are engaged with the system. The more sovereign your toroidal fields, the less you will be impacted by this correction. When your toroidal fields are sovereign, you are aerodynamic, moving in accordance with the flow of nature and therefore running with, rather than against, the wind.

## THE MAP HOME

Every individual contains numerous energy centers in the form of toroidal fields. Every cell, organ, and chakra expresses at the quantum level through these tori, as does the entire human body. Each of these toroidal fields requires a balance of positive, negative, neutral and motion in order to function.

FIG. 9.1 MAP HOME LOGO

The Map Home symbol you have been repeatedly exposed to throughout this book (Fig. 9.1) represents these toroidal fields, with each shape signifying a different component.

Heart = neutral.

Top = masculine/positive.

Left = masculine/positive.

Bottom = feminine/negative.

Right = feminine/negative.

Figure eights or infinity signs = motion.

Pyramids or triangles are the ley lines of power created by the field.

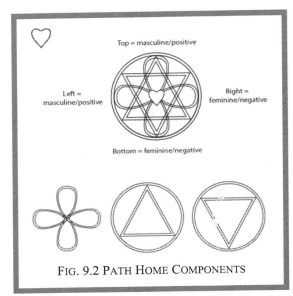

Top = masculine/positive

Left = masculine/positive

Right = feminine/negative

Bottom = feminine/negative

FIG. 9.2 PATH HOME COMPONENTS

An individual's personal power is proportional to the free functioning of their toroidal fields. The system or machine dismantles their fields, using portions of them to run its own agenda. The single masculine/positive pyramid is an example of this imbalanced appropriation of power.

Without the counterbalance of the feminine/negative pyramid in place, (Fig. 9.4) the system can be hacked into and exploited.

This exploitation is made possible by the mind ruling without the counterbalance of the heart.

FIG. 9.3

Eagle Mind

Much Information Shared By Few

Much Money/Power Shared By Few

CEO
Executives
Supervisors
Managers
Working Masses

Little Information Shared By Many

Little Money/Power Shared By Many

Condor Heart

FIG. 9.4

Conversely, in the ages of extreme feminine that border and include the Age of Scorpio, (Fig. 9.5) the heart rules without the counterbalance of the mind. This is represented by the single feminine/negative pyramid (Fig. 9.4) without the counterbalance of the masculine. During this age, passion rules without logic—exploitation of the individual is once again the result.

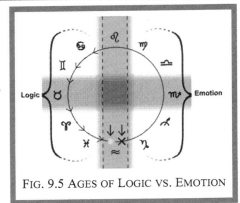

Logic

Emotion

FIG. 9.5 AGES OF LOGIC VS. EMOTION

## DETHRONING THE MIND

During the transition from being predominantly mental beings to becoming balanced physical, emotional, mental and spiritual beings, we may experience depression; we may feel as if nothing we have accomplished is worthwhile. Often there is a feeling of a total loss of direction and purpose. Nothing is looking like we expected, and none of the old rules seem to apply. Vision for the future may have disappeared, along with our passion.

During the long dark era surrounding the age of Taurus, when we were operating at a much lower or less-expansive frequency, and lost direct spiritual connection, our minds had to take over the job of guiding us. At that time, things were moving and changing very slowly. We could use our linear mind to evaluate events of the past and superimpose them onto the present or future and come up with a pretty good idea of what to expect. This was very useful during the denser times when we had no direct access to intuition or spiritual information. Our entire educational system was built upon this premise. We stored information in the mind to draw upon when it was needed to guide us through life. Our minds became so important to survival that we put everything else on the back burner. We judged against emotions as interfering with our ability to reason. The body was thought of as a house for the mind, and spirit was left in the care of the church, which through the natural devolution of the times became dogmatic.

While necessary and useful, the mind-centered way of operating has several disadvantages. Without the checks and balances of the other three aspects of our beings—physical, emotional, and spiritual—the mind is subject to illusion, which makes it subject to programming and control. We have seen that we are now controlled by society's imposed concepts and realities that actually dictate our addictions—programming our wants and needs. The mind is totally identified with its place in this false reality, and we are identified with our minds.

Another disadvantage of the mind-centered approach to life is that, logic, by its very nature, is somewhat linear, polarized and mono-dimensional. Life is not polarized, but cyclical, which puts our linear minds out of touch with nature, and as we have seen, the only law that holds true over time is the law of nature.

When the mind rules all, the rest of our being languishes. We equate this languishing as longing for love, for something to complete us. Because we are trapped in linear, polarized reality, we have lost touch with All-That-Is. We are compartmentalized and unable to complete ourselves in order to connect with spirit. Self-longing is not understood, so it is translated as longing for others. We find ourselves looking for love in all the wrong places.

Anyone wanting something badly enough becomes easily controlled and manipulated. We may think that money or sex drives our culture, but if we look deeply enough into it, the real reason we want money is to buy love. We think we need sex to connect and find fulfillment. Yet, it is wholeness we truly seek, and wholeness is something we cannot get from others.

Now, as we enter the new era, this old format no longer serves. As we find ourselves subject to the increasingly expansive frequencies, everything is moving at much greater speeds, and the old "knowledge" that we so prided ourselves in collecting no longer applies. Furthermore, by the time the mind has figured out what is going on and is getting ready to project it onto the future, the present changes and, seemingly, so do all the rules. The entire system we have identified with is rapidly failing us, leaving us with a deep sense of personal failure. The mind-centered way of being is dying, and, because we are so identified with the mind, we feel as if we also are dying. The mind has ruled for so long that it has become an entity unto itself, and it is going down kicking and screaming, which results in much suffering among us.

Now is the time to dust off our long-dormant instincts that are present within our bodies, listen to the natural direction provided by our emotions and reconnect our spirits to All-That-Is. The almighty mind needs to get over itself and take on its rightful job of receiving and translating information from the body, heart, and spirit.

Trust, faith, spontaneity, and living in the moment are paramount in order to navigate through these changing times.

One of the challenges is that, much like an unoccupied room in a home, anything left dormant becomes a storage place for unprocessed stuff. In order to access and use our physical, emotional, and spiritual beings, we need to dig in and deal with our unprocessed garbage.

We need to unclutter the mind from past information that no longer serves us, release it from past duties it can no longer perform, and make it live in the present. As long as the mind is projecting old information and dictating our actions accordingly, we have no hope of being spontaneous—in other words—taking action appropriate to the present moment.

We are all burdened by unprocessed, denied emotions that cloud present issues. It is very difficult to discern feelings generated by our present circumstances from those that are triggers into past unprocessed feelings still harbored in our emotional realm. When we cannot trust our feelings, we simply cannot trust.

The mental concept of faith is the assumption that things will turn out according to our visions. Yet we now find that our vision is based in illusion, which we experience as a loss of faith. Faith at the more expansive frequencies is faith in our rightful and natural place in the circle of life.

If we can find wholeness and completeness in ourselves, we can find contentment in all circumstances, which is ours for the taking, once we process through our old limiting beliefs and identifications. Only then can we truly embrace all that we truly are.

At present, while we are still trying to clear our old baggage from all four levels and become flight worthy, it is still difficult to tell triggers from perceptions. The clearer and more processed we become, the easier it is to tell insight from judgment. While evolving, it is important to be gentle with ourselves and each other. We are all works in process and doing the best we can with what we carry. Nature is our model for healing; natural law is our map home.

## The Multidimensional Life

When we live from our heart as well as our mind, the eagle of the north and the condor of the south can once again fly together. Our experience becomes multidimensional rather than linear. Many options can open up through healing. We can take back our power from the system. Our lives can be ours to create rather than a programmed set of events to be endured.

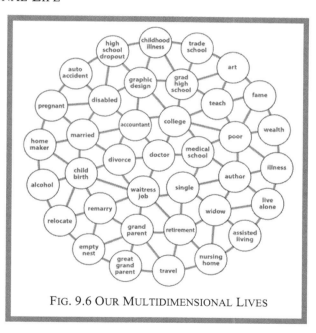

FIG. 9.6 OUR MULTIDIMENSIONAL LIVES

Soul retrieval can reconnect us to the options that are our birthright, granting us increasing mobility, creativity, and independence.

## Changing Worlds

Much like a woman in the last stages of labor, the pressure of these times is intense. Multiple factors are all coming together in this perfect moment (Fig. 9.7).

1) Age of Aquarius

2) Reentrance into the Photon Band

3) Earth's proximity to neighboring galaxies

4) Apex of the Mayan calendar

5) Precession of equinoxes leading our North Pole towards galactic center

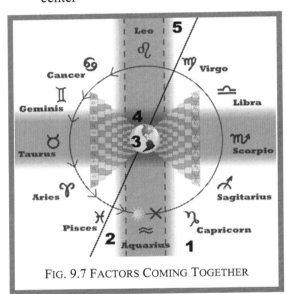

FIG. 9.7 FACTORS COMING TOGETHER

We are being birthed by life itself into an entire new way of being. Birth is a process best met with yielding and cooperation rather than resistance. It is the resistance to the process that creates suffering.If we can let go of resistance and fear, if we can embrace the changes now upon us, we can evolve into a level of power and proficiency beyond our wildest dreams.

## DYING WORLD

So how do we escape this old world breaking up? There has been talk about building personal toroidal space ships and escaping Earth to find a brave new world. On some level this is probably more than physically possible, but it may not be the optimal answer. Instead, we can become toroidal ships of evolution and bring the new Heaven and the new Earth here.

*~ FOR, BEHOLD, I CREATE NEW HEAVENS AND A NEW EARTH:*
*AND THE FORMER SHALL NOT BE REMEMBERED,*
*NOR COME INTO MIND. ~*
*~ ISAIAH 65:17 ~*

## STAIRWAY TO HEAVEN

In "A Magic Temple," I introduced the chakra system and discussed how each chakra expresses in the form of a differentiated toroidal field (see Fig. 9.8).

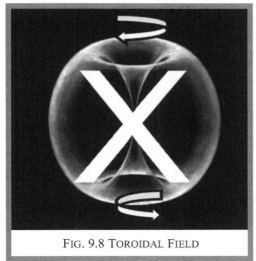

FIG. 9.8 TOROIDAL FIELD

We also touched on how each chakra presents a crossover place—the eye of a needle. The progression through these chakric eyes of the needle travels both above and below the physical body into infinity. As we evolve, we increasingly gain access to the portion of our chakra system that extends above and below the physical body. Each esoteric chakra, or the portion of the chakra system existing above and below the body, also expresses as a toroidal field and must be activated in order for us to open up to more expansive realities. The activation of these toroidal fields requires positive, negative, and neutral, combined with movement. The positive "light" we channel from above the body, the negative "light" from below.

FIG. 9.9 CHAKRIC EYES OF THE NEEDLE

In other words, in order for chakric evolution to take place, we must embrace both the positive/masculine/light and negative/feminine/dark in equal measure. As in the story of the "Tree that Grew Tall," the point is not to go higher and higher, but to expand equal distances in either direction. For this reason, we don't just keep activating the chakras above our body in order to evolve. Evolution is acquired through activating *sets* of chakras that are distanced equally but in opposite directions from the heart.

This *is* our stairway to heaven and is represented by the feathered serpent Quetzalcoatl as it ascends and descends the nine terraces of the pyramid on the spring equinox in Chichen Itza (see Fig. 9.10).

Every time a set of these esoteric chakras (one from above and the other from below) is activated, it is necessary to clear the unprocessed emotions, thoughts/beliefs and physical restrictions that the increasing frequency brings to light. Conversely, it is through clearing unprocessed emotions, thoughts/beliefs, and restrictions that our overall frequency rises to a point where another level of our esoteric chakra system can be activated or engaged.

FIG. 9.10 ASCENDING/
DESCENDING SNAKE OF
CHICHEN ITZA

Plants and trees don't just grow straight up, but rather spiral into the earth and toward the sun. The same is true of humankind. In order to grow or evolve, we must spiral through all four levels —physical, emotional, mental and spiritual—both upward and downward each time another set of esoteric chakras is activated. The spiral configuration is one of the major keys. All four levels must be addressed at each stage of evolution to enable forward movement while still maintaining integrity. We must clear our miasms on all four levels before progressing to the next transition, or we will evolve beyond our integrity and like the tree, come crashing down.

Freedom of movement is another necessary ingredient. At each crossover we must address the restrictions on all four levels that show up as the frequencies increase, which can involve further refining our diet or physically aligning with natural law. It may require processing out stored emotions, letting go of judgments and reframing our reality. Correcting fragmentation through shamanic healing may be necessary.

*~ OUR CHAKRAS, AS WELL AS OUR AURAS,
EXTEND WELL BEYOND THE PHYSICAL BODY, TRAVELING OUT INTO INFINITY.
THIS IS OUR STAIRWAY TO HEAVEN. ~*

By evolving in all directions, we are including our present life rather than rising above it. We become progressively more multidimensional until we are actually intergalactic beings, without having to leave our bodies or the planet. We can be of the Earth and dance in the stars, which is true ascension. This is the garden where "man was one with God."

## PIECES PARTS

Personal power and our ability to evolve through the stairway of the chakra systems are totally dependent upon one thing—whole health. Yet, for the most part, western medicine practices compartmentalized health care. Modern medicine predominantly treats on one level— the physical. Within that they have broken the physical down into parts, and various practices treat those parts in a vacuum.

In an attempt to treat on one level only, medicine has gotten increasingly coarse, clearly adhering to the "bigger hammer" school of thought. This approach has resulted in creating medications by taking elements out of their natural order or made from synthetic chemicals. That failing, we start cutting on the body and removing what is judged to be an offending body part.

## NOT MY DEPARTMENT

Whole health is the unified connection to the entirety of our being—body, emotions, mind and spirit—in synergy and balance. Years ago, before the concept of whole health was as well known as it is today, I had been going to the same dentist for years. Gum disease runs in my family, and I have had a history of it myself. I was very clear with my dentist and his hygienist about my tendency to periodontal disease. Religiously, every three months I would have my teeth cleaned.

My hygienist was very chatty. I knew about all of her family-drama trauma, and I got an update every visit. I sometimes wondered how she could talk so much and still pay attention to what she was doing. As it turned out, she could not.

I started noticing that a tooth was becoming very sensitive to temperature. I made an appointment with my dentist, who assured me that the tooth was fine. Over time, the discomfort got more pronounced. I returned, complaining of the increase in discomfort. He took an X-ray, and then reassured me that all was well with the tooth. He suggested that I take aspirin for pain and use toothpaste for sensitive teeth.

Finally I had a full-blown toothache. In desperation, I went to a dentist one of my friends recommended. He took one look in my mouth and sent me to a gum specialist. The specialist informed me I had deep pockets where my gums had pulled away from my teeth, exposing the root and developing an infection. He did deep scaling and put me on very strong antibiotics in an attempt to save the tooth, but it was too late. It had gone on for too long. He sent me to an oral surgeon to get the tooth pulled, after which, the surgeon sent me home with more antibiotics to clear up any residual infection.

Not long thereafter, I went to my family doctor, complaining of stomach aches, bloating and constipation. He gave me a strong antacid and laxative. Soon I developed irritable bowel syndrome. After my blood tests came back inconclusive, my family doctor sent me to an internist, who gave me an antispasmodic drug. Over time, the condition worsened, and I was failing to digest my food. My internist informed me that I might have to have part of my colon removed if we didn't get the condition under control.

Meanwhile, I acquired food allergies. The internist sent me to an allergist who, after more testing, took me off of wheat and dairy. My symptoms persisted, and the food allergies increased. Soon eggs and soy were added to the list. I started to feel exhausted all of the time. I went to my family doctor, who diagnosed me with chronic-fatigue syndrome and depression. He warned me that if things worsened, I might need to go on disability. He sent me to a psychiatrist, who put me on antidepressants.

I was at my chiropractor for an adjustment and happened to mention my worsening digestion. He asked if I had been on antibiotics recently. Remembering the dental adventure, I answered in the affirmative. He suggested that I might have a candida overgrowth, and he sent me home with a printout of the condition and a diet to treat it. He suggested that I follow up with a series of supplements to rebuild my intestinal flora and vitamins to replace what I had lost while being unable to digest.

I followed the recommendations for three months and was much improved. Next, I went off all the medications by first replacing them with herbs and supplements, then moving to homeopathic remedies. My chiropractor suggested a cleanse to detox all the drugs out of my system. After the cleanse, all of my symptoms cleared, and I was able to go off of the homeopathic remedies. I was left with acquired food allergies and one less tooth. I counted myself lucky, for I still had my colon and my job.

I went back to my original dentist and asked him how, with my having cleanings and checkups every three months, they managed to miss the pockets forming.

"Gums aren't my department," he replied in a huff.

I decided to seek out a more holistic dental clinic for my future dental care.

One again, to be fair, this experience was in 1981, and since then there has been remarkable advancement in holistic approaches in western medicine. I am currently a preceptor for the University Of Colorado School Of Medicine, where I provide instruction to medical doctors on the modern interface between shamanism and allopathic medicine for the University's School of Medicine Complementary and Alternative Medicine course. To say we have come a long way is an understatement. Unfortunately, the scenario I described is still fairly common in modern medicine.

*~ THE PROBLEM WITH THE CURRENT MEDICAL SYSTEM IS NOT A LACK OF CARING, COMPETENT, WELL-TRAINED PRACTITIONERS, BUT THE COMPARTMENTALIZED, LINEAR APPROACH OF THE WESTERN MIND. ~*

Many of us are suffering from a labyrinth of illness and chemical/surgical corrections that greatly compromise our health and frequency. At the same time, we are pouring our hard-earned cash into the food, drug, diet, and insurance empires. If you want to know where you might stand in this happy little equation, just get on the scales—count the prescription drugs you are on. The higher the number, the more ensnared you are.

However, lest we start pointing too many fingers at the doctors, it is grossly unreasonable to fill our bodies with chemicals and processed food, use them to store our unprocessed emotions, refuse to reevaluate our reality one iota, and then go to our doctors and expect them to be able to correct the results of our negligence with pills. The poor physician has no choice but to pull out the big guns to deal with that level of lock down.

*~ THERE ARE NO INCURABLE DISEASES, ONLY INCURABLE PEOPLE. ~*
*DR. JOHN RAY CHRISTOPHER*

## THE CURE IS WORSE THAN THE DISEASE

Many of the symptoms we label as disease are not the actual problem but rather our bodies' attempt to correct the imbalances at the root of the problem. Most of western medicine is based on treating symptoms rather than correcting the imbalances causing them. By treating the symptoms, we are actually crippling our body's ability to regain and maintain the very balance necessary for health and longevity. All illness, whether it be physical, emotional, mental, or spiritual, can be summed up as an imbalance in our toroidal fields.

It has taken me years, but I have finally learned that when I become "ill," I need to embrace the illness as a cure rather than fighting the symptoms. I have finally realized that if I don't want to be "sick," I need to avoid doing sick or imbalanced things.

By eating predominantly organic food, avoiding genetically modified/ refined foods, and drinking plenty of pure water, one can avoid the discomfort of our bodies having to detox what they can't use.

Any "illness" is best met by supporting the body through the process with supplements, herbs, homeopathic remedies, and essential oils rather than masking the symptom with drugs.

*~ SHE WAS NEVER SICK A DAY OF HER LIFE UNTIL SHE DIED OF CANCER ~*

We are constantly being exposed to things that compromise our balance. Now, more than ever, our bodies struggle to overcome all the pollutants that impact them on a daily basis. We are also expected to be at peak performance at all times—no one wants a sickly employee. When our bodies attempt to correct themselves through detoxing, we are more likely to pop some cold medicine and go to work, or school rather than take a day of rest to support the healing process.

Over time, such actions actually drive the imbalance deeper into the body. We can only do this for so long before a much more violent clearing is necessary to regain the balance needed to maintain true health. We treat these more intense clearings with drugs, driving the imbalance yet deeper and adding the imbalance of the drugs to the equation.

Everyone's body has cancer cells at any given time. Cancer is not the problem. Compromising the body's ability to correct imbalance renders it incapable of keeping the growth of cancerous cells in check.

Emotionally, we all have overwhelming feelings or imbalanced thoughts from time to time. The same holds true here. If we try to drive them down rather than take the time to process them out, we become increasingly imbalanced, which results in mental and emotional illness.

*~ NATURE HOLDS THE KEY TO BALANCE. ~*

Constant exposure to violent, imbalanced television programs or inflammatory polarized news reports increases the imbalances in our thoughts and emotions. Our time is much better spent taking a walk in the park or petting our dog.

## BUILDING YOUR STAIRWAY

It may appear that I am anti-medication and against western medicine. Actually, I am not. There have been several holistically minded medical doctors in my life that have literally saved my life. It is a matter of employing the proper tool at the proper time, while keeping an eye on the goal—evolution and personal empowerment.

I like to think of the healing process as a car with a standard transmission. If you are stopped at a light, you can't start out in fifth gear. It doesn't have enough power or torque, and the engine will stall. You must use first gear to get the vehicle rolling. Yet, after reaching a certain speed, you need a higher gear if you want to go faster. First gear, while having the most power, only goes so fast. If you continue to push first gear beyond its limit, it will burn out the engine.

This is how it is with drugs versus homeopathic remedies. If your frequency is extremely low, if you are ill and depleted, treating with homeopathic remedies will have little to no effect (remember, you can't shovel poop with a feather). A person who is addicted to salt, sugar, artificial flavorings and chemical additives, and who has been treated allopathically all their lives, may need to start out by fighting fire with fire. It is usually necessary to use the proper combination of drugs to stabilize an individual whose frequency is severely compromised.

The key is to physically stabilize the person and then add support on the other three levels. By adding the appropriate support to the emotional, mental, and spiritual levels, we have gained some leeway, enabling us to revisit the medications and start replacing some of them with less invasive drugs and herbal remedies, which are of a more refined and balanced frequency than prescription drugs. After replacing some of the coarser meds, we can once again make the appropriate adjustments to the emotional, mental, and spiritual levels.

> *Methods for physical frequency adjustments include but are not limited to:*
>
> *In order of lesser to greater refinement*
>
> *Surgery*
> *Prescription drugs*
> *Herbal remedies*
> *Supplements*
> *Essential oils*
> *Homeopathic remedies*
> *Foods*
> *Sound*
> *Light*
> *Intent*

When choosing what level to use in initiating any correction, a good rule of thumb is to start with the least invasive level that will effect a positive change. Once people heal enough to move beyond their programmed addictions, they become sensitive to the needs of their bodies. At this point they begin to simply crave the food they need to maintain balance at any given time, which is the instinctual provision we see operating in pregnant women and their notorious tendency to crave different foods at differing stages of their pregnancy

There is a story about a horse who knew exactly what to do that illustrates this quite well:

*Instinctual Healing*

*In 1840, Quaker horse farmer John Hoxsey discovered a malignant tumor on one of his favorite horses. Knowing the horse's time was limited, he put it out to pasture to die.*

*After the horse had been in the pasture for several weeks, John noticed the animal grazing on weeds that were not part of its normal diet. Upon inspection, he found the tumor stabilizing. Three months later the tumor had noticeably shrunken.*

*Mr. Hoxsey, fascinated by the development, began to experiment with the herbs his horse had instinctually been eating. He devised three formulas he then used to treat the animal.*

*A year later the horse was completely healed. Jon Hoxsey went on to become well known in his area for successfully treating animals with cancer.*

Just as there is a frequency below which we can no longer maintain health, there is one above which we regain it. By systematically cycling through the physical, emotional, mental, and spiritual levels and refining the frequency of the corrections every time, we can evolve our overall frequency, which reestablishes health and well-being at all four levels.

Once physical health has been reestablished, continuing this process not only results in health and well-being, but also spiritual evolution and personal empowerment. For more detailed instructions on this process see: Map Home Workbook 1: Stairway to Heaven: (see "Appendix," on page 225).

## THE FRONT LINE

On the front line of good health is a healthy immune system. We tend to consider the immune system to be on the physical level only. Actually, the immune system is present on all four levels and beyond.

The master of the immune system is the thymus gland. This endocrine gland is the seat of one of our newest developing chakras, the turquoise. It is located just below the throat chakra, but well above the heart, and it is responsible for the protective function of our auric field. Like all chakras, it has its own differentiated toroidal field. At the quantum level, this field modulates in order to attune to helpful frequencies and field those that would be harmful to us. The more functional our immune system is on all levels, the more mobility, and therefore, adaptability we have, which translates as resistance to imbalance or disease, as we are able to quickly adjust our frequency to deal with substances that are harmful to us. The more rapidly we adapt to any given situation, the less our overall frequency is compromised. For this reason, immune function is directly related to evolution.

When we function at lower frequencies, we need coarser corrections to regain balance, such as pharmaceuticals. When we operate at higher frequencies, these adjustments can be achieved through intent alone.

## TOKAYA

In 2006, I contracted West Nile disease while teaching Path Home Shamanic Arts School's wilderness program. My immune system was fairly strong, so I was able to heal in about two weeks.

My daughter Laura's red-tailed hawk, Tokaya, also contracted the disease later that year and was failing rapidly. At first, Tokaya couldn't fly, but soon she was even having difficulty sitting on her perch. We contacted the raptor-rescue centers for advice, only to be told that thus far, there had been a 100% mortality rate in the raptors that had contracted West Nile disease. Our local veterinarian gave us little hope. He told us that there was no known way to treat Tokaya beyond keeping her well fed and letting nature take its course. Soon it became clear that we were losing her.

In desperation, Laura asked me to do shamanic work on Tokaya's behalf. I entered a journey trance and was reminded that I too had suffered from West Nile and had recovered. The answer to Tokaya's illness was in a frequency signature now held in my immune system. While still in journey trance, I offered this frequency to Tokaya's immune system. In two days, she showed improvement. At the end of the week she was on the mend. Tokaya ended up fully recovering. At that time she was the only known raptor in the area to have survived the disease.

Not long thereafter, Laura's fiancé also came down with West Nile. His philosophy leaned toward Western medicine, so that is the route he took. After three months, he was still ill, couldn't eat, and his fever was dangerously high. Laura took him to the hospital several times, only to be told that they couldn't help beyond treating the fever. Both times they just gave him ibuprofen and IV fluids, and then sent him home.

Since I don't work without permission, I was greatly relieved the day he looked at Laura with one bloodshot eye and asked, "Do you suppose your mother has anything in that medicine pouch of hers?"

I journeyed and offered his immune system the frequency I held from overcoming the disease. I was also instructed to do several soul retrievals for him, which I did. His fever broke the next day. In three days he was up and walking for the first time in three months. He had lost 35 pounds.

## THESE AND GREATER THINGS

With over 30 years of living in the shamanic way, I have reached a level of mastery that allows me to refine my intent to shift my frequency at any of the four levels. If I am in a shopping mall (a very unfriendly environment for the empathic) I adjust my spiritual level to filter out unwanted input. When it is being filtered at the spiritual level, the emotional bleed off of the people around me no longer impacts my personal emotional realm. If I so choose, I can extend this protective field to include those around me.

When I am in a mosquito-infested area, I adjust the frequency of my auric field at the physical level and emit the frequency of "not food." The mosquitoes will swarm around me but not land on my body.

Any time one of my shamanic clients or students asks me a question, I shift the frequency of my mental realm to attune to the Akashic Records to access the answer.

Am I exceptional? Yes, but then, so are you. We are living in exceptional times. These abilities and more are yours for the taking, just on the other side of the healing and processing that will unlock your potential and set you free.

## HEARTBREAK HOTEL

One of the down sides of evolving is the recognition of how abusive our system and society really is. Adjusting to living in this system is a process of fragmenting in order to be able to tolerate its coarseness and brutality. This compartmentalization allows us to numb out, detaching us from our emotions to the point that we can often witness atrocities and consider them common place. The common acceptance of war and even promoting it as the patriotic mission to save our country are other examples of this disconnect.

As we evolve into unity, we start to recognize all the beings on Earth and beyond as our relatives. This comes with a price—from animal testing to children starving in third world countries, we are surrounded with the suffering of all of our relations. It is necessary to wake up to this suffering in order to change it. On the other hand, it is important not to become polarized against it, or it will take us out of our own process.

We have discussed how unprocessed emotion from past traumas can cloud our perceptions of present events. If we get too wrapped up in the injustices of our current system, we run the risk of projecting our own damage onto the events around us, rather than processing it out in a dispassionate way.

At first this new emotional awareness can be overwhelming. I liken it to having my fingers numb from the cold. When they first start to thaw out they hurt like the dickens. Yet, the only way out is through. Unless I go through the painful thawing process, my fingers will freeze, die, and be lost altogether.

*~ YOU CAN CHOOSE TO EVOLVE WITHOUT HEALING AND PROCESSING: IT IS KNOWN AS DEATH, AND IT IS A PROCESS ALL ITS OWN. ~*

Waking to the pain of our world is at first almost overwhelming. Yet, if you stick with it, instead of shutting down or projecting your feelings, soon you can evolve to a higher perspective—the one of detached compassion so eloquently represented by the deity Kuan-Yin. From this perspective, we are able to trust life and its process, understanding that all of our relations are on their own path to wholeness, regardless of what it looks like in the moment. We can be in the world but not of it, standing for a better way while not condoning or participating in the abomination.

## EXPANDING REALITIES

Reality is directly related to chakra expansiveness. The more levels of our chakra system we have access to, the more expansive is our reality and the further reaching is our influence. Another way of viewing this is that the more chakras we have active, the larger and more influential our toroidal fields become. Soul retrieval and other shamanic healing modalities work on the quantum level and are able to clear restrictions in our chakra system.

We are blocked from expanding our reality by our restrictions, miasms, denials, and lack of processing. In order to heal into greater expansion, these blocks must be removed, thus granting us access to all the levels of reality we have evolved through.

This increased mobility is what allows me to meet my clients and students in their reality before helping them embrace a more expanded one. Evolution is not a matter of "rising above it all," isolating ourselves on a mountain top, and contemplating our navels. We can have little influence from there, nor be of service, as there is no translation point. We truly evolve by expanding while maintaining access to all the levels we have experienced. We don't need to be subject to the limitations of the less expansive realities as we interact with them, for we have the larger picture, but we can still relate to those residing there.

A transducer maintains contact with all levels of reality. It is a device that converts energy from one form into another. This expansiveness allows us to convert higher-level information and energy into the mundane. The ability to transduce expansive energy into the mundane empowers us to manifest on the physical plane. This book is a result of that very process.

I will delve deeper into the concept of manifestation in book 2 of The Map Home Series: *These and Greater Things*.

## THE EVOLUTION OF SPIRIT

Can you evolve without the benefit of shamanism? Yes, absolutely—to a point. You can address the things that compromise your physical, emotional, and mental frequencies. Ultimately, unless you also address the energetic push and pull operating on the quantum level of life, you will hit a wall. You can flog it all you like, but a three-legged horse is still just a three-legged horse, and it can only go so far, so fast.

You can recite positive affirmations until you are blue in the face. While they can be very helpful in integrating shamanic healing, unless you correct the frozen polarities that are recreating the dysfunction in your life, affirmations become just another form of denial.

You can employ guided meditation, receive Reiki, or use any number of modalities, and, while they all have value, if you are fragmented, you cannot really take full advantage of any of them.

*~ THERE IS A REASON SHAMANISM HAS BEEN SYSTEMATICALLY ERADICATED ON THE PLANET TO NEAR EXTINCTION—THE LAST THING A SYSTEM BENT ON EXPLOITING ITS PEOPLE WANTS IS SOMETHING THAT WILL GIVE THOSE PEOPLE ACCESS TO TRUTH, MUCH LESS TO THE POWER OF THE UNIVERSE. ~*

Through shamanic healing and processing we can overcome not only our personal limitations but also those imposed upon us by our current system. We can heal our physical body to the point of refinement, and maintain that balance through intent directed through the shamanic interface with the quantum level. The human body can once again become an anchor for spirit in the mundane rather than the totality of our experience.

It is possible to evolve our reality through shamanic healing to the point where we are no longer subject to the agreed-upon beliefs of our culture. This evolution of reality gives us the ability to work spiritual principals on the physical plane. In so doing, we can accomplish things once thought to be miracles. We can begin to actually manifest the things we want in our life, rather than rely on the system to provide for us.

*~ MIRACLE ENERGY IS ALREADY AMONG US. ~*

As our toroidal fields expand through shamanic healing, we are no longer restricted to third-dimensional physical reality. We will once again be able to access the information held in the Akashic records and commune with our relations from the stars.

## EVOLVING TORI AND UNITY

Every fully functioning torus within a system increases the power and functioning of the whole. As the tori of our cells gain power, the entire body becomes more sovereign. As the body gains integrity, it becomes at the same time more grounded and more expansive, which encourages the opening and activation of our esoteric chakras that exist above and below our physical bodies. The scope of our overall toroidal field increases with every level of our chakra system that we access.

There comes a point when each individual on the planet acts as an evolving cell or torus for their society. Each society comprises the individualized tori of the organism Earth, which herself is a torus in the toroidal field of the solar system. In turn, the solar system is a functioning torus in the toroidal system known as the Milky Way Galaxy. In this way, each of us is participating in the evolutionary process that expands us ever outward towards unity.

~ *UNITY, ONENESS, JOY, PEACE, PROSPERITY, LONGEVITY, AND PERSONAL EMPOWERMENT ARE A FOREGONE CONCLUSION. THE ONLY QUESTION IS, "WHERE ON THE CONTINUUM DO YOU CHOOSE TO PARTICIPATE?"* ~

During this process, we must first see to ourselves. In so doing, self-service becomes world-service. Each thing we clear as an individual blazes a frequency trail in the morphogenetic field for others to follow. While this is indeed an inside job, our work also affects the whole. This *is* our service.

## STEWARDS OF THE STAIRWAY

For years I have believed that we all had to participate in the evolutionary process in order for evolution to take place. I would look around me in despair, judging the progress of humanity as a whole and think, "We are all doomed."

Then one day I was laboring myself up the stairs from my basement with a large basket of freshly folded laundry only to find a cat lounging across one of the steps. I tried to skip the step he occupied by taking the one above. Seeing my unstable form looming over him with the laundry basket, he gave up his position and bolted. I lost my balance and ended back at the bottom of the stairs, bruised and covered with scattered laundry.

Ah, one must love those humbling moments of sentience! It was then, lying flat on my back, gazing up the stairs, that I realized that each step must remain present in order for anyone to ascend. In my arrogance, I had judged what other people's process needed to look like, based on my own.

It is vital to trust another's path. We are all a valuable and indispensable part of the whole, regardless of where we choose to participate at any given time. We can relax in knowing that all people, including ourselves, are exactly where they need to be, when they need to be there. Everything is in divine order. Without the presence of stewards holding the frequency for every step, there can be no stairway.

## STAR GAZING

Myths, legends, and prophecies from many lineages speak of our stellar ancestry. From ancient Egyptian ceremonies to the Zuñi Kachina dances, provisions have been in place to commune with the Star Nations who offer guidance during times of upheaval and change. Stellar communion is simply a matter of frequency limited only by our ability to accommodate it. Shaman have been accessing stellar guidance through the shamanic trance for millennia.

*~ WE ARE THE KEYS TO THE UNIVERSE—*
*OUR BODIES ARE THE VEHICLES FOR INTERGALACTIC TRAVEL. ~*

Those of us who choose to evolve during this era of accelerated frequencies have the opportunity to reach a level of processing that enables direct communication with our stellar relations, which is reputed to be where the Mayan Calendar came from—beings from the stars who came down to impart wisdom, bred with the people, and then returned to the stars. Is that literal? Metaphorical? I strongly suspect it is both, but that is another whole subject, yet another that I will address in book 2 of the Map Home series, *These and Greater Things.*

## THE GIANT TORUS IN THE SKY

Who, pray tell, is smart enough to run this perfectly synchronized machinery we call life? Certainly no one here—we humans could not even consciously run the basic functioning of our own bodies if they were not automatic. We would overlook some vital function like remembering to breathe, and we would die, if it were left to our almighty conscious mind to run things. Who, then, is breathing the universe?

*~ ALL MATTER ORIGINATES AND EXISTS ONLY BY VIRTUE OF A FORCE THAT*
*BRINGS THE PARTICLES OF AN ATOM TO VIBRATION, WHICH HOLDS*
*THE ATOM TOGETHER. WE MUST ASSUME THAT BEHIND THIS FORCE*
*IS THE EXISTENCE OF A CONSCIOUS AND INTELLIGENT MIND.*
*THIS MIND IS THE MATRIX OF ALL MATTER. ~*
*—MAX PLANCK, ONE OF THE FATHERS OF QUANTUM THEORY ~*

The cosmos is run by the same one managing the very breath of our bodies: Breath in; breath out—positive and negative—expansion and contraction—masculine and feminine—the alpha and the omega—the beginning and the end—Mother/Father God in sacred marriage of the heart.

## GRATITUDE

Nothing can be received, absorbed, or transmuted in the absence of gratitude. Yet in our culture, we rarely take time for it. In our frantic rush to fill the emptiness, we run from one acquisition or activity to the next in hopes that something out there will "make us happy." Naturally, nothing ever does, at least not for long, so we toss the latest distraction into our growing pile of acquisitions. Then judging the last distraction as the cause of our discontent, we then seek out the latest-greatest in hopes

FIG. 9.11 THE MAP HOME

that once we acquire it we will be happy, which is the enchantment of the consumer-driven system in which we live. This enchantment assures that we are always hungry and unfulfilled—forever seeking more.

*~ GRATITUDE IN ALL THINGS ~*

A little-known function of gratitude is transmutation. If we can find something to be grateful for in the most horrific experiences in our lives, we can transmute the pain and suffering into growth and evolution.

This transmutation can't be done by denying our pain, but rather through being willing to stay in process—to ride the joy-and-sorrow sine wave. By embracing both joy and sorrow in equal measure—neither seeking one nor avoiding the other—we establish freedom of movement, which generates the power to transmute our experience into one of contentment in all circumstances. This contentment allows us to live in the present moment, where infinite possibility resides.

# 10

# Power Tools

The process of evolution requires support. Yet, we are all unique—each of us requires different support at any given time. There is no one canned answer. The following are various tools you can use in building and customizing your map home to spiritual evolution and personal empowerment:

THERE'S YOUR SIGN

Astrology can be a powerful tool to aid your evolutionary process. Having your chart done by a competent astrologer can be extremely useful in helping you direct your intent and consciously create your experience. When we remember that our astrological sign is simply a map of where we are in the current of life, it can be used to help us ride the wave rather than be tossed around by it.

An astrologer can map out the influences different heavenly bodies will have on the currents running through your life at any given time. I like to have my chart done annually on my birthday. I request a month-by-month reading of my chart for the following year and mark significant influences on my personal calendar. When I am planning on initiating a project, I will consult my calendar and take these currents into consideration.

Educating yourself on the basics of astrology can also be quite useful. There are very basic planetary influences that, when observed, can support our activities. A perfect example is that when Mercury is in retrograde, new endeavors are not being supported and communication may be difficult. This is a time better spent cleaning up things from our past, as introspective backward movement is enhanced.

I have found, however, that as I become more processed and evolved, I am more in tune with these currents and have less need to physically consult my horoscope. The practice of following the horoscope has become a subroutine that I automatically take into consideration by listening to my intuition. However, I had to first build the subroutine through the discipline of following the horoscope so my intuition could automatically factor in the astrological currents.

## THE ART OF CEREMONIES

Across the ages, shaman have been responsible for performing ceremonies at auspicious times in order to propel the intent of their people. From planting to harvest, the art of collaboration with nature has been practiced with favorable results. Ceremonies are designed to cooperate with the laws of nature. Combined with group agreement, they allow the intent of the people to be propelled by natural law.

*~ THE MASTER IS ONE WHO HAS LEARNED HOW TO RIDE THE TIDES OF NATURE. ~*

While I do not advocate appropriating ceremonies from other cultures, there are universal principles that all cultures have adhered to when building their ceremonies. Through journeywork, these ancient principles can be used today to design living ceremonies that are better suited to our modern purpose and culture. At the same time, by adhering to the ancient tried-and-true principles, these modern ceremonies are grounded in the way life works. Ceremonies built in this way fulfill the needs of today while still carrying all the checks and balances that have held true over the ages.

Ceremony can only be as effective as the one wielding it. As an organized set of rituals designed to help focus the practitioner's intent, the true power of ceremony is totally dependent on the power of the practitioner's toroidal fields, which can only be as clear as his/her conscious intent. Ceremony is not a replacement for processing and healing, nor is it a power source in and of itself. The true power of ceremony lies in how it assists the practitioner in aligning with natural law.

## OF PURE INTENT

Before performing ceremony, it is very important to be sure that your intent is pure and direct. Ask yourself some questions:

Will my intent result in appropriating energy rightfully belonging to another?

Am I imposing energy or my agenda onto another?

Am I working without permission?

Is my intent ultimately to best serve all concerned? (remember nature works in synergistic win-win scenarios)

## BOTTOM LINE

The concept of bottom-line intent was discussed in "Shamanism 101." and it is one of the most important concepts to master. It is your bottom-line intent, whether it is conscious or unconscious that drives all manifestation in your life. It also dictates your experience. We all have bottom lines that drive the events of our lives. Unfortunately, due to our damage, programming and the resulting denials, our bottom lines are mostly unconscious ones.

*~ IF YOU ARE NOT PLEASED WITH WHAT IS MANIFESTING IN YOUR LIFE, RATHER THAN POINT THE FINGER, LOOK TO YOUR OWN PERSONAL BOTTOM LINE. ~*

As with all things, the bottom line must evolve as you do. As I look back on my past bottom lines, it is easy to see where I was trying to create solutions to perceived problems rather than state what I truly wanted. Be forewarned: When you set a bottom line, suddenly, everything that stands between you and achieving it is up in your face to be cleared. More simply, "Watch what you ask for."

## TERRORIZING

I had an appointment with a client who was also a student in my school. When she arrived, I could see she was uncharacteristically agitated.

"What's up for you?" I inquired.

"Everything is conspiring to terrorize me," she stated heatedly.

"How so?" I wanted to know.

She proceeded to relay numerous incidents over the previous week that did indeed sound terrifying. From being stalked, to several near accidents, I could see that she had been having a rough time of it. She had even been experiencing nightmares that were quite hair-raising, which was not normal for her.

After sitting with the information for a while, I finally asked, "Have you added anything to your bottom line lately?"

"Why, yes," she responded. "Just before this all started I added that I never wanted to be afraid again."

I burst out laughing, but she was not amused.

Adding "I never want to be afraid again" to her bottom line necessitated confronting all of her fears at once in order to clear them. She was also creating solutions. She had judged against all fear and decided that if she didn't have to feel fear, she would be more comfortable. Her solution was to abolish fear. Yet, the problem wasn't fear in the first place. Fear is a valuable and necessary emotion in any given moment—especially if you are being stalked. It is designed to warn us when we are engaging in a dangerous situation. The problem was all the unprocessed fear from her past that was being projected onto her present experience. This projection was being implemented so she could avoid remembering the original trauma.

Once she got over her snit at my apparent insensitivity to her suffering, we reworked her bottom line. We finally agreed to change her bottom line from, "I never want to be afraid again" to "Given that I don't want to be overwhelmed in the process, I intend to heal the past damage that is causing me to experience unnecessary fear in the present." This change in wording clarified her intent, making her process much more comfortable and effective.

The more you work on refining your bottom line, the easier it gets. The more you process and heal, the less you need in your bottom line. At first, our bottom lines have to work around our unconscious bottom lines. In this woman's case, her unconscious bottom line was, "I don't want to feel any fear, because it will remind me of my trauma."

## SUNRISE, SUNSET

Ceremonies are basically subroutines. When combining these subroutines with our intent and bottom line, the simplest ceremony can carry great power. By working with the natural rhythms of the day/night cycles, we can propel our intent by aligning it with the spin of the Earth.

1) Start your day by taking a moment to set your intent as to what you wish to accomplish.

2) At mid-morning again take time to make sure your actions are aligned with your intent and make the proper adjustments to make it so. (Given my bottom line, am I taking the proper actions to improve my relationships at work?)

3) In mid-afternoon, evaluate your progress and sort through what is serving you and what you need to let go of or temporarily set aside. (Given my bottom line, what is supporting my intent, and what behaviors or attitudes are not working for me?)

4) At night give gratitude for all you have gained and embrace a willingness to let go of what no longer serves. (I am grateful for the progress I have made toward improving my relationships at work. Given my bottom line, I intend to release any unnecessary behavior, beliefs and attitudes that do not serve that purpose.)

This simple ritual can exponentially increase your productivity and efficiency. By aligning your intent with the natural rhythms of the Earth, you are being reminded to be conscious and deliberate in your thoughts and actions, which increases the power of your intent by bringing you back to the present moment periodically throughout your day. It also further supports your intent by aligning it with the powerful flow of nature.

*~ THE ONLY PLACE WE CAN WIELD TRUE POWER*
*IS IN THE PRESENT MOMENT. ~*

## SINGING DOWN THE MOON

❖ Ceremonies can also be built to take advantage of the differentiated power of moon phases, so mark the phases of the moon on your calendar. (Found in "The Natural Law.")

❖ Decide on and write down what you wish to accomplish during the month.

❖ Compose your bottom line as it applies to the intent.

❖ At each phase of the moon you may choose to light a candle to help focus your ceremony. Then state the following:

❖ New Moon: "Given my bottom line, I wish to initiate_____, and I intend to release the unnecessary things blocking me from accomplishing my goal."

❖ First Quarter: "Given my bottom line, with courage, clarity and balance, I wish to take proper action to achieve my intent."

❖ Full Moon: "Given my bottom line, I wish to examine my intent with increased clarity, self-awareness and truth and refine it accordingly."

❖ Last Quarter: "I give gratitude for all I have received this month. I intend to look within to seek harmony and maintain balance before making final decisions upon my next actions, intents, and bottom line."

*~ GRATITUDE IS THE FERTILIZER FOR THE SEEDS OF LIFE. ~*

## FOUR SEASONS

The seasons also carry great power, which when aligned with our intent, can greatly propel our purpose.

❖ Mark the year's solstices and equinoxes on your calendar. (Found in "The Natural Law.".)

❖ Decide on and write down what you wish to accomplish during the next year.

❖ Compose your bottom line as it applies to the intent.

At each solstice and equinox you may choose to light a candle to help focus your ceremony then state the following:

❖ *Spring Equinox*: "Given my bottom line, I wish to initiate the following_____."

❖ *Summer Solstice*: "Given my bottom line, I wish to grow and cultivate the following_____."

❖ *Fall Equinox*: "Given my bottom line, I wish to harvest what I have produced. I choose to discern and release what no longer serves my purpose."

❖ *Winter Solstice*: "I embrace the lessons and wisdom gained during the past year and give gratitude for all I have received." (Make a comprehensive list of these things)

These ceremonies can be performed by your entire family. By sharing these simple concepts with your children, you will empower them in ways you cannot even imagine. Unlike us, they will grow up with the subroutines in place. Working with life will come natural to them, enhancing all they do for the rest of their lives. Agreeing on what you wish to accomplish as a family and coming together at appointed times also engages group intent and strengthens the foundation of your family.

There are ceremonies that I perform alone to direct my personal intent, ceremonies that I share with my family, and others that I share with my community. It is important that the bottom line for each ceremony is built through the collaboration of all the participants. I will also sit down before each phase and determine if the bottom line or intent needs refinement. Then I make the appropriate adjustments before performing it again. This process, when shared with your family or group, can deepen your understanding of how life works. It also enables you to come out of the victim stance and participate in the construction of your experience. When you take time to see how your intent and bottom line are directing your life, you can choose to be a co-creator rather than a passenger of fate.

JUST A SUGGESTION

Given that this book is about spiritual evolution and personal empowerment, I humbly suggest the following for your ceremonies:

❖ Intend to take the next step toward healing what stands between you and your personal power in _____ situation.

❖ Intend to heal what stands between you and your next step in your evolutionary process.

❖ Intend to take the next step toward healing what keeps you subject to the system in an individual area of your life. Examples: your current finances, a specific relationship, a particular health issue, a specific addiction, etc.

It is usually best to keep your intent simple and contained, as there is ever so much more involved in every issue than meets the eye. I suggest that you ask to *take the next step* toward healing what stands between you and your personal power in a *specific* situation rather than just heal what stands between you and your personal power. In our current state there is so much standing between us and all of our potential power, that to intend to heal it all would likely blow us out of the water. We could not hope to be able to understand or process all of the healing required to fulfill such a broad-spectrum intent.

Any time you start to feel under duress or overwhelmed while working with ceremony, look to your bottom line and intent. You may need to reevaluate what you are asking for. You can just about be assured that you have inadvertently bitten off more than you can chew.

Another problem that you may run into is that your conscious intent can be diametrically opposed to an underlying unconscious one. People may intend to lose weight while not realizing that on a deeper level of their consciousness, they believe that their life depends on not being attractive. To complicate this, they may have no memory of a traumatic incident that created that belief. To remember the incident at this time in their life might be too overwhelming. For instance, there may still be a teenager living within who is reliant upon the perpetrator. Denial has its purposes. We have to be mindful to pick our battles.

When working with ceremony, action is required on your part in order to fulfill your intent. We don't just set our intent and sit on our hands, expecting it to magically happen. Instead, we watch our promptings and pay attention to opportunities that present themselves. Ceremony and intent simply align us with the opportunities necessary to accomplish our goal. It is up to us to recognize and take advantage of those opportunities as they arise.

Once having set my intent, I have learned to see many of the things coming my way as examples of these opportunities.

## THE WINDOWLESS ROOM

I had just gone through a divorce and had ended up owning a large house in the country with a large mortgage and a lot of debt. I still had two children to raise. I was a shamanic practitioner and teacher by trade with a limited income. I had put the country home on the market in order to sell it and pay off my debt. I had also contracted for a smaller home to be built in town. It was difficult to know how much to put into the new home, as I didn't know what the current house would sell for, or, for that matter, when. Being conservative, I had contracted for a relatively small, windowless room to be finished in the basement, in which to hold my classes.

Having set my intent to procure a good home in which to finish raising my children, I composed my bottom line:

❖ The house needs to be affordable and yet have space to hold my practice.

❖ The home, and the building of it, are to best serve the needs of all concerned.

Setting up an altar to help focus my intent, I put the piece of paper containing my intent and bottom line under the candle. I lit the candle morning and night taking care to refine my intent and bottom line as needed.

One day I was holding a class in the large, well-lit walkout basement of the country home. While drumming for the students' journey, my mind began to wander. Deeply appreciating the large sunlit room we were in, I was concerned about the smaller, windowless, north-facing room in the new home that was to replace it.

At one point, the phone rang upstairs, but I let it go to voicemail in order to finish the morning portion of the class. During the lunch break I retrieved a message from my builder. He told me that, due to the water table on the lot, he could not dig deep enough to give me the eight-foot ceilings I had contracted for in the basement. He assured me that he would still hold to our contract, even though, in order to do so, he would need to absorb the additional expense of raising the foundation to garden level on the south side. He was calling to see if, given the new elevation, I would like him to install windows in the south-garden level wall of the basement. To do so would require adding cost to the contract price of the house.

I didn't even have to consider my answer. I instructed him to not only put three windows in the south wall, but also change the plans to finish the larger south-facing portion of the basement, rather than the small north corner I originally planned on.

How did I know that I could afford the three new windows, much less finish the much larger room? I had put "affordable" in my bottom line, and I recognized the opportunity being presented.

After years of setting my intent and bottom line and then empowering them with ceremony, I have noted how the raw materials for fulfilling my intent mysteriously show up. I have also experienced how following up on these promptings and opportunities leads directly to my intent within the parameters of my bottom line. Over time, I have learned to trust the process.

## Suggested Journeys

Hopefully you have been practicing your journey skills and are becoming fairly proficient. If not, a quick review of "Shamanism 101." and the guidelines for responsible journeys, may be in order before performing the suggested journeys.

## Some Reminders:

### Intent

When performing the shamanic journey, assure that your intent is clean and direct. In order to do so, ask yourself the same questions from the section "Of Pure Intent."

### Question

A journey can only be as good as the question that starts it. You can review the proper wording for journey questions in "The Divination Journey" on page 177.

### Bottom Line

Compose a bottom line appropriate to the journey at hand. Again, until you feel confidant, refer to the instructions in "The Divination Journey" on page 177.

15-minute journey[1]

Limit your questions to one per journey.

## Physical Evolution

Given my bottom line,

1) What is my next step in freeing my *physical* body to participate in the evolutionary process available to me at this time?

2) What do I need to know, do, or heal, in order to accomplish this?

4) What tools or modalities will best serve my physical evolution at this time?

3) How can I support my *physical* body in adjusting to the increasing frequency of the new era?

---

1. *Track 4 on "On Wings of Spirit" or "Betwixt and Between" CDs/MP3s*

## EMOTIONAL EVOLUTION

Given my bottom line,

1) What is my next step in freeing my *emotional* body to participate in the evolutionary process available to me at this time?

2) What do I need to know, do, or heal, in order to accomplish this?

4) What tools or modalities will best serve my *emotional* evolution at this time?

3) What unprocessed emotions from the past am I projecting onto my present experiences?

## MENTAL EVOLUTION

Given my bottom line,

1) What is my next step in freeing my *mental* body to participate in the evolutionary process available to me at this time?

2) What do I need to know, do, or heal, in order to accomplish this?

3) What tools or modalities will best serve my *mental* evolution at this time?

4) What beliefs do I hold that are blocking my *mental* evolutionary process?

## SPIRITUAL EVOLUTION

Given my bottom line,

1) What is my next step in freeing my *spiritual* body to participate in the evolutionary process available to me at this time?

2) What do I need to know, do, or heal, in order to accomplish this?

3) What tools or modalities will best serve my *spiritual* evolution at this time?

4) How can I better access the *spiritual* information/guidance available to me at this time?

## FINAL REMINDERS

❖ Journal and interpret your journeys upon your return, rather than trying to figure out what you are being told while on the journey.

❖ Keep a log of your journeys to track your progress in the evolutionary process.

❖ Refer back to past journeys to deepen your understanding and further support your process.

❖ Take notes on how you have implemented the suggestions from your journeys and the results you experience.

❖ Repeat this set of journeys often throughout your evolutionary process.

So we end where we began, at this precipice of a remarkable adventure, the adventure of human evolution.

As we participate in the evolutionary process, we increasingly reenter the circle of life where we are one with All That Is. From this place of unity we support, and are supported by, all of our relations. Synergy, symbiosis and win-win scenarios are the norm. The flow of life becomes the river that carries us home.

Along your sacred path to wholeness, it's my sincere hope that this work may contribute in some small way to your well being as you embrace the glory of who you are, as you walk hand in hand with All-That-Is.

Until the other side of tomorrow:

*May you walk in beauty.*

> ### *May You Walk In Beauty*
>
> *Beauty above you*
> *Beauty below you*
> *To your right*
> *To your left*
> *Beauty behind you*
> *Beauty before you*
> *Walk in beauty*
> *Walk in beauty*
> *Walk in beauty*
>
> *~ StarFaihre ~*
> *(Song based on a*
> *Native American Prayer)*

# About the Author

Gwilda Wiyaka is the founder, director and head instructor of the Path Home Shamanic Arts School, which is a one-of-a-kind, Colorado state-certified, occupational school of the shamanic arts that trains and certifies shamanic practitioners.

She is also a preceptor for the University of Colorado School of Medicine, where she provides instruction to medical doctors on the modern interface between shamanism and allopathic medicine for the University's School of Medicine's Complementary and Alternative Medicine course.

In her private practice she began interfacing with psychotherapists, psychiatrists, chiropractors and medical doctors from whom she still receives many of her referrals. Her medical intuitive skills have been corroborated by MRIs and CT scans, validating consistent accuracy.

Born in the United States, Gwilda grew up overseas, attending grade school in Saudi Arabia, and obtaining most of her higher education in Switzerland. She holds a B.S. in Psychology and Religious Studies and later became a Certified Massage Therapist. Her background with different societies and locations around the world, and her on-going fascination with the way life works, prompted her life-long immersion into shamanism. She has studied with many Native American healers, including the Seneca, Lakota, Navajo, Arapaho and Choctaw. She also received training in Tibetan, Core and Celtic Shamanism.

Gwilda has studied Shamanism for over 38 years and has been a practitioner for over 20. She has taught the shamanic arts for 15 years.

She teaches workshops and seminars throughout the world and is an inspirational speaker and an accomplished singer/songwriter, with four CDs to date.

# Glossary - Definitions

**Akashic Records**: *akasha is a Sanskrit word meaning "sky, space, or ether." The Akashic Records are often described as a library or a collection of knowledge encoded in a non-physical plane of existence. This automatically updated compilation contains all the knowledge of human experience and the history of the universe.*

**Astrology:** *The study of the positions and aspects of celestial bodies and the influence the resulting frequencies have on the course of natural earthly occurrences and human affairs.*

**Aura:** *a multilayered field of subtle, luminous radiation surrounding a person or object, which is created by energy systems such as meridians and chakras, and which follows the laws of harmonic inductance and sympathetic resonance.*

**Chakras:** *(from the Sanskrit word for "wheel" or "turning") the main energy centers found throughout the body that are connected to major governing organs or glands. Like a toroidal field, a chakra interacts with anything encountered at the quantum level at its band of frequency.*

**Decay:** *to break down into constituent parts.*

**Defense Mechanisms**: *expressions taken out of their natural order and used to prevent the reoccurrence of circumstances. Defense mechanisms maintain frozen polarities, impinging upon mobility.*

**Depossession:** *the casting out of possessing spirits.*

**Dogma:** *an established belief or doctrine held by a religion, or a particular group or organization that is authoritative and not to be disputed, doubted, or diverged from.*

**Elements:** *traditionally reflect the simplest known essential parts, principles, and the fundamental powers of which anything consists. Traditional beliefs are based on natural observation of the phases of matter, rather than chemistry or atomic theory.*

***Endocrine glands:*** *glands of the endocrine system in the human body that secrete hormones directly into the blood.*

***Equinox:*** *an astronomical event occurring twice a year when the tilt of the Earth's axis is inclined neither away from nor towards the Sun, resulting in days and nights of equal length. (see also Solstice)*

***Esoteric Chakra****: The portion of the chakra system existing both above and below the body.*

***Extraction:*** *a shamanic-healing technique whereby practitioners remove incompatible frequencies from their clients that may be causing pain and illness.*

***Genesis:*** *the origin or mode of formation of something.*

***Ions:*** *are molecules that have gained or lost an electrical charge, resulting in negative or positive ions. They are created in nature as air molecules, and break apart due to sunlight, radiation, and moving air and water.*

***Integration:*** *the process of unifying or making into a whole by bringing all parts together on all four levels: physical, emotional, mental and spiritual.*

***Light:***
*a. increasing levels of multidimensionality in both the "dark-light" feminine frequencies and "light-light" masculine frequencies. Any increase in one without an equal but opposite increase in the other results in imbalance. (The reference to light-light and dark-light is not to be confused with the ages of greater light, Leo and Aquarius, and ages of the long dark in Taurus and Scorpio. In the ages of greater light both light-light and dark-light are increased while in the long dark both light-light and dark-light are diminished.)*
*b. electromagnetic radiation formed by a changing magnetic field combined with changing electric fields.*

***Long Dark:*** *Time in the astrological ages characterized by extreme polarization and lack of balanced masculine/feminine frequencies.*

***Magnetic Pole - North:*** *a point on the surface of the Earth, located in the Northern Hemisphere, at which at any given time, the Earth's magnetic field is vertical.*

***Magnetic Pole - South:*** *a point on the surface of the Earth, located in the Southern Hemisphere, where at any given time, the Earth's magnetic field is vertical.*

***Miasm:*** *A restriction in the physical, emotional, mental, or spiritual body that is caused by a frozen polarity reversal in the toroidal field of same. Miasms are the energetic root of all illnesses.*

**Middle World:** *the reality we live in, but existing outside of time and space.*

**Multidimensionality:** *having access to multiple frequencies and therefore multiple realities at the same time. All of us are multidimensional to one degree or another.*

**Non-ordinary Reality:** *the shamanic metaphorical representation of reality as it expresses at the quantum level.*

**Parasite:** *an organism that lives on or in a host organism and gets its food from or at the expense of its host.*

**Prism:** *a transparent optical element that refracts light.*

**Process:** *a systematic series of actions directed at achieving a purpose.*

**Psychopomp:** *a person who conducts spirits or souls to the other world. The term is derived from the Greek word meaning "conductor of souls."*

**Quantum Physics:** *The branch of physics that uses quantum theory to describe and predict the properties of a physical system. Quantum physics provides a mathematical description of much of the dual particle-like and wave-like behavior and interactions of energy and matter.*

**Religion:** *a collection of cultural belief systems and moral values.*

**Shamanism:** *an organized set of rituals designed to focus the practitioner's natural ability to manage energy and matter at the quantum level. (Note: this is my personal definition, not the commonly accepted one).*

**Socialization:** *the process of learning one's culture and how to live within it.*

**Solstice:** *an astronomical event occurring twice a year when the tilt of the Earth's north axis is most steeply inclined either away from or directly towards the sun. This results in the shortest day and longest day in the year, respectively, in the Northern Hemisphere. (See also Equinoxes)*

**Sorcery:** *Use of supernatural power over others and their affairs without their permission; appropriation and misuse of natural law.*

**Soul:** *the energetic aspect or expression of person, place, or thing that operates at the quantum level.*

**Soul Loss:** *disconnection from natural expression or options at the quantum level due to trauma, judgment, or programming that creates frozen polarization.*

**Soul Retrieval:** *a shamanic healing practice whereby the practitioner, through use of shamanic ritual and the altered state of consciousness known as the shamanic journey trance, locates and corrects restrictions in their client's toroidal field.*

**Sound:** *vibrations or pressure disturbances in the form of mechanical waves that travel through a medium by means of particle-to-particle interaction, with frequencies in the approximate range of 20 to 20,000 hertz.*

**Spirit:** *the unifying force of all nature; the interrelatedness of all things.*

**Spirit World:** *a metaphoric representation created by the practitioner's imagination to represent actual interactions of life (to the mind) at the quantum level.*

**Spiritual Healing:** *realignment with natural law at the quantum level of life.*

**Spiritual level:** *the higher-frequency, more unified realms found at the quantum level; not to be confused with religion. It is from the spiritual level that humans obtain broader understanding, inspiration, creativity, sovereignty, and the ability to manifest for themselves.*

**Subculture:** *a subset or group of people within a culture differentiated from the larger culture to which they belong.*

**Subroutine:** *a set of instructions for performing some task which, when repeatedly applied, forms a unified action.*

**Symbiotic:** *living in symbiosis, or having an interdependent, mutually beneficial relationship.*

**Torus:** *A surface generated by a closed curve rotating about, but not intersecting or containing, an axis in its own plane.*

**Transducer:** *a device that converts one form of energy to another.*

**Trigger:** *An event that precipitates other events, setting into motion a course of action.*

**Whole Health:** *the unified connection to the entirety of our being—body, emotions, mind, and spirit—in synergy and balance.*

# Appendix

# Map Home

## More Tools to Build Your Map Home

For more in-depth instructions on personalizing your evolutionary
process don't miss:

---

## The Map Home Workshop:

Many of the ancients, from the Mayans to the Hopis, long expected the
"Fourth World" of greed, war and competition to begin to transform into the
"Fifth World" of love, balance and spiritual strength at about this point in
time. While this transition is a joyous one, it is not without its challenges, for
we must shed the remains of an old world dying as we endeavor to embrace
the new one now being born.

The Map Home is designed to offer guidance as we undergo this transformation. It is comprised of leading edge information in the form of books, vid-
eos, interviews, healings, teachings, workshops, and experiential retreats. The
Map Home was created by Gwilda Wiyaka to help individuals engage in the
evolution that is available to us all during these intensely transformative
times. Through this evolutionary process you can access your health, longevity and personal power in order to live a life of abundance, joy and ease.

Tune in to the following website to enjoy books, retreats, classes, articles
and interviews with Map Home's founder, Gwilda Wiyaka and her guests as
we explore the potential and future of the human race.

Let us help you build your personal Map Home.
tinyurl.com/PathMapHome

## MAP HOME WORKBOOK 1:

*Stairway to Heaven: Tools for Spiritual Evolution and Personal Empowerment:* Gwilda Wiyaka

(Accompanying workbook for: *So, We're Still Here. Now What?)*

Full of tools for the evolving human, *Stairway to Heaven* includes step-by-step instructions to help you customize your healing process at all four levels—physical, emotional mental and spiritual. Ceremonies, journeys and innumerous resources are presented to walk you through your next levels of enlightenment and personal empowerment.

Available at:

tinyurl.com/PathHomeStore

or

Amazon.com

## SHAMANIC HEALING

Path Home offers long-distance shamanic healing sessions. All Path Home Long Distance Practitioners are certified shamanic practitioners who, in addition, have been specifically trained by Gwilda Wiyaka to support the evolutionary process of their clients.

To schedule an appointment:
tinyurl.com/PathHomeLD

## CDS AND MP3S

These journey CDs and MP3s were specifically designed for Path Home Shamanic Arts School classes and certification programs. They are approved to accompany the journey portion of this text as well as the companion workbook: *Stairway to Heaven.*

*On Wings of Spirit*: Gwilda Wiyaka performs quad drumming for the shamanic journey. Available at:
tinyurl.com/PathHomeStore,
 Amazon.com
or iTunes.

*Betwixt and Between*: Gwilda Wiyaka performs double drumming for the shamanic journey.

Available at:
tinyurl.com/PathHomeStore,
or Amazon.com
or
iTunes.

## BOOKS

Book 2 in the Map Home Series, coming in 2014:

*These and Greater Things: Unlocking Your Power to Manifest and Thrive through Shamanism.*

by Gwilda Wiyaka

Coming soon to:

tinyurl.com/PathHomeStore, or

Granite-Planet.net

## SHAMANIC TRAINING

Path Home Shamanic Arts School is a Colorado State Certified Occupational School designed to bring into modern times and practices ancient, tried and true shamanic skills. Path Home specializes in training and certifying shamanic practitioners and teach-

ers providing quality spiritual healers and stewards for our modern communities.

FindYourPathHome.com

touchin@findyourpathhome.com

## CLASSES AND RETREATS:

### MAP HOME: RETREATS FOR THE EVOLVING HUMAN

tinyurl.com/PathMapHome

### OTHER BOOKS, CDS, AND MP3S BY GWILDA WIYAKA

Available at:tinyurl.com/PathHomeStore or Amazon.com

*In Touch With Spirit, The Shamanic Journey: Workbook 1*

The shamanic journey is the cornerstone of all shamanic divination practices. Mastering this ancient form can effectively connect you to your own spiritual information and guidance.

*In Touch With Spirit* was written by Gwilda Wiyaka, CSI, founder and director of Path Home Shamanic Arts School, as a text to accompany the School's Shamanic Journey and Power Animals/ Helping Spirits classes.

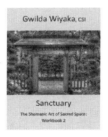

*Sanctuary, The Shamanic Art of Sacred Space: Workbook 2*

The easily understood shamanic principles and techniques found in *Sanctuary* offer step-by-step instruction on creating sacred space for the home or workplace. This book is a must read for anyone seeking peace and personal empowerment.

### MUSIC BY STARFAIHRE

StarFaihre is a unique musical group performing ancient and original world/shamanic music. During these times of intense shifts and deep transformation, we may find ourselves at the precipice of life changing revelations. **StarFaihre** produces powerful shamanic works designed to assist this transformation.

Their music is healing and transformative, offering the opportunity to transmute our experience. What was seen as deep suffering can be perceived as joy, hopelessness as hope disguised, the alpha and the omega, the beginning and the end coexisting in one moment of time.

Through complex harmonies and counter melodies, and accompanied by multicultural instrumentation, StarFaihre's stunning vocalists, Gwilda Wiyaka and Cody Wigle, create the sound of the soul that carries down the millennia on the winds of time.

*Winds of Time: StarFaihre*

Music designed to inspire and support the evolutionary process. During these times of intense shifts and deep transformation, we may find ourselves standing at the precipice of life-changing revelations. *Winds of Time* is a channeled work designed to assist this transformation. Experience music that truly heals through these songs created and performed by StarFaihre's Gwilda Wiyaka and Cody Wigle.

Available in CD or MP3 at

tinyurl.com/PathHomeMusic

or amazon.com

or iTunes

*One People One Nation: Ancient and Modern Shamanic Songs*: Gwilda Wiyaka

From the innocence of Earth-connected tribal life, journey through the Trail of Tears and beyond the polarized industrial era. Through deep processing we shed that which is not true and enter into personal healing to once again find "The Way" in a new way stewarded by the old way. **One People One Nation** is a map to the future we all hope to create—one of joy, unity and abundance, living in sacred harmony on our beloved planet Earth. Available on CD

tinyurl.com/PathHomeMusic or

amazon.com

# Index

# List of Figures

**Granite Publishing L.L.C.**

info@granitepublishing.us

POB 1429,

Columbus NC 28722

828.894.8444

ON THE WEB AT: GRANITE-PLANET.NET

| GRANITE PUBLISHING: | | SOLID GROUND IN A SHIFTING WORLD | |
|---|---|---|---|
| **Common Sense in Uncommon Times:** Survival Techniques for a Changing World | Dr. Brian Crissey and Rev. Pam Crissey | | |
| WILD FLOWER PRESS: | | DOCUMENTING THE UNEXPECTED | |
| **A Time of Change:** Akashic Guidance for Spiritual Transformation | Aingeal Rose O'Grady | | |
| SWAN-RAVEN & CO.: | | ANCIENT WISDOM IN MODERN TIMES | |
| **These and Greater Things:** Unlocking Your Power to Manifest and Thrive through Shamanism | Coming in 2014 Gwilda Wiyaka | | |
| NOTMADEBYHANDS.COM: | | Cosmic Crop-Circle Energy Essences | |
| **Energized Water from out of this world:** Unique, Powerful Transformative | Collected by Barbara Lamb Decoded by Aingeal Rose O'Grady via the Akashic Records | | |

Made in the USA
Charleston, SC
27 February 2014